REA's Test Prep Books Are The Best!

(a sample of the <u>hundreds of letters</u> REA receives each year)

" I did well because of your wonderful prep books... I just wanted to thank you for helping me prepare for these tests. "

Student, San Diego, CA

" My students report your chapters of review as the most valuable single resource they used for review and preparation. "

Teacher, American Fork, UT

" Your book was such a better value and was so much more complete than anything your competition has produced (and I have them all!). "

Teacher, Virginia Beach, VA

" Compared to the other books that my fellow students had, your book was the most useful in helping me get a great score. "

Student, North Hollywood, CA

" Your book was responsible for my success on the exam, which helped me get into the college of my choice... I will look for REA the next time I need help. "

Student, Chesterfield, MO

" Just a short note to say thanks for the great support your book gave me in helping me pass the test... I'm on my way to a B.S. degree because of you! "

Student, Orlando, FL

(more on next page)

" I just wanted to thank you for helping me get a great score on the AP U.S. History exam... Thank you for making great test preps! "
Student, Los Angeles, CA

" Your Fundamentals of Engineering Exam book was the absolute best preparation I could have had for the exam, and it is one of the major reasons I did so well and passed the FE on my first try. "
Student, Sweetwater, TN

" I used your book to prepare for the test and found that the advice and the sample tests were highly relevant... Without using any other material, I earned very high scores and will be going to the graduate school of my choice. "
Student, New Orleans, LA

" What I found in your book was a wealth of information sufficient to shore up my basic skills in math and verbal... The section on analytical ability was excellent. The practice tests were challenging and the answer explanations most helpful. It certainly is the Best Test Prep for the GRE! "
Student, Pullman, WA

" I really appreciate the help from your excellent book. Please keep up the great work. "
Student, Albuquerque, NM

" I am writing to thank you for your test preparation... your book helped me immeasurably and I have nothing but praise for your GRE preparation."
Student, Benton Harbor, MI

(more on back page)

THE BEST TEST PREPARATION FOR THE
SAT II: Subject Test

LITERATURE

Joseph Alvarez, Ph.D.
Chairperson, English & Foreign Languages
Central Piedmont Community College,
Charlotte, NC

Ellen Davis, M.A.
English Instructor
Clearlake High School
Houston, TX

Pauline Beard, Ph.D.
Instructor of English
Portland State University
Portland, OR

Philip Harmon, Ph.D.
Professor of English
Ricks College
Rexburg, ID

Research & Education Association
61 Ethel Road West • Piscataway, New Jersey 08854

The Best Test Preparation for the
SAT II: SUBJECT TEST IN LITERATURE

Year 2003 Printing

Printed in the United States of America

Library of Congress Control Number 99-75147

International Standard Book Number 0-87891-846-9

Research & Education Association
61 Ethel Road West
Piscataway, New Jersey 08854

REA supports the effort to conserve and
protect environmental resources by
printing on recycled papers.

ACKNOWLEDGMENTS

We wish to thank the following for permission to reprint copyrighted materials:

From *Death of a Salesman* by Arthur Miller. Copyright 1949, renewed copyright © 1977 by Arthur Miller. Reprinted by permission of the publisher, Viking Penguin, a division of Penguin Books USA Inc.

"Shooting an Elephant" from *Shooting an Elephant and Other Essays* by George Orwell, copyright 1950 by Sonia Bromwell Orwell and renewed 1978 by Sonia Pitt-Rivers, reprinted by permission of Harcourt Brace Jovanovich, Inc.

Excerpts from "Hamlet and His Problems" in *Selected Essays* by T.S. Eliot, copyright 1950 by Harcourt Brace Jovanovich, Inc., and renewed 1978 by Esme Valerie Eliot, reprinted by permission of the publisher.

From *Cat's Cradle* by Kurt Vonnegut, Jr. Reprinted by permission from Kurt Vonnegut, Jr., Delacourte Press.

From "Musee des Beaux Arts" by W.H. Auden. Copyright 1940 and renewed 1968 by W. H. Auden. Reprinted from *W.H. Auden; Collected Poems* edited by Edward Mendelson, by permission of Random House, Inc.

Reprinted with permission of Charles Scribner's Sons, an imprint of Macmillan Publishing Company from "The Rich Boy" by F. Scott Fitzgerald. Copyright 1925, 1926 by Consolidated Magazines Corporation, renewal copyright 1953, 1954 by Frances Scott Fitzgerald Lanahan.

Reprinted with permission of Charles Scribner's Sons, and imprint of Macmillan Publishing Company from *Cry, the Beloved Country* by Alan Paton. Copyright © 1948 Alan Paton, copyright renewed 1976 Alan Paton.

From *Waiting for Godot* by Samuel Beckett. Reprinted with permission by Grove Press, Inc.

Copyright 1951 by Langston Hughes. Reprinted from *The Panther and the Lash* by Langston Hughes, by permission of Alfred A. Knopf Inc.

Excerpt from *Slaughterhouse-Five* by Kurt Vonnegut, Jr., copyright 1968, 1969 by Kurt Vonnegut, Jr. Reprinted by permission of Delacourte Press/Seymour Lawrence, a division of Bantam, Doubleday, Dell Publishing Group, Inc.

From *Time Wars* by Jeremy Rifkin. Copyright © 1987 by Jeremy Rifkin. Reprinted by permission of Henry Holt and Company, Inc.

"The Rainbow" by D.H. Lawrence. Copyright © 1964 by D.H. Lawrence. Reprinted with permission of Viking Penguin, Inc.

From *The Seven Pillars of Wisdom* by T.E. Lawrence. Reprinted by permission of Doubleday, a division of Bantam, Doubleday, Dell Publishing Group, Inc.

"The Lovers of the Poor" by Gwendolyn Brooks. Harper and Row Publishers, Inc. Reprinted by permission of Gwendolyn Brooks, Chicago.

Research & Education Association would like to express gratitude to the following professionals for their contributions to the SAT II: Subject Test in Literature Course Review:

Joanne Miller, M.A., Chairperson of English Department, Harrison High School, West Lafayette, IN

Peter Trenouth, Ph.D. Teacher of English, Silverlake Regional High School, Kingston, MA

ABOUT RESEARCH & EDUCATION ASSOCIATION

Research & Education Association (REA) is an organization of educators, scientists, and engineers specializing in various academic fields. Founded in 1959 with the purpose of disseminating the most recently developed scientific information to groups in industry, government, high schools, and universities, REA has since become a successful and highly respected publisher of study aids, test preps, handbooks, and reference works.

REA's Test Preparation series includes study guides for all academic levels in almost all disciplines. Research & Education Association publishes test preps for students who have not yet completed high school, as well as high school students preparing to enter college. Students from countries around the world seeking to attend college in the United States will find the assistance they need in REA's publications. For college students seeking advanced degrees, REA publishes test preps for many major graduate school admission examinations in a wide variety of disciplines, including engineering, law, and medicine. Students at every level, in every field, with every ambition can find what they are looking for among REA's publications.

While most test preparation books present practice tests that bear little resemblance to the actual exams, REA's series presents tests that accurately depict the official exams in both degree of difficulty and types of questions. REA's practice tests are always based upon the most recently administered exams, and include every type of question that can be expected on the actual exams.

REA's publications and educational materials are highly regarded and continually receive an unprecedented amount of praise from professionals, instructors, librarians, parents, and students. Our authors are as diverse as the fields represented in the books we publish. They are well-known in their respective disciplines and serve on the faculties of prestigious high schools, colleges, and universities throughout the United States and Canada.

CONTENTS

ABOUT THE BOOK ix

ABOUT THE TEST ix

ABOUT THE REVIEW SECTION x

ABOUT THE INDEX OF LITERARY WORKS x

SCORING THE EXAMINATION x

LITERATURE COURSE REVIEW 1

CHAPTER 1 - PROSE 1

    Reading Novels 3

    Reading Short Stories 8

    Reading Essays 12

    Reading Satire 15

CHAPTER 2 - POETRY 18

    Verse and Meter 24

    Figurative Language and Poetic Devices 28

    Types of Poetry 36

CHAPTER 3 - DRAMA AND THEATER 40

    Plot Structure 42

    Character 43

    Reading the Play 46

    Types of Plays 48

    History 54

    Modern Drama 56

SIX PRACTICE EXAMS

Test 1 59
Answer Sheet 60
Answer Key 82
Detailed Explanations to Answers 83

Test 2 93
Answer Sheet 94
Answer Key 122
Detailed Explanations to Answers 123

Test 3 137
Answer Sheet 138
Answer Key 160
Detailed Explanations to Answers 161

Test 4 169
Answer Sheet 170
Answer Key 192
Detailed Explanations to Answers 193

Test 5 209
Answer Sheet 210
Answer Key 232
Detailed Explanations to Answers 233

Test 6 243
Answer Sheet 244
Answer Key 268
Detailed Explanations to Answers 269

LITERATURE INDEX 282

ABOUT THE BOOK

This book provides an accurate and complete representation of the SAT II: Subject Test in Literature. It is composed of six complete practice tests based on the most recently administered Literature tests. Each test is modeled after the actual exam and takes one hour to complete. The tests cover every type of question that can be expected to appear on the exam. Following each test is an answer key complete with detailed explanations designed to clarify the material for the student.

By studying the review sections, completing all six tests, and studying the answer explanations, students can discover their strengths and weaknesses and prepare themselves for the actual exam in Literature.

ABOUT THE TEST

The SAT II: Subject Test in Literature is designed to test the student's ability to read and understand literature in English. Each exam consists of approximately sixty multiple-choice questions based on six to eight short reading comprehension passages.

The passages are drawn from:
>English literature (40-50%)
>American literature (40-50%)
>Other Literature written in English (0-10%)

Each test covers material from:
>Renaissance and 17th century (30%)
>18th and 19th centuries (30%)
>20th century (40%)

Each test contains:
>poetry selections (45-50%)
>prose selections (45-50%)
>drama and other selections (0-10%)

The Literature test does not require any specific knowledge of literature in English. The student is expected to possess a working knowledge of basic literary terms and to use analytical skills derived from high school literature studies to answer the test questions. The questions are divided into sets of about four to twelve questions. The number of questions in a set is related to the length and complexity of the poem or passage. Generally, each group of questions based on a passage or poem consists of several questions about meaning, including effect and argument or theme, and several questions about form, including structure, generic properties, and method of organization. Where appropriate, the questions may also consider the narrative voice and the tone. The questions have five answer choices, and they can be categorized into three types: the regular multiple-choice question, the NOT/EXCEPT question, and the Roman numeral question.

ABOUT THE REVIEW SECTIONS

The reviews in this book are designed to further students' understanding of the test material. Each review includes techniques students can use to enhance their reading and analyzing abilities to earn higher scores on the exam. The reviews also discuss extensively the variety of literary genres, terms, and devices which the student will be required to know for the exam. The three review sections in this book correspond with the three topics covered on the SAT II exam:

READING PROSE This review covers the various forms of prose the student may encounter on the SAT II exam, including novels, short stories, essays, and satire. Also included is a section covering general rules and ideas about fiction and non-fiction, as well as tips on how to analyze prose passages for the test.

READING POETRY Every type of poetry the student can encounter on the SAT II exam is described in detail with examples. Genre, structure, convention, and poetic form are all given ample discussion. Definitions and examples appear in this section for such terms as onomatopoeia, masculine/feminine rhyme, paradox, allusion, and many others, as well as study hints to help the student analyze poetry for the test.

READING DRAMA This review gives extensive examples of the types of questions which could be asked about drama on the SAT II exam. The various types of drama, including conflict, character, and types of plays are discussed at length with examples. Classic works such as *Antigone*, *The Glass Menagerie*, and *Death of a Salesman* are used to illustrate the topics covered.

ABOUT THE INDEX OF LITERARY WORKS

In the back of this book you will find an extensive index which lists all of the literary works which are mentioned in this book. In addition to helping you find where specific works are located in the test, this index also serves as a suggested reading list of many of the literary classics you should read to help familiarize yourself with all the terms and genres you will need to know. Reading these works is excellent preparation for taking the SAT II: Literature Test.

SCORING THE EXAM

The exam is scored by crediting each correct answer and deducting one-fourth of a point for each wrong answer. Unanswered questions receive neither credit nor a deduction.

THE RAW SCORE

Use this formula to calculate your raw score:

_____ − (_____ x 1/4) = _____ (round to the nearest whole number)

number   number   raw
right   wrong   score

This number is your raw score.

THE COMPOSITE SCORE

Now take your raw score and locate it in the left hand column on the chart below. The corresponding number in the right hand column on the chart is your composite score.

SCORE CONVERSION CHART					
LITERATURE SUBJECT TEST					
Raw Score	Scaled Score	Raw Score	Scaled Score	Raw Score	Scaled Score
60	800	35	630	10	430
59	800	34	620	9	420
58	800	33	610	8	410
57	800	32	600	7	400
56	800	31	590	6	390
55	790	30	580	5	390
54	780	29	580	4	380
53	770	28	570	3	370
52	760	27	560	2	360
51	750	26	550	1	350
50	740	25	540	0	340
49	730	24	530	-1	340
48	720	23	530	-2	330
47	710	22	520	-3	320
46	710	21	510	-4	310
45	700	20	500	-5	300
44	690	19	490	-6	290
43	680	18	480	-7	290
42	670	17	480	-8	280
41	670	16	470	-9	270
40	670	15	460	-10	270
39	660	14	450	-11	270
38	650	13	440	-12	270
37	640	12	430	-13	270
36	630	11	430	-14	270
				-15	270

Although some colleges require SAT II: Subject Tests as part of the admission process, most colleges use the scores from the tests for placement and administrative purposes. Registration forms for the SAT II: Subject Tests can be obtained from the school guidance office.

COURSE REVIEW

CHAPTER 1

PROSE

GENERAL RULES AND IDEAS

Why do people write prose? Certainly such a question has a built-in counter: As opposed to writing what, poetry? One possible answer is that the person is a poor poet. The requirements and restrictions of the various genres make different demands upon a writer; most writers find their niche and stay there, secure in their private "comfort zone." Shakespeare did not write essays; Hemingway did not write poetry. If either did venture outside of his literary domain, the world took little note.

Students are sometimes confused as to what exactly is prose. Basically, prose is **not** poetry. Prose is what we write and speak most of the time in our everyday intercourse: unmetered, unrhymed language. Which is not to say that prose does not have its own rhythms—language, whether written or spoken, has cadence and balance. And certainly prose can have instances of rhyme or assonance, alliteration or onomatopoeia. Language is, after all, **phonic.**

Furthermore, **prose** may be either **fiction** or **non-fiction.** A novel (like a short story) is fiction; an autobiography is non-fiction. While a novel (or short story) may have autobiographical elements, an autobiography is presumed to be entirely factual. Essays are usually described in other terms: expository, argumentative, persuasive, critical, narrative. Essays may have elements of either fiction or non-fiction, but are generally classed as a separate subgenre.

Satire, properly speaking, is not a genre at all, but rather a **mode,** elements of which can be found in any category of literature—from poetry and drama to novels and essays. Satire is a manifestation of authorial attitude (tone) and purpose. Our discussion of satire will be limited to its use in prose.

But we have not addressed the initial question: "Why do people write prose?" The answer depends, in part, on the writer's intent. If he wishes to tell a rather long story, filled with many characters and subplots, interlaced with motifs, symbols, and themes, with time and space to develop interrelationships and to present descriptive passages, the writer generally chooses the novel as his medium. If he believes he can present his story more compactly and less complexly, he may choose the novella or the short story.

These subgenres require from the reader a different kind of involvement than does the essay. The essay, rather than presenting a story from which the reader may discern meaning through the skillful analysis of character, plot, symbol, and language, presents a relatively straightforward account of the writer's opinion(s) on an endless array of topics. Depending upon the type of essay, the reader may become informed (expository), provoked (argumentative), persuaded, enlightened (critical), or, in the case of the narrative essay, better acquainted with the writer who wishes to illustrate a point with his story, whether it is autobiographical or fictitious.

Encountering satire in prose selections demands that the reader be sensitive to the nuances of language and form, that he detect the double-edged sword of irony, and that he correctly assess both the writer's tone and his purpose.

Readers of prose, like readers of poetry, seek aesthetic pleasure, entertainment, and knowledge, not necessarily in that order. Fiction offers worlds—real and imagined—in which characters and ideas, events and language, interact in ways familiar and unfamiliar. As readers, we take delight in the wisdom we fancy we have acquired from a novel or short story. Non-fiction offers viewpoints which we may find comforting or horrifying, amusing or sobering, presented by the author rather than by his once-removed persona. Thus, we are tempted to believe that somehow the truths presented in non-fiction are more "real" than the truths revealed by fiction. But we must resist! **Truth** is not "genre-specific."

Reading prose for the SAT II: Literature is really no different from reading prose for your own purposes, except for the time constraints, of course! Becoming a competent reader is a result of practicing certain skills. Probably most important is acquiring a broad reading base. Read widely; read eclectically; read actively; read avidly. The idea is not that you might stumble onto a familiar prose selection on the SAT II and have an edge in writing about it; the idea is that your familiarity with many authors and works gives you a framework upon which to build your understanding of **whatever** prose selection you encounter on the SAT II: Literature exam. So read, read, read!

READING NOVELS

Most literary handbooks will define a novel as an extended fictional prose narrative, derived from the Italian *novella*, meaning "tale, piece of news." The term "novelle," meaning short tales, was applied to works such as Boccaccio's *The Decameron*, a collection of stories which had an impact on later works such as Chaucer's *Canterbury Tales*. In most European countries, the word for **novel** is **roman**, short for **romance**, which was applied to longer verse narratives (Malory's *Morte d'Arthur*), which were later written in prose. Early romances were associated with "legendary, imaginative, and poetic material"—tales "of the long ago or the far away or the imaginatively improbable"; novels, on the other hand, were felt to be "bound by the facts of the actual world and the laws of probability" (*A Handbook to Literature*, C. Hugh Holman, p. 354).

The novel has, over some 600 years, developed into many special forms which are classified by subject matter: detective novel, psychological novel, historical novel, regional novel, picaresque novel, Gothic novel, stream-of-consciousness novel, epistolary novel, and so on. These terms, of course, are not exhaustive nor mutually exclusive. Furthermore, depending on the conventions of the author's time period, his style, and his outlook on life, his *mode* may be termed **realism**, **romanticism, impressionism, expressionism, naturalism**, or **neo-classicism** (Holman, p. 359).

Our earlier description of a novel ("...a rather long story, filled with many characters and subplots, interlaced with motifs, symbols, and themes, with time and space to develop interrelationships and to present descriptive passages") is satisfactory for our purposes here. The works generally included on the SAT II are those which have stood the test of time in significance, literary merit, and reader popularity. New works are incorporated into the canon which is a reflection of what works are being taught in literature classes. And teachers begin to teach those works which are included frequently among the questions. So the process is circular, but the standards remain high for inclusion.

Analyzing novels is a bit like asking the journalist's five questions: what? who? why? where? and how? The **what?** is the story, the narrative, the plot and subplots. Most students are familiar with Freytag's Pyramid, originally designed to describe the structure of a five-act drama but now widely used to analyze fiction as well. The stages generally specified are **introduction** or **exposition, complication, rising action, climax, falling action**, and **denouement** or **conclusion**. As the novel's events are charted, the "change which structures the story" should emerge. There are many events in a long narrative; but generally only one set of events comprises the "real" or "significant" story.

However, subplots often parallel or serve as counterpoints to the main plot line, serving to enhance the central story. Minor characters sometimes have essentially the same conflicts and goals as major characters, but the consequences of the outcome seem less important. Sometimes the parallels involve reversals of characters and situations, creating similar yet distinct differences in the outcomes. Nevertheless, seeing the parallels makes understanding the major plot line less difficult.

Sometimes an author divides the novel into chapters—named or unnamed, perhaps just numbered. Or he might divide the novel into "books" or "parts," with chapters as subsections. Readers should take their cue from these divisions; the author must have had some reason for them. Take note of what happens in each larger section, as well as within the smaller chapters. Whose progress is being followed? What event or occurrence is being foreshadowed or prepared for? What causal or other relationships are there between sections and events? Some writers, such as Steinbeck in *The Grapes of Wrath*, use intercalary chapters, alternating between the "real" story (the Joads) and peripheral or parallel stories (the Okies and migrants in general). Look for the pattern of such organization; try to see the interrelationships of these alternating chapters.

Of course, plots cannot happen in isolation from characters, the **who?** element of a story. Not only are there major and minor characters to consider; we need to note whether the various characters are **static** or **dynamic**. Static characters do not change in significant ways—that is, in ways which relate to the story which is structuring the novel. A character may die, i.e., change from alive to dead, and still be static, unless his death is central to the narrative. For instance, in Golding's *Lord of the Flies*, the boy with the mulberry birthmark apparently dies in a fire early in the novel. Momentous as any person's death is, this boy's death is not what the novel is about. However, when Simon is killed, and later Piggy, the narrative is directly impacted because the reason for their deaths is central to the novel's theme regarding man's innate evil. A dynamic character may change only slightly in his attitudes, but those changes may be the very ones upon which the narrative rests. For instance, Siddhartha begins as a very pure and devout Hindu but is unfulfilled spiritually. He eventually does achieve spiritual contentment, but his change is more a matter of degree than of substance. He is not an evil man who attains salvation, nor a pious man who becomes corrupt. It is the process of his search, the stages in his pilgrimage, which structure the novel *Siddhartha*.

We describe major characters or "actors" in novels as **protagonists** or **antagonists**. Built into those two terms is the Greek word **agon**, meaning "struggle." The *pro*tagonist struggles **toward** or for someone or something; the *ant(i)*agonist struggles **against** someone or something. The possible conflicts are usually cited as man against himself, man against man, man against society, man against nature. Sometimes more than one of these conflicts appears in a story, but usually one is dominant and is the structuring device.

A character can be referred to as **stock**, meaning that he exists because the plot demands it. For instance, a Western with a gunman who robs the bank will require a number of **stock** characters: the banker's lovely daughter, the tough but kindhearted barmaid, the cowardly white-shirted citizen who sells out the hero to save his own skin, and the young freckle-faced lad who shoots the bad guy from a second-story hotel window.

Or a character can be a **stereotype**, without individuating characteristics. For instance, a sheriff in a small Southern town; a football player who is all brawn; a librarian clucking over her prized books; the cruel commandant of a POW camp.

Characters often serve as **foils** for other characters, enabling us to see one or more of them better. A classic example is Tom Sawyer, the Romantic foil for Huck Finn's Realism. Or, in Lee's *To Kill a Mockingbird*, Scout as the naive observer of events which her brother Jem, four years older, comes to understand from the perspective of the adult world.

Sometimes characters are **allegorical**, standing for qualities or concepts rather than for actual personages. For instance, Jim Casey (initials "J. C.") in *The Grapes of Wrath* is often regarded as a Christ figure, pure and self-sacrificing in his aims for the migrant workers. Or Kamala, Siddhartha's teacher in the art of love, whose name comes from the tree whose bark is used as a purgative; she purges him of his ascetic ways on his road to self-hood and spiritual fulfillment.

Other characters are fully three-dimensional, "rounded," "mimetic" of humans in all their virtue, vice, hope, despair, strength and weakness. This verisimilitude aids the author in creating characters who are credible and plausible, without being dully predictable and mundane.

The interplay of plot and characters determines in large part the **theme** of a work, the **why?** of the story. First of all, we must distinguish between a mere topic and a genuine theme or thesis; and then between a theme and contributing *motifs*. A **topic** is a phrase, such as "man's inhumanity to man"; or "the fickle nature of fate." A **theme**, however, turns a phrase into a statement: "Man's inhumanity to man is barely concealed by 'civilization.'" Or "Man is a helpless pawn, at the mercy of fickle fate." Many writers may deal with the same topic, such as the complex nature of true love; but their themes may vary widely, from "True love will always win out in the end," to "Not even true love can survive the cruel ironies of fate."

To illustrate the relationship between plot, character, and theme, let's examine two familiar fairy tales. In "The Ugly Duckling," the structuring story line is "Once upon a time there was an ugly duckling, who in turn became a beautiful swan." In this case, the duckling did nothing to merit either his ugliness nor his eventual transformation; but he did not curse fate. He only wept and waited, lonely and outcast. And when he became beautiful, he did not gloat; he eagerly joined the other members of his flock, who greatly admired him. The theme here essentially is: "Good things come to him who waits," or "Life is unfair—you don't get what you deserve, nor deserve what you get"? What happens to the theme if the ugly duckling remains an ugly duckling: "Some guys just never get a break"?

Especially rewarding to examine for the interdependence of plot and theme is "Cinderella": "Once upon a time, a lovely, sweet-natured young girl was forced to labor for and serve her ugly and ungrateful stepmother and two stepsisters. But thanks to her fairy godmother, Cinderella and the Prince marry, and live happily ever after."

We could change events (plot elements) at any point, but let's take the penultimate scene where the Prince's men come to the door with the single glass slipper. Cinderella has been shut away so that she is not present when the other women in the house try on the slipper. Suppose that the stepmother or either of the two stepsisters tries on the slipper—and it fits! Cinderella is in the back room doing the laundry, and her family waltzes out the door to the palace and she doesn't even get an invitation to the wedding. And imagine the Prince's dismay when the ugly, one-slippered lady lifts her wedding veil for the consummating kiss! Theme: "There is no justice in the world, for those of low or high station"; or "Virtue is not its own reward"?

Or let's say that during the slipper-test scene, the stepsisters, stepmother, and finally Cinderella all try on the shoe, but to no avail. And then in sashays the Fairy Godmother, who gives them all a knowing smirk, puts out her slipper-sized foot and cackles hysterically, like the mechanical witch in the penny arcade. Theme: "You can't trust anybody these days"; or, a favorite statement of theme, "Appearances can be deceiving." The link between plot and theme is very strong, indeed.

Skilled writers often employ **motifs** to help unify their works. A motif is a detail or element of the story which is repeated throughout, and which may even become symbolic. Television shows are ready examples of the use of motifs. A medical show, with many scenes alternately set in the hospital waiting room and operating room, uses elements such as the pacing, anxious parent or loved one, the gradually filling ashtray, the large wall clock whose hands melt from one hour to another. And in the operating room, the half-masked surgeon whose brow is frequently mopped by the nurse; the gloved hand open-palmed to receive scalpel, sponge, and so on; the various oscilloscopes giving read-outs of the patient's very fragile condition; the expanding and collapsing bladder manifesting that the patient is indeed breathing; and, again, the wall clock, assuring us that this procedure is taking forever. These are all **motifs**, details which in concert help convince the reader that this story occurs in a hospital, and that the mood is pretty tense, that the medical team is doing all it can, and that Mom and Dad will be there when Junior or Sissy wakes up.

But motifs can become symbolic. The oscilloscope line quits blipping, levels out, and gives off the ominous hum. And the doctor's gloved hand sets down the scalpel and shuts off the oscilloscope. In the waiting room, Dad crushes the empty cigarette pack; Mom quits pacing and sinks into the sofa. The door to the waiting room swings shut silently behind the retreating doctor. All these elements signal "It's over, finished."

This example is very crude and mechanical, but motifs in the hands of a skillful writer are valuable devices. And in isolation, and often magnified, a single motif can become a controlling image with great significance. For instance, Emma Bovary's shoes signify her obsession with material things; and when her delicate slippers become soiled as she crosses the dewy grass to meet her lover, we sense the impurity of her act as well as its futility. Or when wise Piggy, in *Lord of the Flies,* is reduced to one lens in his specs, and finally to no specs at all, we see the loss of insight and wisdom on the island, and chaos follows.

Setting is the **where?** element of the story. But setting is also the **when** element: time of day, time of year, time period or year; it is the dramatic moment, the precise intersection of time and space when this story is being told. Setting is also the atmosphere: positive or negative ambiance, calm, chaotic, Gothic, Romantic. The question for the reader to answer is whether the setting is ultimately essential to the plot/theme, or whether it is incidental; i.e., could this story/theme have been told successfully in another time and/or place? For instance, could the theme in *Lord of the Flies* be made manifest if the boys were not on an island? Could they have been isolated in some other place? Does it matter whether the "war" which they are fleeing is WWII or WWIII or some other conflict, in terms of the theme?

Hopefully, the student will see that the four elements of plot, character, theme, and setting are intertwined and largely interdependent. A work must really be read as a whole, rather than dissected and analyzed in discrete segments.

The final question, **how?**, relates to an author's style. Style involves language (word choice), syntax (word order, sentence type and length), the balance between narration and dialogue, the choice of narrative voice (first person participant, third person with limited omniscience), use of descriptive passages, and other aspects of the actual words on the page which are basically irrelevant to the first four elements (plot, character, theme, and setting). Stylistic differences are fairly easy to spot among such diverse writers as Jane Austen, whose style is—to today's reader—very formal and mannered; Mark Twain, whose style is very casual and colloquial; William Faulkner, whose prose often spins on without punctuation or paragraphs far longer than the reader can hold either the thought or his breath; and Hemingway, whose dense but spare, pared-down style has earned the epithet, "Less is more."

READING SHORT STORIES

The modern short story differs from earlier short fiction such as the parable, fable, and tale, in its emphasis on character development through scenes rather than summary: through *showing* rather than *telling*. Gaining popularity in the 19th century, the short story generally was realistic, presenting detailed accounts of the lives of middle-class personages. This tendency toward realism dictates that the plot be grounded in *probability*, with causality fully in operation. Furthermore, the characters are human with recognizable human motivations, both social and psychological. Setting—time and place—is realistic rather than fantastic. And, as Poe stipulated, the elements of plot, character, setting, style, point of view, and theme all work toward a single *unified* effect.

However, some modern writers have stretched these boundaries and have mixed in elements of nonrealism—such as the supernatural and the fantastic—sometimes switching back and forth between realism and nonrealism, confusing the reader who is expecting conventional fiction. Barth's "Lost in the Funhouse" and Allen's "The Kugelmass Episode" are two stories which are not, strictly speaking, *realistic*. However, if the reader will approach and accept this type of story on its own terms, he will be better able to understand and appreciate them fully.

Unlike the novel, which has time and space to develop characters and interrelationships, the short story must rely on flashes of insight and revelation to develop plot and characters. The "slice of life" in a short story is of necessity much narrower than that in a novel; the time span is much shorter, the focus much tighter. To attempt anything like the panoramic canvas available to the novelist would be to view fireworks through a soda straw: occasionally pretty, but ultimately not very satisfying or enlightening.

The elements of the short story are those of the novel, discussed earlier. However, because of the compression of time and concentration of effect, probably the short story writer's most important decision is **point of view**. A narrator may be *objective*, presenting information without bias or comment. Hemingway frequently uses the objective *third-person* narrator, presenting scenes almost dramatically, i.e., with a great deal of dialogue and very little narrative, none of which directly reveals the thoughts or feelings of the characters. The third-person narrator may, however, be less objective in his presentation, directly revealing the thoughts and feelings, of one or more of the characters, as Chopin does in "The Story of an Hour." We say that such a narrator is fully or partially *omniscient*, depending on how complete his knowledge is of the characters' psychological and emotional makeup. The least objective narrator is the *first-person* narrator, who presents information from the perspective of a single character who is a participant in the action. Such a narrative choice allows the author to present the discrepancies between the writer's/reader's perceptions and those of the narrator.

One reason the choice of narrator, the point of view from which to tell the story, is immensely important in a short story is that the narrator reveals character and event in ways which affect our understanding of theme. For instance, in Faulkner's "A Rose for Emily," the unnamed narrator who seems to be a townsperson recounts the story out of chronological order, juxtaposing events whose causality and significance are uncertain. The narrator withholds information which would explain events being presented, letting the reader puzzle over Emily Grierson's motivations, a device common in detective fiction. In fact, the narrator presents contradictory information, making the reader alternately pity and resent the spinster. When we examine the imagery and conclude that Miss Emily and her house represent the decay and decadence of the Old South which resisted the invasion of "progress" from the North, we see the importance of setting and symbol in relation to theme.

Similarly, in Mansfield's "Bliss," the abundant description of setting creates the controlling image of the lovely pear tree. But this symbol of fecundity becomes ironic when Bertha Young belatedly feels sincere and overwhelming desire for her husband. The third-person narrator's omniscience is limited to Bertha's thoughts and feelings; otherwise we would have seen her husband's infidelity with Miss Fulton.

In O'Connor's "Good Country People," the narrator is broadly omniscient, but the reader is still taken by surprise at the cruelty of the Bible salesman who seduces Joy-Hulga. That he steals her artificial leg is perhaps poetic justice, since she (with her numerous degrees) had fully intended to seduce him ("just good country people"). The story's title, the characters' names—Hopewell, Freeman, Joy; the salesman's professed Christianity, the Bibles hollowed out to hold whiskey and condoms, add to the irony of Mrs. Freeman's final comment on the young man: "Some can't be that simple... I know I never could."

The *initiation story* frequently employs the first-person narrator. To demonstrate the subtle differences which can occur in stories which ostensibly have the same point of view and general theme, let's look at three: "A Christmas Memory" (Capote), "Araby" (Joyce), and "A & P" (Updike).

Early in "A Christmas Memory," Capote's narrator identifies himself:

The person to whom she is speaking is myself. I am seven; she is sixty-something. We are cousins, very distant ones, and we have lived together—well, as long as I can remember. Other people inhabit the house, relatives; and though they have power over us, and frequently make us cry, we are not, on the whole, too much aware of them. We are each other's best friend. She calls me Buddy, in memory of a boy who was formerly her best friend. The other Buddy died in the 1880's, when she was still a child. She is still a child.

Buddy and his cousin, who is called only "my friend," save their meager earnings throughout the year in order to make fruitcakes at Christmas to give mainly to "persons we've met maybe once, perhaps not at all... Like President Roosevelt.... Or Abner Packer, the driver of the six o'clock bus from Mobile, who exchanges waves with us everyday...." Their gifts to one another each year are always handmade, often duplicates of the year before, like the kites they present on what was to be their last Christmas together.

Away at boarding school, when Buddy receives word of his friend's death, it "merely confirms a piece of news some secret vein had already received, severing from me an irreplaceable part of myself, letting it loose like a kite on a broken string. That is why, walking across a school campus on this particular December morning, I keep searching the sky. As if I expected to see, rather like hearts, a lost pair of kites hurrying toward heaven."

Buddy's characterizations of his friend are also self-revelatory. He and she are peers, equals, despite their vast age difference. They are both totally unselfish, joying in the simple activities mandated by their economic circumstances. They are both "children."

The story is told in present tense, making the memories from the first paragraphs seem as "real" and immediate as those from many years later. And Buddy's responses from the early years ("Well, I'm disappointed. Who wouldn't be? With socks, a Sunday school shirt, some handkerchiefs, a hand-me-down sweater and a year's subscription to a religious magazine for children. *The Little Shepherd*. It makes me boil. It really does.") are as true to his seven-year-old's perspective, as are those when he, much older, has left home ("I have a new home too. But it doesn't count. Home is where my friend is, and there I never go.").

The youthful narrator in "A & P" also uses present tense, but not consistently, which gives his narrative a very colloquial, even unschooled flavor. Like Buddy, Sammy identifies himself in the opening paragraph: "In walks these three girls in nothing but bathing suits. I'm in the third checkout slot, with my back to the door, so I don't see them until they're over by the bread." And later, "Stokesie's married, with two babies chalked up on his fuselage already, but as far as I can tell that's the only difference. He's twenty-two, and I was nineteen this April." The girls incur the wrath of the store manager, who scolds them for their inappropriate dress. And Sammy, in his adolescent idealism, quits on the spot; although he realizes that he does not want to "do this" to his parents, he tells us "... it seems to me that once you begin a gesture it's fatal not to go through with it." But his *beau geste* is ill-spent: "I look around for my girls, but they're gone, of course.... I could see Lengel in my place in the slot, checking the sheep through. His face was dark gray and his back stiff, as if he'd just had an injection of iron, and my stomach kind of fell as I felt how hard the world was going to be to me hereafter."

Like Buddy, Sammy tells his story from a perch not too distant from the events he recounts. Both narrators still feel the immediacy of their rites of passage very strongly. Buddy, however, reveals himself to be a more admirable character, perhaps because his story occurs mainly when he is seven—children tend not to be reckless in the way that Sammy is. Sammy was performing for an audience, doing things he knew would cause pain to himself and his family, for the sake of those three girls who never gave him the slightest encouragement and whom he would probably never even see again.

In "Araby," the unnamed narrator tells of a boyhood crush he had on the older sister of one of his chums: "I thought little of the future. I did not know whether I would ever speak to her or not or, if I spoke to her, how I could tell her of my confused adoration. But my body was like a harp and her words and gestures were like fingers running upon the wires." She asks the boy if he is going to Araby, a "splendid bazaar," and reveals that she cannot. He promises to go himself and bring her something. But his uncle's late homecoming delays the boy's excursion until the bazaar is nearly closed for the night, and he is unable to find an appropriate gift. Forlornly, "I turned away slowly and walked down the middle of the bazaar.... Gazing up into the darkness I saw myself as a creature driven and derided by vanity; and my eyes burned with anguish and anger." This narrator is recounting his story from much further away than either Buddy or Sammy tells his own. The narrator of "Araby" has the perspective of an adult, looking back at a very important event in his boyhood. His "voice" reflects wisdom born of experience. The incident was very painful then; but its memory, while poignant, is no longer devastating. Like Sammy, this narrator sees the dichotomy between his adolescent idealism and the mundane reality of "romance." However, the difference is in the narrator's ability to turn the light on himself; Sammy is still so close to the incident that he very likely would whip off his checker's apron again if the girls returned to the A & P. The "Araby" narrator has "mellowed," and can see the futility—and the necessity—of adolescent love.

READING ESSAYS

Essays fall into four rough categories: **speculative**, **argumentative**, **narrative**, and **expository**. Depending on the writer's purpose, his essay will fit more or less into one or these groupings.

The **speculative** essay is so named because, as its Latin root suggests, it *looks* at ideas; explores them rather than explains them. While the speculative essay may be said to be *meditative*, it often makes one or more points. But the thesis may not be as obvious or clear-cut as that in an expository or argumentative essay. The writer deals with ideas in an associative manner, playing with ideas in a looser structure than he would in an expository or argumentative essay. This "flow" may even produce *intercalary* paragraphs, which present alternately a narrative of sorts and thoughtful responses to the events being recounted, as in White's "The Ring of Time."

The purposes of the **argumentative** essay, on the other hand, are always clear: to present a point and provide evidence, which may be factual or anecdotal, and to support it. The structure is usually very formal, as in a debate, with counterpositions and counterarguments. Whatever the organizational pattern, the writer's intent in an argumentative essay is to persuade his reader of the validity of some claim, as Bacon does in "Of Love."

Narrative and **expository** essays have elements of both the speculative and argumentative modes. The narrative essay may recount an incident or a series of incidents and is almost always autobiographical, in order to make a point, as in Orwell's "Shooting an Elephant." The informality of the storytelling makes the narrative essay less insistent than the argumentative essay, but more directed than the speculative essay.

Students are probably most familiar with the **expository** essay, the primary purpose of which is to explain and clarify ideas. While the expository essay may have narrative elements, that aspect is minor and subservient to that of explanation. Furthermore, while nearly all essays have some element of persuasion, argumentation is incidental in the expository essay. In any event, the four categories—speculative, argumentative, narrative, and expository—are neither exhaustive nor mutually exclusive.

As non-fiction, essays have a different set of elements from novels and short stories: **voice**, **style**, **structure**, and **thought**.

Voice in non-fiction is similar to the narrator's tone in fiction; but the major difference is in who is "speaking." In fiction, the author is not the speaker—the **narrator** is the speaker. Students sometimes have difficulty with this distinction, but it is necessary if we are to preserve the integrity of the fictive "story." In an essay, however, the author speaks directly to the reader, even if he is presenting ideas which he may not actually espouse personally—as in a satire. This directness creates the writer's **tone**, his attitude toward his subject.

Style in non-fiction derives from the same elements as style in fiction: word choice, syntax, balance between dialogue and narration, voice, use of description—those things specifically related to words on the page. Generally speaking, an argumentative essay will be written in a more formal style than will a narrative essay, and a meditative essay will be less formal than an expository essay. But such generalizations are only descriptive, not prescriptive.

Structure and **thought**, the final elements of essays, are so intertwined as to be inextricable. We must be aware that to change the structure of an essay will alter its meaning. For instance, in White's "The Ring of Time," to abandon the *intercalary* paragraph organization, separating the paragraphs which narrate the scenes with the young circus rider from those which reflect on the circularity and linearity of time, would alter our understanding of the essay's thesis. Writers signal structural shifts with alterations in focus, as well as with visual clues (spacing), verbal clues—(*but, therefore, however*), or shifts in the kind of information being presented (personal, scientific, etc).

Thought is perhaps the single element which most distinguishes non-fiction from fiction. The essayist chooses his form not to tell a story but to present an idea. Whether he chooses the speculative, narrative, argumentative, or expository format, the essayist has something on his mind that he wants to convey to his readers. And it is this idea which we are after when we analyze his essay.

Often anthologized is Orwell's "Shooting an Elephant," a narrative essay recounting the writer's (presumably) experience in Burma as an officer of the British law that ruled the poverty-ridden people of a small town. Orwell begins with two paragraphs which explain that, as a white, European authority figure, he was subjected to taunts and abuse by the natives. Ironically, he sympathized with the Burmese and harbored fairly strong anti-British feelings, regarding the imperialists as the oppressors rather than the saviors. He tells us that he felt caught, trapped between his position of authority which he himself resented, and the hatred of those he was required to oversee.

The body of the essay—some eleven paragraphs—relates the incident with an otherwise tame elephant gone "must" which had brought chaos and destruction to the village. Only occasionally does Orwell interrupt the narrative to reveal his reactions directly, but his descriptions of the Burmese are sympathetically drawn. The language is heavily connotative, revealing the helplessness of the villagers against both the elephant and the miserable circumstances of their lives.

Orwell recounts how, having sent for an elephant gun, he found that he was compelled to shoot the animal, even though its destruction was by now unwarranted and even ill-advised, given the value of the elephant to the village. But the people expected it, demanded it; the white man realized that he did not have dominion over these people of color after all. They were in charge, not he.

To make matters worse, Orwell bungles the "murder" of the beast, which takes half an hour to die in great agony. And in the aftermath of discussions of the rightness or wrongness of his action, Orwell wonders if anyone realizes he killed the elephant only to save face. It is the final sentence of the final paragraph which directly reveals the author's feelings, although he has made numerous indirect references to them throughout the essay. Coupled with the opening paragraphs, this conclusion presents British imperialism of the period in a very negative light: "the unable doing the unnecessary to the ungrateful."

Having discovered Orwell's main idea, we must look at the other elements (voice, style, structure) to see *how* he communicates it to the reader. The voice of the first-person narrative is fairly formal, yet remarkably candid, using connotation to color our perception of the events. Orwell's narrative has many complex sentences, with vivid descriptive phrases in series, drawing our eye along the landscape and through the crowds as he ponders his next move. Structurally, the essay first presents a premise about British imperialism, then moves to a gripping account of the officer's reluctant shooting of the elephant; and ends with an admission of his own culpability as an agent of the institution he detests. Orwell frequently signals shifts between his role as officer and his responses as a humane personage with *but*, or with dashes to set off his responses to the events he is recounting.

READING SATIRE

Satire, is a *mode* which may be employed by writers of various genres: poetry, drama, fiction, non-fiction. It is more a perspective than a product.

Satire mainly exposes and ridicules, derides and denounces vice, folly, evil, stupidity, as these qualities manifest themselves in persons, groups of persons, ideas, institutions, customs, or beliefs. While the satirist has many techniques at his disposal, there are basically only two types of satire: gentle or harsh, depending on the author's intent, his audience, and his methods.

The terms *romanticism*, *realism*, and *naturalism* can help us understand the role of *satire*. Romanticism sees the world idealistically, as perfectible if not perfect. Realism sees the world as it is, with healthy doses of both good and bad. Naturalism sees the world as imperfect, with evil often triumphing over good. The satirist is closer to the naturalist than he is to the romantic or realist, for both the satirist and the naturalist focus on what is wrong with the world, intending to expose the foibles of man and his society. The difference between them lies in their techniques. The naturalist is very direct and does not necessarily employ humor; the satirist is more subtle, and does.

For instance, people plagued with overpopulation and starvation is not, on first glance, material for humor. Many works have treated such conditions with sensitivity, bringing attention to the plight of the world's unfortunate. Steinbeck's *Grapes of Wrath* is such a work. However, Swift's "A Modest Proposal" takes essentially the same circumstances and holds them up for our amused examination. How does the satirist make an un-funny topic humorous? And why would he do so?

The satirist's techniques—his weapons—include **irony, parody, reversal** or **inversion, hyperbole, understatement, sarcasm, wit, invective**. By exaggerating characteristics, by saying the opposite of what he means, by using his cleverness to make cutting or even cruel remarks at the expense of his subject, the writer of satire can call the reader's attention to those things he believes are repulsive, despicable, or destructive.

Whether he uses more harsh (Juvenalian) or more gentle (Horatian) satire depends upon the writer's attitude and intent. Is he merely flaunting his clever intellect, playing with words for our amusement or to inflate his own sense of superiority? Is he probing the psychological motivations for the foolish or destructive actions of some person(s)? Is he determined to waken an unenlightened or apathetic audience, moving its members to thought or action? Are the flaws which the satirist is pointing out truly destructive or evil, or are they the faults we would all recognize in ourselves if we glanced in the mirror, not admirable but not really harmful to ourselves or society? Is the author amused, sympathetic, objective, irritated, scornful, bitter, pessimistic, mocking? The reader needs to identify the satirist's purpose and tone. Its subtlety sometimes makes satire a difficult mode to detect and to understand.

Irony is perhaps the satirist's most powerful weapon. The basis of irony is inversion or reversal, doing or saying the opposite or the unexpected. Shakespeare's famous sonnet beginning "My mistress' eyes are nothing like the sun..." is an ironic tribute to the speaker's beloved, who, he finally declares is "as rare/As any she belied with false compare." At the same time, Shakespeare is poking fun at the sonnet form as it was used by his contemporaries—himself included—to extol the virtues of their ladies. By selecting a woman who, by his own description, is physically unattractive in every way imaginable, and using the conventions of the love sonnet to present her many flaws, he has inverted the sonnet tradition. And then by asserting that she compares favorably with any of the other ladies whose poet-lovers have lied about their virtues, he presents us with the unexpected twist. Thus, he satirizes both the love sonnet form and its subject by using irony.

Other notable poetic satires include Koch's "Variations on a Theme by William Carlos Williams," in which he parodies Williams "This is Just to Say." Koch focuses on the simplicity and directness of Williams' imagery and makes the form and ideas seem foolish and trivial. In "Boom!," Nemerov takes issue with a pastor's assertion that modern technology has resulted in a concomitant rise in religious activities and spiritual values. Nemerov catalogues the instant, disposable, and extravagant aspects of Americans' lifestyles, which result in "pray as you go... pilgrims" for whom religion is another convenience, commercial rather than spiritual.

Satire in drama is also common; Wilde's "The Importance of Being Earnest" is wonderfully funny in its constant word play (notably on the name *Ernest*) and its relentless ridiculing of the superficiality which Wilde saw as characteristic of British gentry. Barrie's "The Admirable Chrichton" has a similar theme, with the added assertion that it is the "lower" or servant class which is truly superior— again, the ironic reversal so common in satire. Both of these plays are mild in their ridicule; the authors do not expect or desire any change in society or in the viewer. The satire is gentle; the satirists are amused, or perhaps bemused at the society whose foibles they expose.

Classic novels which employ satire include Swift's *Gulliver's Travels* and Voltaire's *Candide*, both of which fairly vigorously attack aspects of the religions, governments, and prevailing intellectual beliefs of their respective societies. A modern novel which uses satire is Heller's *Catch-22*, which is basically an attack on war and the government's bureaucratic bungling of men and materiel, specifically in WWII. But by extension, Heller is also viewing with contempt the unmotivated, illogical, capricious behavior of all institutions which operate by that basic law: "catch-22." Like Swift and Voltaire, Heller is angry. And although his work, like the other two, has humor and wit, exaggeration and irony, his purpose is more than intellectual entertainment for his readers. Heller hopes for reform.

Heller's attack is frontal, his assault direct. Swift had to couch his tale in a fantastic setting with imaginary creatures in order to present his views with impunity. The audience, as well as the times, also affect the satirist's work. If the audience is hostile, the writer must veil his theme; if the audience is indifferent, he must jolt them with bitter and reviling language if he desires change. If he does not fear reprisals, the satirist may take any tone he pleases.

We can see satire in operation in two adaptations of the biblical story of King Solomon, who settled the dispute between two mothers regarding an infant: Cut the baby in two and divide it between you, he told them. The rightful mother protested, and was promptly awarded the child. The story is meant to attest to the King's wisdom and understanding of parental love, in this case.

However, Twain's Huck Finn has some difficulty persuading runaway slave Jim that Solomon was wise. Jim insists that Solomon, having fathered "'bout five million chillen," was "waseful.... *He* as soon chop a chile in two as a cat. Dey's plenty mo'. A chile er two, mo' er less, warn't no consekens to Solermun, dad fetch him!" Twain is ridiculing not only Jim's ingenuousness, as he does throughout the novel; he is also deflating time-honored beliefs about the Bible and its traditional heroes, as he earlier does with the account of Moses and the "bulrushers." While Twain's tone is fairly mild, his intent shows through as serious; Twain was disgusted with traditional Christianity and its hypocritical followers, as we see later in *Huck Finn* when young Buck Grangerford is murdered in the feud with the Shepherdsons: "I wished I hadn't ever come ashore that night to see such things."

A second satiric variation on the Solomon theme appears in Asprin's *Myth Adventures*, in the volume *Hit or Myth*. Skeeve, the narrator, realizes that he, as King pro-tem, must render a decision regarding the ownership of a cat. Hoping to inspire them to compromise, he decrees that they divide the cat between them: "Instead they thanked me for my wisdom, shook hands, and left smiling, presumably to carve up their cat." He concludes that many of the citizens of this realm "don't have both oars in the water," a conclusion very like Huck's: "I never see such a nigger. If he got a notion in his head once, there warn't no getting it out again." The citizens' unthinking acceptance of the infallibility of authority is as laughable as Jim's out-of-hand rejection of Solomon's wisdom because no wise man would "want to live in the mids' er sich a blim-blammin' all de time" as would prevail in the harem with the King's "million wives."

CHAPTER 2

POETRY

Opening a book to study for an examination is perhaps the worst occasion on which to read poetry, or about poetry, because above all, poetry should be enjoyed; it is definitely "reading for pleasure." This last phrase seems to have developed recently to describe the reading we do other than for information or for study. Perhaps you personally would not choose poetry as pleasure reading because of the bad name poetry has received over the years. Some students regard the "old" poetry such as Donne's or Shelley's as effete (for "wimps" and "nerds" only, in current language), or modern poetry as too difficult or weird. It is hard to imagine that poetry was the "current language" for students growing up in the Elizabethan or Romantic eras. Whereas in our world information can be retrieved in a nano-second, in those worlds time was plentiful to sit down, clear the mind and let poetry take over. Very often the meaning of a poem does not come across in a nanosecond and for the modern student this proves very frustrating. Sometimes it takes years for a poem to take on meaning—the reader simply knows that the poem sounds good and it provokes an emotional response that cannot be explained. With time, more emotional experience, more reading of similar experiences, more life, the reader comes to a meaning of that poem that satisfies for the time being. In a few more years that poem may take on a whole new meaning.

This is all very well for reading for pleasure but you are now called upon, in your present experience, to learn poetry for an important examination. Perhaps the first step in the learning process is to answer the question, "Why do people write poetry?" An easy answer is that they wish to convey an experience, an emotion, an insight, or an observation in a startling or satisfying way, one that remains in the memory for years. But why not use a straightforward sentence or paragraph? Why wrap up that valuable insight in fancy words, rhyme, paradox, meter, allusion, symbolism and all the other seeming mumbo-jumbo that explicators of poetry use? Why not just come right out and say it like "normal people" do? An easy answer to these questions is that poetry is not a vehicle for conveying meaning alone. Gerard Manley Hopkins, one of the great innovators of rhythm in poetry, claimed that poetry should be "heard for its own sake and interest even over and above its interest or meaning." Poetry provides intellectual stimulus of course, one of the best ways of studying a poem is to consider it a jigsaw puzzle presented to you whole, an integral work of art, which can be taken apart piece by piece (word by word), analyzed scientifically, labelled, and put back together again into a whole, and then the meaning is complete. But people write poetry to convey more than meaning.

T.S. Eliot maintained that the meaning of the poem existed purely to distract us "while the poem did its work." One interpretation of a poem's "work" is that it changes us in some way. We see the world in a new way because of the way the poet has seen it and told us about it. Maybe one of the reasons people write poetry is to encourage us to *see* things in the first place. Simple things like daffodils take on a whole new aspect when we read the way Wordsworth saw them. Why did Wordsworth write that poem? His sister had written an excellent account of the scene in her journal. Wordsworth not only evokes nature as we have never seen it before, alive, joyous, exuberant, he shows nature's healing powers, its restorative quality as the scene flashes "upon that inward eye/Which is the bliss of solitude." Bent over your books studying, how many times has a similar quality of nature's power in the memory come to you? Maybe for you a summer beach scene rather than daffodils by the lake is more meaningful, but the poet captures a moment that we have all experienced. The poet's magic is to make that moment new again.

If poets enhance our power of sight they also awaken the other senses as powerfully. We can hear Emily Dickinson's snake in the repeated "s" sound of the lines:

His notice sudden is—
The Grass divides as with a Comb—
A spotted shaft is seen—

and because of the very present sense of sound, we experience the indrawn gasp of breath of fear when the snake appears. We can touch the little chimneysweep's hair "that curled like a lamb's back" in William Blake's poetry and because of that tactile sense we are even more shocked to read that the child's hair is all shaved off so that the soot will not spoil its whiteness. We can smell the poison gas as Wilfred Owen's soldiers fumble with their gas masks; we can taste the blood gurgling in the poisoned lungs.

Poets write, then, to awaken the senses. They have crucial ideas but the words they use are often more important than the meaning. More important still than ideas and sense awakening is the poet's appeal to the emotions. And it is precisely this area that disturbs a number of students. Our modern society tends to block out emotions—we need reviews to tell us if we enjoyed a film, a critic's praise to see if a play or novel is worth our time. We hesitate to laugh at something in case it is not the "in" thing to do. We certainly do not cry—at least in front of others. Poets write to overcome that blocking (very often it is their own blocking of emotion they seek to alleviate), but that is not to say that poetry immediately sets us laughing, crying, loving, hating. The important fact about the emotional release in poetry is that poets help us explore our own emotions, sometimes by shocking us, sometimes by drawing attention to balance and pattern, sometimes by cautioning us to move carefully in this inner world.

Poets tell us nothing really new. They tell us old truths about human emotions that we begin to restructure anew, to reread our experiences in light of theirs, to reevaluate our world view. Whereas a car manual helps us understand the workings of a particular vehicle, a poem helps us understand the inner workings of human beings. Poets frequently write to help their emotional life—the writing then becomes cathartic, purging or cleansing the inner life, feeding that part of us that separates us from the animal. Many poets might paraphrase Byron, who claimed that he had to write or go mad. Writer and reader of poetry enter into a collusion, each helping the other to find significance in the human world, to find safety in a seemingly alien world.

This last point brings any reader of poetry to ask the next question: Why read poetry? One might contend that a good drama, novel or short story might provide the same emotional experience. But a poem is much more accessible. Apart from the fact that poems are shorter than other genres, there is a unique directness to them which hinges purely on language. Poets can say in one or two lines what may take novelists and playwrights entire works to express. For example, Keats' lines—

Beauty is truth, truth beauty,—that is all
Ye know on earth, and all ye need to know—

studied, pondered, open to each reader's interpretations, linger in the memory with more emphasis than George Eliot's *Middlemarch*, or Ibsen's *The Wild Duck*, which endeavor to make the same point.

In your reading of poems remember that poetry is perhaps the oldest art and yet surrounds us without our even realizing it. Listeners thrilled to Homer's poetry; tribes chanted invocations to their gods; today we listen to pop-song lyrics and find ourselves, sometimes despite ourselves, repeating certain rhythmic lines. Advertisements we chuckle over or say we hate have a way of repeating themselves as we use the catchy phrase or snappy repetition. Both lyricists and advertisers cleverly use language, playing on the reader's/listener's/watcher's ability to pick up on a repeated sound or engaging rhythm or inner rhyme. Think of a time as a child when you thoroughly enjoyed poetry: nursery rhymes, ball-game rhythms, jump-rope patterns. Probably you had no idea of the meaning of the words ("Little Miss Muffet sat on a tuffet..." a tuffet?!) but you responded to the sound, the pattern. As adults we read poetry for that sense of sound and pattern. With more experience at reading poetry there is an added sense of pleasure as techniques are recognized: alliteration, onomatopoeia; forms of poetry become obvious—the sonnet, the rondelle. Even greater enjoyment comes from watching a poet's development, tracing themes and ideas, analyzing maturity in growth of imagery, use of rhythm.

To the novice reader of poetry, a poem can speak to the reader at a particular time and become an experience in itself. A freshman's experience after her mother's death exemplifies this. Shortly after the death, the student found Elizabeth Jenning's poem "Happy Families." Using the familiar names of the cards, Mrs. Beef and Master Bun, the poet describes how strangers try to help the family carry on their lives normally although one of the "happy family" is "missing." The card game continues although no one wants it to. At the end the players go back to their individual rooms and give way to their individual grief. The student described the relief at knowing that someone else had obviously experienced her situation where everyone in the family was putting up a front, strangers were being very kind, and a general emptiness prevailed because of that one missing family member. The poem satisfied. The student saw death through another's eyes; the experience was almost the same, yet helped the reader to reevaluate, to view a universal human response to grief as well as encourage her to deal with her own.

On reading a poem the brain works on several different levels: it responds to the sounds; it responds to the words themselves and their connotations; it responds to the emotions; it responds to the insights or learning of the world being revealed. For such a process poetry is a very good training ground—a boot camp—for learning how to read literature in general. All the other genres have elements of poetry within them. Learn to read poetry well and you will be a more accomplished reader, even of car manuals! Perhaps the best response to reading poetry comes from a poet herself, Emily Dickinson, who claimed that reading a book of poetry made her feel "as if the top of [her] head were taken off!"

Before such a process happens to you, here are some tips for reading poetry before and during the examination.

Before the exam

1) Make a list of poets and poems you remember; analyze poems you liked, disliked, loved, hated, and were indifferent to. Find the poems. Reread them and for each one analyze your *feelings*, first of all, about the poetry itself. Have your feelings changed? Now what do you like or hate? Then paraphrase the *meaning* of each poem. Notice how the "magic" goes from the poem, i.e., "To Daffodils:" the poet sees many daffodils by the side of a lake and then thinks how the sight of them later comforts him.

2) Choose a poem at random from an anthology or one mentioned in this introduction. Read it a couple of times, preferably aloud, because the speaking voice will automatically grasp the rhythm and that will help the meaning. Do not become bogged-down in individual word connotation or the meaning of the poem—let the poetry do its "work" on you; absorb the poem as a whole jigsaw puzzle.

3) Now take the puzzle apart. Look carefully at the title. Sometimes a straightforward title helps you focus. Sometimes a playful title helps you get an angle on the meaning. "Happy Families," of course, is an ironic title because the family playing the card game of that name is not happy.

4) Look carefully at the punctuation. Does the sense of a line carry from one to

another? Does a particular mark of punctuation strike you as odd? Ask why that mark was used.

5) Look carefully at the words. Try to find the meaning of words with which you are not familiar within the context. Familiar words may be used differently: ask why that particular use. Having tapped into your memory bank of vocabulary and you are still at a loss, go to a dictionary. Once you have the *denotation* of the word, start wondering about the *connotation*. Put yourself in the poet's position and think why that word was used.

6) Look carefully at all the techniques being used. You will gain these as you progress through this section and through the test preparation. As soon as you come across a new idea—"caesura" perhaps—learn the word, see how it applies to poetry, where it is used. Be on the lookout for it in other poetry. Ask yourself questions such as why the poet used alliteration here; why the rhythm changes there; why the poet uses a sonnet form and which sonnet form is in use. Forcing yourself to ask the WHY questions, and answering them, will train the brain to read more perceptively. Poetry is not accidental; poets are deliberate people; they do things for specific reasons. Your task under a learning situation is to discover WHY.

7) Look carefully at the speaker. Is the poet using another persona? Who is that persona? What is revealed about the speaker? Why use that particular voice?

8) Start putting all the pieces of the puzzle together. The rhythm helps the meaning. The word choice helps the imagery. The imagery adds to the meaning. Paraphrase the meaning. Ask yourself simple questions: What is the poet saying? How can I relate to what is being said? What does this poet mean to me? What does this poem contribute to human experience?

9) Find time to read about the great names in poetry. Locate people within time areas and analyze what those times entailed. For example, the Elizabethans saw a contest between secular love and love of God. The Romantics (Wordsworth, Coleridge, Keats, Shelley, Byron) loved nature and saw God within nature. The Victorians (Tennyson, Blake) saw nature as a threat to mankind and God, being replaced by the profit cash-nexus of the Industrial Age. The moderns (T.S. Eliot, Pound, Yeats) see God as dead and man as hollow, unwanted and unsafe in an alien world. The Post-Moderns see life as "an accident," a comic/cosmic joke, fragmented, purposeless—often their topics will be political: apartheid, abortion, unjust imprisonment.

10) Write a poem of your own. Choose a particular style; use the sonnet form; parody a famous poem; express yourself in free verse on a crucial, personal aspect of your life. Then analyze your own poetry with the above ideas.

During the exam

You will have established a routine for reading poetry, but now you are under pressure, must work quickly, and will have no access to a dictionary. You cannot read aloud but you can:

1) Internalize the reading—hear the reading in your head. Read through the poem two or three times following the absorbing procedure.

2) If the title and poet are supplied, analyze the title as before and determine the era of the poetry. Often this pushes you toward the meaning.

3) Look carefully at the questions which should enable you to be able to "tap into" your learning process. Answer the ones that are immediately clear to you: form, technique, language perhaps.

4) Go back for another reading for those questions that challenge you—theme or meaning perhaps—analyze the speaker or the voice at work— paraphrase the meaning—ask the simple question "What is the poet saying?"

5) If a question asks you about a specific line, metaphor, opening or closing lines, highlight or underline them to force your awareness of each crucial word. Internalize another reading emphasizing the highlighted area—analyze again the options you have for your answers.

6) Do not waste time on an answer that eludes you. Move onto another section and let the poetry do its "work." Very often the brain will continue working on the problem on another level of consciousness. When you go back to the difficult question, it may well become clear.

7) If you still are not sure of the answer, choose the option that you *feel* is the closest to correct.

Go home, relax, forget about the examination—read your favorite poem!

VERSE and METER

As children reading or learning poetry in school, we referred to each section of a poem as a verse. We complained we had ten verses to learn for homework. In fact the word **verse** strictly refers to a line of poetry, perhaps from the original Latin word "versus": a row or a line, and the notion of turning, "vertere," to turn or move to a new idea. In modern use we refer to poetry often as "verse" with the connotation of rhyme, rhythm and meter but we still recognize verse because of the positioning of lines on the page, the breaking of lines that distinguish verse from prose.

The verses we learned for homework are in fact known as **stanzas:** a grouping of lines with a metrical order and often a repeated rhyme which we know as the **rhyme scheme.** Such a scheme is shown by letters to show the repeating sounds. Byron's "Stanzas" will help you recall the word, see the use of a definite rhyme and how to mark it:

"Stanzas"

(When a man hath no freedom to fight for at home)

When a man hath no freedom to fight for at home,	*a*
Let him combat for that of his neighbors;	*b*
Let him think of the glories of Greece and of Rome,	*a*
And get knocked on the head for his labors.	*b*
To do good to mankind is the chivalrous plan,	*c*
And is always as nobly requited;	*d*
Then battle for freedom wherever you can,	*c*
And, if not shot or hanged, you'll get knighted.	*d*

The rhyme scheme is simple: *abab* and your first question should be "Why such a simple, almost sing-song rhyme?" The simplicity reinforces the **tone** of the poem: sarcastic, cryptic, cynical. There is almost a sneer behind the words "And get knocked on his head for his labors." It is as if the poet sets out to give a lecture or at least a homily along the lines of: "Neither a lender nor a borrower be," but then undercuts the seriousness. The **irony** of the poem rests in the fact that Byron joined a freedom fighting group in Greece and died, not gloriously, but of a fever. We shall return to this poem for further discussion.

Certain types of rhyme are worth learning. The most common is the **end rhyme,** which has the rhyming word at the end of the line, bringing the line to a definite stop but setting up for a rhyming word in another line later on, as in "Stanzas": home… Rome, a perfect rhyme. **Internal rhyme** includes at least one rhyming word within the line, often for the purpose of speeding the rhythm or making it linger. Look at the effect of Byron's internal rhymes mixed with half-rhymes: "combat… for that"; "Can/And… hanged" slowing the rhythm, making the reader dwell on the harsh long "a" sound, prolonging the sneer which almost becomes a snarl of anger. **Slant rhyme**, sometimes referred to as half, off, near or approximate rhyme, often jolts a reader who expects a perfect rhyme; poets thus use such a rhyme to express disappointment or a deliberate let-down. **Masculine rhyme** uses one-syllable words or stresses the final syllable of polysyllabic words, giving the feeling of strength and impact. **Feminine rhyme** uses a rhyme of two or more syllables, the stress not falling upon the last syllable, giving a feeling of softness and lightness, one can see that these terms for rhyme were written in a less enlightened age! The terms themselves for the rhymes are less important than realizing or at least appreciating the effects of the rhymes.

If the lines from "Stanzas" had been unrhymed and varying in metrical pattern, the verse would have been termed **free**, or to use the French term, *"Vers libre,"* not to be confused with **blank verse**, which is also unrhymed but has a strict rhythm. The Elizabethan poets Wyatt and Surrey introduced blank verse, which Shakespeare uses to such good effect in his plays, and later, Milton in the great English epic, *Paradise Lost*. Free verse has become associated with "modern" poetry, often adding to its so-called obscurity because without rhyme and rhythm, poets often resort to complicated syntactical patterns, repeated phrases, awkward cadences and parallelism. Robert Frost preferred not to use it because, as he put it, "Writing free verse is like playing tennis with the net down," suggesting that free verse is easier than rhymed and metrical. However, if you have ever tried writing such verse, you will know the problems. (Perhaps a good exercise after your learning about meter is to write some "free" verse.) T.S. Eliot, who uses the form most effectively in "The Journey of the Magi," claimed that no *"vers"* is *"libre"* for the poet who wanted to do a good job.

Such a claim for the artistry and hard work behind a poem introduces perhaps the most difficult of the skills for a poet to practice and a reader to learn: meter. This time the Greeks provide the meaning of the word from *"metron,"* meaning measure. **Meter** simply means the pattern or measure of stressed or accented words within a line of verse. When studying meter a student should note where stresses fall on syllables—that is why reading aloud is so important, because it catches the natural rhythm of the speaking voice—and if an absence of stressed syllables occurs there is always an explanation why. We "expect" stressed and unstressed syllables because that is what we use in everyday speech. We may stress one syllable over another for a certain effect, often using the definite article "THE well known author..." or the preposition "Get OUT of here!" Usually, however, we use a rising and falling rhythm, known as **iambic rhythm**. A line of poetry that alternates stressed and unstressed syllables is said to have **iambic meter**. A line of poetry with ten syllables of rising and falling stresses is known as **iambic pentameter**, best used by Shakespeare and Milton in their blank verse. The basic measuring unit in a line of poetry is called a **foot**. An **iambic foot** has one unstressed syllable followed by a stressed marked by ◡ ╱. Pentameter means "five-measure." Therefore **iambic pentameter** has five groups of two syllables, or ten beats, to the line. Read aloud the second and fourth, sixth and eighth lines of "Stanzas," tapping the beat on your desk or your palm, and the ten beat becomes obvious. Read again with the stresses unstressed and stressed (or soft and loud, short or long, depending on what terminology works for you) and the iambic foot becomes clear .

Tapping out the other alternate lines in this poem you will not find ten beats but twelve. The term for this line is **hexameter**, or six feet, rather than five. Other line-length names worth learning are:

monometer	one foot	**dimeter**	two feet
trimeter	three feet	**tetrameter**	four feet
heptameter	seven feet	**octameter**	eight feet

Other foot names worth learning are:

the **anapest** marked ∪ ∪ /, the most famous anapestic line being:

∪ ∪ / ∪ ∪ / ∪ ∪ / ∪ ∪ / ∪ ∪ /

"Twas the night before Christmas, when all through the house..."

the **trochee**, marked / ∪, the most memorable trochaic line being:

/ ∪ / ∪ / ∪ / ∪

"Double double toil and trouble..."

the **dactyl** marked / ∪ ∪, the most often quoted dactylic line being:

/ ∪ ∪ / ∪ ∪

"Take her up tenderly..."

Old English poetry employs a meter known as **accentual meter,** with four stresses to the line without attention to the unstressed syllables. Contemporary poets tend not to use it, but one of the greatest innovators in rhythm and meter, Gerard Manley Hopkins, used it as the "base line" for his counterpointed "Sprung Rhythm." Living in the 19th century, Hopkins produced poetry that even today strikes the reader as "modern," in that the rhymes and rhythms often jar the ear, providing stressed syllables where we expect unstressed and vice versa. The rhythm was measured by feet of from one to four syllables, and any number of unstressed syllables. Underneath the rhythm we hear the "regular" rhythm we are used to in speech, and an intriguing counterpoint develops. One stanza from "The Caged Skylark" will show the method at work:

As a dare-gale skylark scanted in a dull cage
Man's mounting spirit in his bone-house, mean house, dwells—
That bird beyond the remembering his free fells;
This in drudgery, day-labouring-out life's age.

The stress on "That" and "This" works particularly well to draw attention to the two captives: the skylark and Man. The accentual meter in the second line reinforces the wretchedness of the human condition. No reader could possibly read that line quickly, nor fail to put the full length of the syllable on "dwells." The dash further stresses the length and the low pitch of the last word.

If at first the terms for meter are new and strange, remember that what is most important is not that you mindlessly memorize the terminology but are able to recognize the meter and analyze why the poet has used it in the particular context of the poem. For example, Shakespeare did not want the lyrical fall and rise of the iamb for his witches around the cauldron, so he employs the much more unusual trochee to suggest the gloom and mystery of the heath in "Macbeth." Many poets will "mix and match" their meter and your task as a student of poetry is to analyze why. Perhaps the poet sets up the regular greeting card meter, rising and falling rhythm, regular end-stopped rhyme. If the poet abruptly changes that pattern, there is a reason. If the poet subtly moves from a disruptive meter into a smooth one, then analyze what is going on in the meaning. If the poet is doing "a good job" as T.S. Eliot suggested, then the rhyme, rhythm and meter should all work together in harmony to make the poem an integral whole. Answer the test essay questions to practice the points in this section and the integrity of a poem as a single unit will become clearer.

FIGURATIVE LANGUAGE
and POETIC DEVICES

It will be becoming ever more obvious that a poem is not created from mere inspiration. No doubt the initial movement for a poem has something of divine intervention: the ancients talked of being visited by the Muse of Poetry; James Joyce coined the word "epiphany" for the clear moment of power of conception in literature, but then the poet sets to, working at the expression to make it the best it can be.

Perhaps what most distinguishes poetry from any other genre is the use of figurative language—figures of speech—used through the ages to convey the poet's own particular world-view in a unique way. Words have **connotation** and **denotation**, **figurative** and **literal** meanings. We can look in the dictionary for denotation and literal meaning, but figurative language works its own peculiar magic, tapping into shared experiences within the psyche. A simple example involves the word "home." If we free-associated for awhile among a group of twenty students we would find a number of connotations for the word, depending on the way home was for us in our experiences: comforting, scary, lonely, dark, creepy, safety, haven, hell…. However, the denotation is quite straightforward: a house or apartment or dwelling that provides shelter for an individual or family. Poets include in their skill various figures of speech to "plug into" the reader's experiences, to prompt the reader to say "I would have never thought of it in those terms but now I see!"

The most important of these skills is perhaps the **metaphor**, which compares two unlike things, feelings, objects, and the **simile**. Metaphors are more difficult to find than **similes**, which also compare two dissimilar things but always use the words "as if" (for a clause) or "like" (for a word or phrase). Metaphors suggest the comparison, the meaning is implicit. An easy way to distinguish between the two is the simple example of the camel. **Metaphor:** the camel is the ship of the desert. **Simile:** a camel is like a ship in the desert. Both conjure up the camel's almost sliding across the desert, storing up its water as a ship must do for survival for its passengers, and the notion of the vastness of the desert parallels the sea. The metaphor somehow crystallizes the image. Metaphors can be *extended* so that an entire poem consists of a metaphor or unfortunately they can be *mixed*. The latter rarely happens in poetry unless the poet is deliberately playing with his readers and provoking humor.

Start thinking of how many times you use similes in your own writing or speech. The secret is, as Isaac Babel once said, that similes must be "as precise as a slide rule and as natural as the smell of dill." The precision and naturalness coming together perfectly often set up an equation of comparison. A student once wrote "I felt torn apart by my loyalty to my mother and grandmother, like the turkey wishbone at Thanksgiving." We have all experienced divided loyalties.

Using the graphic wishbone-tearing idea, something we have all done at Thanks-giving or have seen done lets us more easily relate to the student's experience. Another student wrote of his friends waiting for the gym class to begin "like so many captive gazelles." Again the visual point of comparison is important but also the sense of freedom in the idea of gazelle, the speed, the grace; juxtaposing that freedom with the word "captive" is a master stroke that makes a simile striking.

The same student went on to an *extended simile* to state precisely and naturally his feelings upon going into a fistfight: "I was like the kid whose parents were killed by the crooked sheriff, waiting for high noon and the showdown that would pit a scared kid with his father's rusty old pistol against the gleaming steel of a matched pair, nestled in the black folds of the sheriff's holsters. I knew there was no way out. Surrounded by friends, I marched out into the brilliant sun, heading for the back fields of the playground, desperately trying to polish the rusty old gun." Although this student was writing in prose, his use of figurative language is poetic. He plugs into readers' movie experience with the central idea of the showdown at high noon, an **allusion** that involves the reader on the same plane as the writer. The notion of the black holster extends the allusion of the old cowboy films where the "baddies" wore black hats and rode black horses. The use of the word "nestled" provokes some interesting connotations of something soft and sweet like a kitten nestling into something. But then the gun is an implement of destruction and death; maybe "nestles" takes on the connotation of how a snake might curl in the sun at the base of a tree. The metaphor then ends with the child going out into the sun. The "rusty gun" in context of the essay was in fact the outmoded ideas and morals his father and old books had inculcated in him. All in all a very clever use of figurative language in prose. If the same concept had been pursued in poetry, the metaphor would have moved more speedily, more subtly—a poet cannot waste words—and of course would have employed line breaks, rhythm and meter.

Personification is a much easier area than metaphor to detect in poetry. Usually the object that is being personified—referred to as a human with the personal pronoun sometimes, or possessing human attributes—is capitalized, as in this stanza from Thomas Gray's "Ode on a Distant Prospect of Eton College":

> Ambition this shall tempt to rise,
> Then whirl the wretch from high,
> To bitter Scorn a sacrifice,
> And grinning Infamy.
> The stings of Falsehood those shall try,
> And hard Unkindness' altered eye,
> That mocks the tear it forced to flow;
> And keen Remorse with blood defiled,
> And moody Madness laughing wild
> Amid severest woe.

As the poet watches the young Eton boys, he envisions what the years have to offer them, and the qualities he sees he gives human status. Thus Ambition is not only capable of tempting, an amoral act, but also of "whirling," a physical act. Scorn is bitter, Infamy grinning, and so on. Coleridge employs a more visual personification in "The Ancient Mariner," for the sun whom he describes as:

> ...the Sun (was) flecked with bars
> (Heaven's Mother send us grace!)
> As if through a dungeon-grate he peered
> With broad and burning face.

More so than with Gray's more formal personification, Coleridge's supplies an image that is precise—we can see the prisoner behind the bars, and what's more this particular prisoner has a broad and burning face... of course because he is the sun! The personification brings us that flash of recognition when we can say "Yes, I see that!"

The word **image** brings us to another important aspect of figurative language. Not a figure of speech in itself, the image plays a large role in poetry because the reader is expected to **imagine** what the poet is evoking, through the senses. The image can be **literal**, wherein the reader has little adjustment to make to see or touch or taste the image; a **figurative image** demands more from readers, almost as if they have to be inside the poet's imagination to understand the image. Very often this is where students of poetry, modern poetry particularly, find the greatest problems because the poetry of **imagism**, a term coined by Ezra Pound, is often intensely personal, delving into the mind of the poet for the comparison and connection with past memories that many readers cannot possibly share. Such an image is referred to as *free*, open to many interpretations. This concept suits the post-modern poet who feels that life is fragmented, open to multi-interpretations— there is no fixed order. Poets of the Elizabethan and Romantic eras saw the world as whole, steady, *fixed*, exactly the word used for their type of images. Readers of this poetry usually share the same response to the imagery. For example, the second stanza of Keats' "Ode to a Nightingale" sets up the taste imagery of a

> draught of vintage that hath been
> Cooled a long age in the deep-delvéd earth,
> Tasting of Flora and the country green,
> Dance, and Provençal song, and sunburnt mirth!
> O for a beaker of the warm South,
> Full of the true, the blushful Hippocrene,
> With beaded bubbles winking at the brim,
> And purple-stainéd mouth;

Even though Flora and Hippocrene are not names we are readily familiar with, the image of the cool wine, the taste, the look, the feeling evoked of the South and warmth, all come rushing into our minds as we enter the poet's imagination and find images in common.

Blake's imagery in "London" works in a similar way but as readers we have to probe a little harder, especially for the last line of the last stanza:

> But, most thro' midnight streets I hear
> How the youthful Harlot's curse
> Blasts the new-born Infant's tear,
> And blights with plagues the Marriage hearse.

Notice how the "Marriage hearse" immediately sets up a double image. Marriage we associate with happiness and joy; hearse we associate with death and sorrow. The image is troubling. We go back to the previous lines. The harlot curses her (?) new-born—the curse of venereal disease—that child marries and carries the disease to marriage? Or the young man consorting with the harlot passes on the disease to his marriage partner? Marriage then becomes death? The image is intriguing and open to interpretation.

Image in figurative language inevitably leads to **symbol**. When an object, an image, a feeling, takes on larger meaning outside of itself, then a poet is employing a symbol, something which stands for something greater. Because mankind has used symbols for so long many have become **stock** or **conventional**: the rose standing for love; the flag standing for patriotism, love of one's country (thus the controversy over flag-burning today); the color yellow standing for corruption (hence Gatsby's Daisy Buchanan—the white-dressed virginal lady with the center core of carelessness); the bird for freedom; the sea for eternity; the cross for suffering and sacrifice. If you are not versed in the Christian tradition it might be useful to read its symbols because the older poetry dwells on the church and the trials of loving God and loving Woman—the latter also has become a symbol deteriorating over the ages from Eve to the Madonna to Whore.

If the symbol is not conventional then it may carry with it many interpretations, depending on the reader's insight. Some students "get carried away" with symbolism, seeing more in the words than the poets do! If the poet is "doing a good job" the poetry will steer you in the "right" direction of symbolism. Sometimes we are unable to say what "stands for" what, but simply that the symbol evokes a mood; it suggests an idea to you that is difficult to explain. The best way to approach symbolism is to understand a literal meaning first and then shift the focus, as with a different camera lens, and see if the poet is saying something even more meaningful. Blake again supplies an interesting example. In his poem "The Chimney Sweeper" he describes the young child's dream of being locked up in "coffins of black." Literally of course coffins are brown wood, the color of mourning is black. Shift the focus then to the young child chimney sweeper, so young he can barely lisp the street cry "Sweep" so it comes out "'weep! 'weep! 'weep! 'weep!" (a symbolic line in itself). Your reading of the Industrial Age's cruelty to children who were exploited as cheap, plentiful, and an expendable labor force will perhaps have taught you that children were used as chimney brushes—literally thrust up the thin black chimneys of Victorian houses and factories, where very often they became trapped, suffocated, sometimes burned to death if fires were set by unknowing owners. Now the black coffins stand for the black-with-soot chimneys the little children had to sweep, chimneys which sometimes became their coffins. The realization of the symbol brings a certain horror to the poem. In the dream an Angel releases the children who then run down "a green plain leaping, laughing.../And wash in a river, and shine in the sun." The action is of course symbolic in that in real life the children's movements were restricted, living in monstrous cities where green plains would be enjoyed only by the rich, and totally limited by the size of the chimneys. They were always black with soot. They rarely saw the sun, never mind shone in it! Again the symbolism adds something to the poem. In many students there have been reactions of tears and anger when they *see* the symbolism behind such simple lines.

The idea of reading about the Industrial Age brings us to an important part of figurative language, briefly mentioned before: **allusion**. Poets tap into previous areas of experience to relate their insights, to draw their readers into shared experiences. Remember how the student writer alluded to old cowboy movies, the classic "High Noon." Poets will refer to history, myth, other older poems, plays, music, heroes, famous people. Allusion is becoming more and more difficult for the modern student because reading is becoming more and more a lost art. Core courses in schools have become hotbeds of controversy about what students should know. Fortunately modern poets are shifting their allusions so that contemporary readers can appreciate and join in with their background of knowledge. However, be aware that for the examination in poetry it will be useful to have a working knowledge of, at least a passing acquaintance with, "oldness." Think of areas of history that were landmarks: the burning of Catharge; Hannibal's elephants; Caesar's greatness; Alexander the Great; the first World War and its carnage of young men; the Second World War and the Holocaust. Think of the great Greek and Roman myths: the giving of fire to the world; the entrance of sin into the world; the labyrinth; the names associated with certain myths: Daedalus, Hercules, the Medusa. You may never have a question on the areas you read but your background for well-rounded college study will already be formulated.

If we now return to more specific figures of speech and other poetic devices, you may feel you can immediately get to grips with these rather than read for background! Alphabetical order may help in your studying:

Alliteration: the repetition of consonants at the beginning of words that are next door to each other or close by. The Hopkins' stanza quoted earlier provides some fine examples: "skylark scanted"; "Man's mounting... mean house"; "free fells"; "drudgery, day-labouring-out life's age." Always try to understand the reason for the alliteration. Does it speed or slow the rhythm? Is it there for emphasis? What does the poet want you to focus on?

Apostrophe: the direct address of someone or something that is not present. Many odes begin this way. Keats' "Ode to a Grecian Urn" for example: "Thou still unravished bride of quietness," and "Ode to Psyche": "O Goddess! hear these tuneless numbers."

Assonance: the repetition of vowel sounds usually internally rather than initially. "Her goodly eyes like sapphires shining bright." Here the poet, Spenser, wants the entire focus on the blue eyes, the crispness, and the light.

Bathos: deliberate anticlimax to make a definite point or draw attention to a falseness. The most famous example is from Pope's "Rape of the Lock": "Here thou, great Anna! whom three realms obey, /Dost sometimes counsel take—and sometimes tea."

The humor in the bathos is the fact that Anna is the Queen of England—she holds meetings in the room Pope describes but also indulges in the venerable English custom of afternoon tea. The fact that tea should rhyme with obey doubles the humor as the elongated vowel of the upper-class laconic English social group is also mocked.

Caesura: the pause, marked by punctuation (/) or not within the line. Sometimes the caesura (sometimes spelled cesura) comes at an unexpected point in the rhythm and gives the reader pause for thought.

Conceits: very elaborate comparisons between unlikely objects. The metaphysical poets such as John Donne were criticized for "yoking" together outrageous terms, describing lovers in terms of instruments, or death in terms of battle.

Consonance: similar to slant rhyme—the repetition of consonant sounds without the vowel sound repeated. Hopkins again frequently uses this as in "Pied Beauty": "All things counter, original, spare, strange;... adazzle, dim."

Diction: the word for word choice. Is the poet using formal or informal language? Does the poetry hinge on slang or a dialect? If so what is the purpose? Are the words "highfalutin" or low-brow? As always, the diction needs examining and questions like these answering.

Enjambment: the running-on of one line of poetry into another. Usually the end of lines are rhymed so there is an end-stop. In more modern poetry, without rhyme, often run-on lines occur to give a speedier flow, the sound of the speaking voice or a conversational tone.

Hyperbole: refers to large overstatement often used to draw attention to a mark of beauty or a virtue or an action that the poet disagrees with. Donne's instruction to the woman he is trying to seduce not to kill the flea, by contrasting her reluctance with "a marriage" of blood within a flea, reinforces the hyperbole used throughout the poem:

Oh stay, three lives in one flea spare,
Where we almost, yea, more than married are.

The example is also good for an unexpected caesura for emphasis at the second pause.

Irony: plays an important role in voice or tone, inferring a discrepancy between what is said and what is meant. A famous example is Shelley's "Ozymandias," which tells of the great ruler who thought that he and his name would last forever, but the traveller describes the huge statue in ruins with the inscription speaking truer than the ruler intended: "My name is Ozymandias, king of kings: / Look on my works, ye Mighty, and despair!"

Metonymy: the name for something closely related to it which then takes on a larger meaning. "You can't fight City Hall" has taken on the meaning of fighting against an entire bureaucracy. "You can't go home again" suggests that you can never emotionally return to your roots.

Onomatopoeia: a device in which the word captures the sound. In many poems the words are those in general use: the whiz of fireworks; the crashing of waves on the shore; the booming of water in a underground sea-cave. However, poets like Keats use the device to superb effect in, for example, " To Autumn," when he describes the gleaner sitting by the cider press watching the last "oozings hours by hours"... one can hear the last minute drops squeezed from the apples.

Oxymoron: a form of paradox in which contradictory words are used next to each other: "painful pleasure," "sweet sorrow."

Paradox: a situation or action or feeling that appears to be contradictory but on inspection turns out to be true or at least make sense. "The pen is mightier than the sword" at first glance is a contradiction of reality. One can hardly die by being stabbed by a pen... but in the larger world view the words of men, the signing of death warrants, the written issuing of commands to the gas chambers have killed. Or reason has prevailed by men writing out their grievances and as a result lives have been saved. Paradox always opens up the doors of thinking.

Pun: a play on words often for humorous or sarcastic effect. The Elizabethans were very fond of them; many of Shakespeare's comedies come from punning. Much of Donne's sexual taunting involves the use of the pun.

Sarcasm: when verbal irony is too harsh it moves into the sarcastic realm. It is the "lowest form of wit" of course but can be used to good effect in the tone of a poem. Browning's dramatic monologues make excellent use of the device.

Synecdoche: when a part of an object is used to represent the entire thing or vice versa. When we ask someone to give us a hand we would be horrified if they cut off the hand, what we want is the person's help, from all of the body!

Syntax: the ordering of words into a particular pattern. If a poet shifts words from the usual word order you know you are dealing with an older style of poetry (Shakespeare, Milton) or a poet who wants to shift emphasis onto a particular word.

Tone: the voice or attitude of the speaker. Remember that the voice need not be that of the poet's. He or she may be adopting a particular tone for a purpose. Your task is to analyze if the tone is angry, sad, conversational, abrupt, wheedling, cynical, affected, satiric, etc. Is the poet including you in a cozy way by using "you," or is he accusing "you" of what he is criticizing? Is the poet keeping you at a distance with coldness and third person pronouns. If so, why? The most intriguing of voices is Browning's in his **dramatic monologues**: poems that address another person who remains silent. Browning brought this type of poetry to an art. Think of all the variations of voices and attitudes and be prepared to meet them in poetry.

TYPES OF POETRY

Having begun to grasp that poetry contains a great deal more than initially meets the eye, you should now start thinking about the various types of poetry. Of course, when reading for pleasure, it is not vital to recognize that the poem in hand is a sonnet or a villanelle, but for the exam you may well be asked to determine what sort of poem is under scrutiny. Certainly in discussing a poem it is also useful to know what "breed" you are dealing with because the form may dictate certain areas of rhyme or meter and may enhance the meaning.

The pattern or design of a poem is known as **form,** and even the strangest, most experimental poetry will have some type of form to it. Allen Ginsberg's "A Supermarket in California" caused a stir because it didn't read like poetry, but on the page there is a certain form to it. Some poets even try to match the shape of the poem to the subject. Find in anthologies John Hollander's "Swan and Shadow," and Dorthi Charles' "Concrete Cat." Such visual poems are not just fun to look at and read but the form adds to the subject and helps the reader appreciate the poet's world view. **Closed form** will be immediately recognizable because lines can be counted, shape determined. The poet must keep to the recognized form, in number of lines, rhyme scheme, and/or meter. **Open form** developed from "vers libre," which name some poets objected to as it suggested that there was little skill or craft behind the poem, simply creativity, as the name suggests, gives a freedom of pattern to the poet.

The most easily recognized closed form of poetry is the **sonnet**, sometimes referred to as a **fixed form**. The sonnet always has fourteen lines but there are two types of sonnets, the Petrarchan or Italian, and the Shakespearean or English. The word sonnet in fact comes from the Italian word "sonnetto" meaning a "little song," and Petrarch, the 14th century Italian poet, took the form to its peak with his sonnets to his loved one Laura. This woman died before he could even declare his love, and such poignant, unrequited love became the theme for many Elizabethan sonnets. As a young man might telephone a young woman for a date in today's society, the Elizabethan would send a sonnet. The Petrarchan sonnet is organized into two groups: eight lines and six: the **octave** and the **sestet**. Usually the rhyme scheme is is abbaabba-cdecde, but the sestet can vary in its pattern. The octave may set up a problem or a proposition, and then the answer or resolution follows in the sestet after a turn or a shift. The Shakespearean sonnet organizes the lines into three groups of four lines: **quatrains** and a **couplet**: two rhyming lines. The rhyming scheme is always abab cdcd efef gg, and the turn or shift can happen at one of three places or leave the resolution or a "twist in the tail" at the end.

Couplet, mentioned earlier, leads us to a closed form of poetry that is very useful for the poet. It is a two-line stanza that usually rhymes with an end rhyme. If the couplet is firmly end-stopped and written in iambic pentameter it is known as an **heroic couplet**, after the use was made of it in the English translations of the great classical or heroic epics such as *The Iliad* and *The Odyssey*. Alexander Pope became a master of the heroic couplet, sometimes varying to the twelve-syllable line from the old French poetry on Alexander the Great. The line became known as the **Alexandrine**. Pope gained fame first as a translator of the epics and then went on to write **mock-heroic** poems like "The Rape of the Lock," written totally in heroic couplets which never become monotonous, as a succession of regularly stepped-out couplets can, because he varied the place of the caesura and masterfully employed enjambment.

Rarely in an exam will you be presented with an **epic** because part of the definition of the word is vastness of size and range. However, you may be confronted with an excerpt and will need to recognize the structure. The translation will usually be in couplets, the meter regular with equal line lengths, because originally these poems were sung aloud or chanted to the beat of drums. Because of their oral quality, repetition plays an important part, so that if the bard, or singer, forgot the line, the audience, who had heard the stories many times before, could help him out. The subject deals with great deeds of heroes: Odysseus (Ulysses), Hector, and Aeneus, their adventures and their trials; the theme will be of human grief or pride, divided loyalties—but all "writ large." The one great English epic, *Paradise Lost* is written by Milton and deals with the story of Adam and Eve and the Fall. Adam thus becomes the great hero. The huge battle scenes of *The Iliad* are emulated in the War of the Heavens when Satan and his crew were expelled into Hell; the divided loyalties occur when Adam must choose between obedience to God and love for his wife.

On much simpler lines are the **ballads**, sometimes the earliest poems we learn as children. Folk or popular ballads were first sung as early as the 15th century and then handed down through generations until finally written down. Usually the ballads are anonymous and simple in theme, having been composed by working folk who originally could not read or write. The stories—a ballad is a story in a song—revolve around love and hate and lust and murder, often rejected lovers, knights, and the supernatural. As with the epic, and for the same reason, repetition plays a strong part in the ballad and often a repeated refrain holds the entire poem together. The form gave rise to the **ballad stanza**, four lines rhyming abcb with lines 1 and 3 having 8 syllables and lines 2 and 4 having 6. Poets who later wrote what are known as **literary ballads** kept the same pattern. Read Coleridge's "Ancient Mariner" and all the elements of the ballad come together as he reconstructs the old folk story but writes it in a very closed form.

The earlier poetry dealt with narrative. The "father of English poetry," Geoffrey Chaucer, told stories within a story for the great *Canterbury Tales*. The Elizabethans turned to love and the humanistic battle between love of the world and love of God. Wordsworth and Coleridge marked a turning point by not only using "the language of men" in poetry but also by moving away from the narrative poem to the **lyric**. The word comes again from the Greek, meaning a story told with the poet playing upon a lyre. Wordsworth moves from story to emotion, often "emotion recollected in tranquillity" as we saw in "Daffodils." Although sometimes a listener is inferred, very often the poet seems to be musing aloud.

Part of the lyric "family" is the **elegy**, a lament for someone's death or the passing of a love or concept. The most famous is Thomas Gray's "Elegy Written in a Country Churchyard," which mourns not only the passing of individuals but of a past age and the wasted potential within every human being, no matter how humble. Often **ode** and elegy become synonymous, but an ode, also part of the lyric family, is usually longer, dealing with more profound areas of human life than simply death. Keats' odes are perhaps the most famous and most beloved in English poetry.

More specialized types of poetry need mentioning so that you may recognize and be able to explicate how the structure of the poem enhances the meaning or theme. For example the **villanelle**: a Courtly Love poem structure from medieval times, built on five three-line stanzas known as **tercets**, with the rhyme scheme aba, followed by a four-line stanza, a **quatrain** which ends the poem abaa. As if this were not pattern and order enough, the poem's first line appears again as the last line of the 2nd and 4th tercets; *and* the third line appears again in the last line of the 3rd and 5th tercets; *and* these two lines appear again as rhyming lines at the end of the poem! The most famous and arguably the best villanelle, as some of the older ones can be so stiff in their pattern that the meaning is inconsequential, is Dylan Thomas' "Do not go gentle into that good night." The poem stands on its own with a magisterial meaning of mankind raging against death, but when one appreciates the structure also, the rage is even more emphatic because it is so controlled. A poem well worth finding for "reading for pleasure." In James Joyce's *A Portrait of the Artist as a Young Man*, writing a villanelle on an empty cigarette packet turns the young boy, Stephen Daedalus, dreaming of being an artist, into a poet, a "real" artist.

Said to be the most difficult of all closed forms is the **sestina**, also French, sung by medieval troubadours, a "song of sixes." The poet presents six six-line stanzas, with six end-words in a certain order, then repeats those six repeated words in any order in a closing tercet. Find Elizabeth Bishop's "Sestina" or W.H. Auden's "Hearing of Harvests Rotting in the Valleys" and the idea of six images running through the poet's head and being skillfully repeated comes across very clearly. You might even try working out a sestina for yourself.

Perhaps at this stage an **epigram** might be more to your liking and time scale because it is short, even abrupt, a little cynical and always to the point. The cynical Alexander Pope mastered the epigram, as did Oscar Wilde centuries later. Perhaps at some stage we have all written **doggerel**, rhyming poetry that becomes horribly distorted to fit the rhymes, not through skill but the opposite. In contrast **limericks** are very skilled: five lines using the anapest meter with the rhyme scheme: aabba. Unfortunately they can deteriorate into types such as "There was a young lady from....," but in artful hands such as Shakespeare's (see Ophelia's mad song in *Hamlet*: "And will he not come again?"), and Edward Lear's, limericks display fine poetry. Finally, if you are trying to learn all the different types of closed-form poetry, you might try an **aubade**—originally a song or piece of music sung or played at dawn—a poem written to the dawn or about lovers at dawn—the very time when poetic creation is extremely high!

Although the name might suggest open-form, **blank verse** is in fact closed-form poetry. As we saw earlier, lines written in blank verse are unrhymed and in iambic pentameter. Open-form poets can arrange words on the page in any order, not confined by any rhyme pattern or meter. Often it seems as if words have spilled onto the page at random with a direct address to the readers, as if the poets are cornering them in their room, or simply chatting over the kitchen table. The lines break at any point—the dash darts in and out—the poets are talking to the audience with all the "natural" breaks that the speaking voice will demonstrate. Open-form poets can employ rhyme, but sometimes it seems as if the rhyme has slipped into the poem quite easily—there is no wrenching of the word "to make it rhyme." Very often there is more internal rhyme as poets play with words, often giving the sensation they are thinking aloud. Open-form poetry is usually thought of as "modern," at least post-World War I, but the use of space on the page, the direct address of the voice and the use of the dash clearly marks Emily Dickinson as an open-form poet, but she lived from 1830-1886.

CHAPTER 3

DRAMA AND THEATER

The Glass Menagerie by Tennessee Williams begins when one of its four characters, Tom, steps into the downstage light and addresses the audience directly as though he were the chorus from a much earlier play. "I have tricks in my pocket, I have things up my sleeve," says Tom. "But I am the opposite of a stage magician. He gives you illusion that has the appearance of truth. I give you truth in the pleasant disguise of illusion."

To sit among the audience and watch a skillful production of *The Glass Menagerie* is to visit Tom's paradoxical world of theater, a magic place in which known imposters and stagecraft trickery create a spectacle which we know is illusion but somehow recognize as truth. Theater, as a performed event, combines the talents and skills of numerous artists and craftspersons, but before the spectacle must come the playwright's work, the pages of words designating what the audience sees and hears. These words, the written script separate from the theatrical performance of them, is what we call *drama*, and the words give the spectacle its significance because without them the illusion has neither frame nor content. Truth requires boundaries and substance. When Shakespeare's Hamlet advises actors just before their performance, he places careful emphasis on the importance of the words, cautioning the players to speak them "trippingly on the tongue." If all actions are not suited to the words, Hamlet adds, the performance will fail because the collaborative purpose combining the dramatist's literary art and the actors' performing art "is to hold as 'twere the mirror up to Nature."

Although drama is literature written to be performed, it closely resembles the other genres. In fact, both poetry and prose also can be performed; but as captivating as these public readings sometimes are, only performed drama best creates the immediate living "illusion as truth" Tom promises. Like fiction and narrative poetry, drama tells a tale—that is, it has plot, characters, and setting—but the author's voice is distant, heard only through the stage directions and perhaps some supplementary notes. With rare exceptions, dialogue dominates the script. Some drama is poetry, such as the works of Shakespeare and Molière, and all plays resemble poems as abstractions because both forms are highly condensed, figurative expressions. Even in Henrik Ibsen's social realism, the dramatic action is metaphorical.

A scene set inside a house, for instance, requires a room with only three walls. No audience complains, just as no movie audience feels betrayed by film characters' appearing ridiculously large. Without a thought, audiences employ what Samuel Taylor Coleridge called "a willing suspension of disbelief"; in other words, they know that the images before them are not real but rather representations, reflections in the mirror of which Hamlet speaks, not the real world ("Nature").

A play contains conflict which can be enacted immediately on the stage without any alterations in the written word. **Enacted** means performed by an actor or actors free to use the entire stage and such theatrical devices as sets, costumes, makeup, special lighting, and props for support. This differs from the oral interpretation of prose or poetry. No matter how animated, the public reader is not acting. This is the primary distinction between drama and other literary forms. Their most obvious similarity is that any form of literature is a linguistic expression. There is, however, one other feature shared by all kinds of narratives: the pulsating energy which pushes the action along is generated by human imperfection. We speak of tragic characters as having "flaws," but the same is true about comic characters as well. Indeed, nothing is more boring either on a stage or in a written text than a consistently flawless personality, because such characters can never be congruent with the real people of our everyday experiences. The most fundamental human truth is human frailty.

Although it can be argued that a play, like a musical composition, must be performed to be realized, the script's linguistic foundation always gives the work potential as a literary experience. Moreover, there is never a "definitive" interpretation. The script, in a sense, remains unfinished because it never stops inviting new variations, and among those invited to participate are individual readers whose imaginations should not be discounted. For example, when *Death of a Salesman* was originally produced, Lee J. Cobb played Willy Loman. Aside from the character's age, Dustin Hoffman's Willy in the revival forty years later bore hardly any physical resemblance to Cobb's. Yet both portrayals "worked." The same could be said about the Willys created by the minds of the play's countless readers. Quite capable of composing its own visions and sounds, the human imagination is the original mirror, the place where all human truths evolve from perceived data.

Hamlet's mirror and Tom's truthful illusions are figures of speech echoing drama's earliest great critic, Aristotle, who believed art should create a **mimesis**, the Greek word for "imitation." For centuries this "mimetic theory" has asserted that a successful imitation is one which reproduces natural objects and actions in as realistic portrayal as possible. Later, this notion of imitation adopted what has been called the "expressive theory," a variation allowing the artist a freer, more individual stylized approach. A drama by Ibsen, for example, attempts to capture experience as unadorned raw sense, the way it normally appears to be. This is realistic imitation. As 20th century drama moved toward examinations of people's inner consciousness as universal representations of some greater human predicament, new expressive styles emerged. The diversity in the works of Eugene O'Neill, Samuel Beckett, and Harold Pinter illustrate how dramatists' imitations can disrupt our sense of the familiar as their plays become more personally expressive. But the theater of Aristotle's time was hardly "realistic" in today's objective sense. Instead, it was highly stylized and full of conventions derived from theater's ritualistic origins. The same is true of medieval morality plays and the rigid formality of Japanese Kabuki theater, yet these differ greatly from each other and from ancient Greek and Roman dramas. In other words, imitating "what's out there" requires only that the form be consistent with itself, and any form is permissible.

PLOT STRUCTURE

As with other narrative types, a play's **plot** is its sequence of events, its organized collection of incidents. At one time it was thought that all the actions within a play should be contained within a single twenty-four hour period. Few lengthy plays have plots which cover only the period of time enacted on the stage. Most plays condense and edit time much as novels do. Decades can be reduced to two hours. Included in the plot is the **exposition**, the revealing of whatever information we need in order to understand the impending conflict. This exposed material should provide us with a sense of place and time (**setting**), the central participants, important prior incidents, and the play's overall mood. In some plays such as Shakespeare's, the exposition comes quickly. Notice, for instance, the opening scenes in *Macbeth, Hamlet*, and *Romeo and Juliet*: not one presents us with a central character, yet each—with its witches or king's ghost or street brawl—clearly establishes an essential tension heralding the main conflict to come. These initial expositions attack the audience immediately and are followed by subsequent events in chronological order. Sophocles' *Oedipus Rex* works somewhat differently, presenting the central character late in the myth from which the play is taken. The exposition must establish what has come previously, even for an audience familiar with the story, before the plot can advance. Like Shakespeare, Sophocles must start his exposition at the beginning, but he takes a longer (though not tedious) time revealing the essential facts. Arthur Miller, in his *Death of a Salesman*, continuously interrupts the central action with dislocated expositions from earlier times as though the past were always in the present. He carefully establishes character, place, mood, and conflict throughout the earliest scenes; however, whatever present he places on stage is always caught in a tension between the audience's anticipation of the future and its suspicions of the past. The plots in plays like *Oedipus Rex* and *Death of a Salesman* tend not to attack us head-on but rather to surround us and gradually close in, the circle made tighter by each deliberately released clue to a mysterious past.

Conflict requires two opposing forces. We see, for instance, how King Lear's irresponsible abdication and conceited anger are countered by Goneril and Regan's duplicity and lusts for power. We also see how Creon's excessive means for restoring order in Thebes is met by Antigone's allegiance to personal conscience. Fairly soon in a play we must experience some incident that incites the fundamental conflict when placed against some previously presented incident or situation. In most plays the conflict's abrasive conditions continuously chafe and even lacerate each other. The play's tempo might provide some interruptions or variations in the pace; nevertheless, conflicts generate the actions which make the characters' worlds worse before they can get better. Any plot featuring only repetitious altercations, however, would soon become tiresome. Potentially, anything can happen in a conflict. The **complication** is whatever presents an element capable of altering the action's direction. Perhaps some new information is discovered or a previously conceived scheme fails, creating a reversal of what had been expected. The plot is not a series of similar events but rather a compilation of related events leading to a culmination, **a crisis.**

In retrospect we should be able to accept a drama's progression of actions leading to the crisis as inevitable. After the crisis comes the **resolution** (or **denouement**), which gives the play its concluding boundary. This does not mean that the play should offer us solutions for whatever human issues it raises. Rather, the playwright's obligation is to make the experience he presents to us seem filled within its own perimeters. George Bernard Shaw felt he had met this obligation when he ended *Pygmalion* with his two principal characters, Higgins and Eliza, utterly incapable of voicing any romantic affection for each other; and the resolution in Ibsen's *A Doll's House* outraged audiences a hundred years ago and still disturbs some people today, even though it concludes the play with believable consequences.

Terms such as **exposition, complication, crisis,** and **resolution,** though helpful in identifying the conflict's currents and directions, at best only artificially define how a plot is molded. If the play provides unity in its revelations, these seams are barely noticeable. Moreover, any successful creative composition clearly shows that the artist accomplished much more than merely plugging components together to create a finished work. There are no rules which all playwrights must follow, except the central precept that the play's unified assortment of actions be complete and contained within itself. *Antigone*, for instance, depicts the third phase of Sophocles' Oedipus trilogy, although it was actually written and performed before *Oedipus Rex* and *Oedipus at Colonus*. And although a modern reader might require some background information before starting, *Antigone* gives a cohesive dramatic impact independent from the other two plays.

CHARACTER

Essential to the plot's success are the characters who participate in it. Midpoint in *Hamlet* when Elsinore Castle is visited by the traveling theater company, the prince joyously welcomes the players, but his mood quickly returns to bitter depression shortly after he asks one actor to recite a dramatic passage in which the speaker recalls the fall of Troy and particularly Queen Hecuba's response to her husband's brutal murder. The player, caught by the speech's emotional power, becomes distraught and cannot finish. Left alone on stage, Hamlet compares the theatrical world created by the player with Hamlet's "real" world and asks: "What's Hecuba to him, or he to Hecuba,/ That he should weep for her!" Under ordinary circumstances Hamlet's anxiety would not overshadow his Renaissance sensibilities, because he knows well that fictional characters always possess the potential to move us. As though by instinct, we know the same. We read narratives and go to the theater precisely because we want to be shocked, delighted, thrilled, saddened, titillated, or invigorated by "a dream of passion." Even though some characters are more complex and interesting than others, they come in countless types as the playwright's delegates to our imaginations and as the imitations of reality seeking our response.

Antigone begins with two characters, Antigone and Ismene, on stage. They initiate the exposition through their individual reactions to a previous event, King Creon's edict following the battle in which Thebes defeated an invading army. Creon has proclaimed Eteocles and the others who recently died defending Thebes as heroes worthy of the highest burial honors; in addition, Creon has forbidden anyone, on penalty of death, from burying Poloneices and the others who fell attacking the city. Since Antigone, Ismene, Polyneices, and Eteocles are the children of Oedipus and Iocaste, the late king and queen, conflict over Creon's law seems imminent. These first two characters establish this inevitability. They also reveal much about themselves as individuals.

ANTIGONE:... now you must prove what you are:
A true sister, or a traitor to your family.

ISMENE: Antigone, are you mad! What could I possibly do?

ANTIGONE: You must decide whether you will help me or not.

ISMENE: I do not understand you. Help you in what?

ANTIGONE: Ismene, I am going to bury him. Will you come?

ISMENE: Bury him! You have just said the new law forbids it.

ANTIGONE: He is my brother. And he is your brother, too.

ISMENE: But think of the danger! Think what Creon will do!

ANTIGONE: Creon is not strong enough to stand in my way.

ISMENE: Ah sister!
Oedipus died, everyone hating him
For what his own search brought to light, his eyes
Ripped out by his own hand; and Iocaste died,
His mother and wife at once: she twisted the cords
That strangled her life; and our two brothers died,
Each killed by the other's sword. And we are left:
But oh, Antigone,
Think how much more terrible than these
Our own death would be if we should go against Creon
And do what he has forbidden! We are only women,
We cannot fight with men, Antigone!
The law is strong, we must give in to the law

In this thing, and in worse. I beg the Dead
To forgive me, but I am helpless: I must yield
To those in authority. And I think it is dangerous business
To be always meddling.

ANTIGONE: If that is what you think,
I should not want you, even if you asked to come.
You have made your choice, you can be what you want to be.
But I will bury him; and if I must die,
I say that this crime is holy: I shall lie down
With him in death, and I shall be as dear
To him as he to me.
It is the dead,
Not the living, who make the longest demands:
We die for ever...
You may do as you like,
Since apparently, the laws of the gods mean nothing to you.

ISMENE: They mean a great deal to me; but I have no strength
To break laws that were made for the public good.

ANTIGONE: That must be your excuse, I suppose. But as for me,
I will bury the brother I love.

ISMENE: Antigone, I am so afraid for you!

ANTIGONE: You need not be:
You have yourself to consider, after all.

ISMENE: But no one must hear of this, you must tell no one!
I will keep it a secret, I promise!

ANTIGONE: Oh tell it! Tell everyone!
Think how they'll hate you when it all comes out
If they learn that you knew about it all the time!

ISMENE: So fiery! You should be cold with fear.

ANTIGONE: Perhaps. But I am doing only what I must.

ISMENE: But can you do it? I say that you cannot.

ANTIGONE: Very well: when my strength gives out, I shall do no more.

ISMENE: Impossible things should not be tried at all.

ANTIGONE: Go away, Ismene:
I shall be hating you soon, and the dead will too,
For your words are hateful. Leave me my foolish plan:
I am not afraid of the danger; if it means death,
It will not be the worst of deaths—death without honor.

ISMENE: Go then, if you feel that you must.
You are unwise,
But a loyal friend to those who love you.

[Exit into the Palace. ANTIONE goes off...]

READING THE PLAY

All we know about Antigone and Ismene in this scene comes from what they
say; therefore, we read their spoken words carefully. However, we must also
remain attentive to dramatic characters, propensity for not revealing all they
know and feel about a given issue, and often characters do not recognize all the
implications in what they say. We might be helped by what one says about the
other, yet these observations are not necessarily accurate or sincere. Even though
the previous scene contains fewer abiguities than some others in dramatic literature,
we would be oversimplifying to say the conflict here is between one character
who is "right" and another who is "wrong." Antigone comes out challenging,
determined and unafraid, whereas Ismene immediately reacts fearfully. Antigone
brims with the self-assured power of righteousness while Ismene expresses vul-
nerability. Yet Antigone's boast that "Creon is not strong enough to stand in my
way" suggests a rash temperament. We might admire her courage, but we question her judgment. Meanwhile, Ismene can evoke our sympathies with her burden
of family woes, at least until she confesses her helplessness and begs the Dead to
forgive her, at which point we realize her objections stem from cowardice and
not conscience.

Although we might remain unsettled by Antigone's single-mindedness, we
soon find ourselves sharing her disdain for Ismene's trepidation, particularly
when Ismene rationalizes her position as the more responsible and labels unau-
thorized intervention in royal decisions as "meddling" against the "public good."
Soon, as we realize the issue here demands moral conscience, we measure Ismene
far short of what is required. Quickly though, Ismene is partly redeemed by her
obvious concern for Antigone's well-being: "I am so afraid for you." Unaffected,
Antigone retorts with sarcasm and threats, but her demeanor never becomes so
impetuously caustic that we dismiss her as a conceited adolescent. In fact, we are
touched by her integrity and devotion, seeing no pretensions when she says: "I
am not afraid of the danger: if it means death,/It will not be the worst of deaths—
death without honor." Ismene's intimation that loyalty and love are unwise counters
Antigone's idealism enough to make us suspect that the stark, cruel world of

human imperfection will not tolerate Antigone's solitary rebellion, no matter how selfless her motivation. At the same time we wonder how long Ismene could remain neutral if Antigone were to clash with Creon.

What immediately strikes us about Antigone and Ismene is that each possesses a sense of self, a conscious awareness about her existence and her connection with forces greater than herself. This is why we can identify with them. It may not always feel reassuring, yet we too can define our existence by saying "I am, and I am not alone." As social creatures, a condition about which they have had no choice, both Antigone and Ismene have senses of self which are touched by their identification with others: each belongs to a family, and each belongs to a civil state. Indeed, much of the play's conflict focuses on which identification should be stronger. Another connection influences them as well—the unbreakable tie to truth. This truth, or ultimate reality, will vary from play to play, and not all characters ever realize it is there, and few will define it the same way. Still, the universe which characters inhabit has definition, even if the resolution suggests a great human absurdity in our insufficient capacity to grasp this definition or, worse, asserts the only definition is the absence of an ultimate reality. With Antigone, we see how her sense of self cannot be severed from its bonds to family obligations and certain moral principles.

Characters with a sense of self and an identity framed by social connections and unmitigated truths dwell in all good narratives. As readers we wander within these connecting perimeters, following the plot and sensing a commentary about life in general. This commentary, the theme, places us within the mirror's image along with the characters and their actions. We look and see ourselves. The characters' universe is ours, the playwright would have us believe, for a while at least. If his art succeeds, we do believe him. But reading literary art is no passive experience; it requires active work. And since playwrights seldom help us decide *how* characters say what they do or interrupt to explain *why* they say what they do, what personal voice he gives through stage directions deserves special attention, because playwrights never tell as much as novelists; instead they show. Our reading should focus on the tone of the dialogue as much as on the information in what is said. Prior to the 19th century, dramatists relied heavily on poetic diction to define their characters. Later playwrights provided stage directions which detail stage activities and modify dialogue. Modern writers usually give precise descriptions for the set and costume design and even prescribe particular background music. But no matter when a play was written or what its expressive style is, our role as readers and audience is to make judgments about characters in action, just as we make judgments about Antigone and Ismene the first time we see them. We should strive to be "fooled" by the truthful illusion by activating our sensitivities to human imperfections and the potential conflicts such flaws can generate. And, finally, as we peer into the playwright's mirror, we seek among the populated reflections shadows of ourselves.

TYPES OF PLAYS

When Polonius presents the traveling players to Hamlet, he reads from the theater company's license, which identifies them as

> The best actors in the world, either for tragedy, comedy, history, pastoral, pastoral-comical, historical-pastoral, tragical-historical, tragical-comical-historical-pastoral, scene individable or poem unlimited...

Shakespeare's sense of humor runs through this speech which sounds like a parody of the license granted Shakespeare's own company by James I, authorizing "the Arte and faculty of playing Comedies, Tragedies, histories, Enterludes, moralls, pastoralls, Stageplaies and Such others..." for the king's subjects and himself. The joke is on those who think all plays somehow can be categorized according to preconceived definitions, as though playwrights follow literary recipes. The notion is not entirely ridiculous, to be sure, since audiences and readers can easily tell a serious play from a humorous one, and a play labeled "tragedy" or "comedy" will generate certain valid expectations from us all, regardless of whether we have read a word by Aristotle or any other literary critic. Still, if beginning playwrights had to choose between writing according to some rigid strictures designating the likes of a "tragical-comical-historical-pastoral" or writing a play unrestricted by such rules (a "poem unlimited"), they would probably choose the latter.

All plays contain thought—its accumulated themes, arguments, and overall meaning of the action—together with a mood or tone, and we tend to categorize dramatic thought into three clusters: the serious, the comic, and the seriocomic. These distinctions echo the primitive rites from which theater evolved, religious observances usually tied to seasonal cycles. In the course of a year numerous situations could arise which would initiate dramatic, communal prayers of supplication or thanksgiving. Indeed, for humanity to see its fate held by the will of a god is to see the intricate unity of flesh and spirit, a paradox ripe for representation as dramatic conflict. And if winter's chill brings the pangs of tragedy and summer's warmth the delight of comedy, the year becomes a metaphor for the overall human condition, which contains both. Thus, in our attempts to interpret life's complexities, it is tempting to place the art forms representing it in precise, fixed designations. From this can come critical practices which ascertain how well a work imitates life by how well it adheres to its designated form. Of course, such a critical system's rigidity would limit the range of possible human experiences expressed on stage to a narrow few, but then the range could be made elastic enough to provide for possible variations and combinations. Like the old Ptolomaic theories which held the earth as the center of the universe, these precepts could work for a while. After a few centuries, though, it would become clear that there is a better way of explaining what a play's form should be—not so much fixed as organic. In other words, we should think of a play as similar to a plant's growing and taking shape according to its own design. This analogy works well because the plant is not a mechanical device constructed from a predetermined plan, yet every plant is a species and as such contains qualities which identify it with others. So just as Shakespeare could ridicule overly precise definitions for dramatic art, he could still write dramas which he clearly identified as tragedies, comedies, or histories, even though he would freely mix two or more of these together in the same play. For the purpose of understanding some of the different perspectives available to the playwright's examining eye, we will look at plays from different periods which follow the three main designations Shakespeare used, followed by a fourth which is indicative of modern American drama. A knowledge of *The Importance of Being Earnest*, *Othello*, *A Man for All Seasons*, and *Death of a Salesman* will be helpful.

Comedy

The primary aim of comedy is to amuse us with a happy ending, although comedies can vary according to the attitudes they project, which can be broadly identified as either **high** or **low**, terms having nothing to do with an evaluation of the play's merit. Generally, the amusement found in comedy comes from an eventual victory over threats or ill fortune. Much of the dialogue and plot development might be laughable, yet a play need not be funny to be comic. **Farce** is low comedy intended to make us laugh by means of a series of exaggerated, unlikely situations that depend less on plot and character than on gross absurdities, sight gags, and coarse dialogue. The "higher" a comedy goes, the more natural the characters seem and the less boisterous their behavior. The plots become more sustained, and the dialogue shows more weighty thought. As with all dramas, comedies are about things that go wrong. Accordingly, comedies create deviations from accepted normalcy, presenting incongruities which we might or might not see as harmless. If these incongruities make us judgmental about the involved characters and events, the play takes on the features of **satire**, a rather high comic form implying that humanity and human institutions are in need of reform. If the action triggers our sympathy for the characters, we feel even less protected from the incongruities as the play tilts more in the direction of **tragi-comedy**. In other words, the action determines a figurative distance between the audience and the play. Such factors as characters' personalities and the plot's predictability influence this distance. The farther away we sit, the more protected we feel and usually the funnier the play becomes. Closer proximity to believability in the script draws us nearer to the conflict, making us feel more involved in the action and less safe in its presence. It is a rare play that can freely manipulate its audience back and forth along this plane and still maintain its unity. Shakespeare's *The Merchant of Venice* is one example.

A more consistent play is Oscar Wilde's *The Importance of Being Earnest*, which opened in 1895. In the following scene, Lady Bracknell questions Jack Worthing, who has just announced that Lady Bracknell's daughter, Gwendolyn, has agreed to marry him. Being satisfied with Jack's answers concerning his income and finding his upper-class idleness and careless ignorance about world affairs an asset, she queries him about his family background. In grave tones, the embarrassed Jack reveals his mysterious lineage. His late guardian, Thomas Cardew—"an old gentleman of a very charitable and kindly disposition"—had found the baby Jack in an abandoned handbag.

LADY BRACKNELL: A hand-bag?

JACK: (very seriously): Yes, Lady Bracknell. I was in a hand-bag—a somewhat large, black leather hand- bag, with handles to it—an ordinary hand-bag in fact.

LADY BRACKNELL: In what locality did this Mr. James, or Thomas, Cardew come across this ordinary hand-bag?

JACK: In the cloak-room at Victoria Station. It was given him in mistake for his own.

LADY BRACKNELL: The cloak-room at Victoria Station?

JACK: Yes. The Brighton line.

LADY BRACKNELL: The line is immaterial, Mr. Worthing. I confess I feel somewhat bewildered by what you have just told me. To be born, or at any rate bred, in a hand-bag, whether it had handles or not, seems to me to display a contempt for the ordinary decencies of family life that reminds one of the worst excesses of the French Revolution. And I presume you know what that unfortunate movement led to? As for the particular locality in which the hand-bag was found, a cloak-room at a railway station might serve to conceal a social indiscretion— has probably, indeed, been used for that purpose before now—but it could hardly be regarded as an assured basis for recognized position in good society.

JACK: May I ask you then what would you advise me to do? I need hardly say I would do anything in the world to ensure Gwendolyn's happiness.

LADY BRACKNELL: I would strongly advise you, Mr. Worthing, to try and acquire some relations as soon as possible, and to make a definite effort to produce at any rate one parent, of either sex, before the season is over.

JACK: Well, I don't see how I could possibly manage to do that. I can produce the hand-bag at any moment. It is in my dressing-room at home. I really think that should satisfy you, Lady Bracknell.

LADY BRACKNELL: Me, sir! What has it to do with me? You can hardly imagine that I and Lord Bracknell would dream of allowing our only daughter—a girl brought up with the utmost care—to marry into a cloak-room, and form an alliance with a parcel. Good morning, Mr. Worthing!

(LADY BRACKNELL sweeps out in majestic indignation.)

This dialogue between Lady Bracknell and Jack is typical of what runs throughout the entire play. It is full of exaggerations, in both the situation being discussed and the manner in which the characters, particularly Lady Bracknell, express their reactions to the situation. Under other circumstances a foundling would not be the focus of a comedy, but we are relieved from any concern for the child since the adult Jack is obviously secure, healthy, and, with one exception, carefree. Moreover, we laugh when Lady Bracknell exaggerates Jack's heritage by comparing it with the excesses of the French Revolution. On the other hand, at the core of their discussion is the deeply ingrained and oppressive notion of English class consciousness, a mentality so flawed it almost begs to be satirized. Could there be more there than light, witty entertainment?

Tragedy

The term "tragedy" when used to define a play has historically meant something very precise, not simply a drama which ends with unfortunate consequences. This definition originated with Aristotle, who insisted that the play be an imitation of complex actions which should arouse an emotional response combining fear and pity. Aristotle believed that only a certain kind of plot could generate such a powerful reaction. Comedy, as we have seen, shows us a progression from adversity to prosperity. Tragedy must show the reverse; moreover, this progression must be experienced by a certain kind of character, says Aristotle, someone whom we can designate as the **tragic hero**. This central figure must be basically good and noble: "good" because we will not be aroused to fear and pity over the misfortunes of a villain, and "noble" both by social position and moral stature because the fall to misfortune would not otherwise be great enough for tragic impact. These virtues do not make the tragic hero perfect, however, for he must also possess **hamartia**—a tragic flaw—the frailty which leads him to make an error in judgment which initiates the reversal in his fortunes, causing his death or the death of others or both. These dire consequences become the hero's **catastrophe**. The most common tragic flaw is **hubris**, an excessive pride that adversely influences the protagonist's judgment.

Often the catastrophic consequences involve an entire nation because the tragic hero's social rank carries great responsibilities. Witnessing these events produces the emotional reaction Aristotle believed the audience should experience, the **catharsis**. Although tragedy must arouse our pity for the tragic hero as he endures his catastrophe and must frighten us as we witness the consequences of a flawed behavior which anyone could exhibit, there must also be a purgation, "a cleansing," of these emotions which should leave the audience feeling not depressed but relieved and almost elated. The assumption is that while the tragic hero endures a crushing reversal somehow he is not thoroughly defeated as he gains new stature though suffering and the knowledge that comes with suffering. Classical tragedy insists that the universe is ordered. If truth or universal law is ignored, the results are devastating, causing the audience to react emotionally; simultaneously, the tragic results prove the existence of truth, thereby reassuring our faith that existence is sensible.

Sophocles' plays give us some of the clearest examples of Aristotle's definition of tragedy. Shakespeare's tragedies are more varied and more modern in their complexities. *Othello* is one of Shakespeare's most innovative and troublesome extensions of tragedy's boundaries. The title character commands the Venetian army and soon becomes acting governor of Cypress. He is also a Moor, a dark-skinned African whose secret marriage to the beautiful Desdemona has infuriated her father, a wealthy and influential Venetian, whose anger reveals a racist element in Venice which Othello tries to ignore. Iago hates Othello for granting a promotion to Cassio which Iago believes should rightfully be his. With unrelenting determination and malicious deception, Iago attempts to persuade Othello that Desdemona has committed adultery with Cassio. The following excerpt catches Iago in the early stages of his successful manipulation:

IAGO: In Venice they [wives] do let heaven see pranks
They dare not show their husbands; their best conscience
Is not to leave 't undone, but keep 't unknown.

OTHELLO: Dost thou say so?

IAGO: She did deceive her father, marrying you;
And when she seem'd to shake and fear your looks,
She lov'd them most.

OTHELLO: And so she did.

IAGO: Why, go to, then;
She that so young could give out such a seeming,
To see her father's eyes up close as oak,
He thought 'twas witchcraft; but I am much to blame;
I humbly do beseech you of your pardon
For too much loving you.

OTHELLO: I am bound to thee for ever.

IAGO: I see, this hath a little dash'd your spirits.

OTHELLO: Not a jot, not a jot.

IAGO: I' faith, I fear it has.
I hope you will consider what is spoke
Comes from my love. But I do see you're mov'd;
I am to pray you not to strain my speech
To grosser issues nor to larger reach
Than to suspicion.

OTHELLO: I will not.

IAGO: Should you do so, my lord,
My speech should fall into such vile success
As my thoughts aim not at. Cassio's my worthy friend—
My lord, I see you're mov'd.

OTHELLO: No, not much mov'd:
I do not think but Desdemona's honest.

IAGO: Long live she so! and long live you to think so!

OTHELLO: And yet, how nature erring from itself,—

IAGO: Ay, there's the point: as, to be bold with you,
Not to affect many proposed matches
Of her own clime, complexion, and degree,
Whereto, we see, in all things nature tends;
Foh! one may smell in such, a will most rank,
Foul disproportion, thoughts unnatural.
But pardon me; I do not in position
Distinctly speak of her, though I may fear
Her will, recoiling to her better judgment,
May fall to match you with her country forms
And happily repent.

OTHELLO: Farewell, farewell:
If more thou dost perceive, let me know more;
Set on thy wife to observe. Leave me, Iago.

IAGO: My lord, I take my leave. (Going)

OTHELLO: Why did I marry? This honest creature, doubtless,
Sees and knows more, much more, than he unfolds.

Notice that Iago speaks much more than Othello. This is typical of their conversations, as though Iago were the superior of the two. Dramatically, for Iago's machinations to compel our interests we must perceive in Othello tragic proportions, both in his strengths and weaknesses; otherwise, *Othello* would slip into a malevolent tale about a rogue and his dupe. Much of the tension in this scene emanates from Othello's reluctance either to accept Iago's innuendos immediately or to dismiss them. This confusion places him on the rack of doubt, a torture made more severe because he questions his own desirability as a husband. Consequently, since Iago is not the "honest creature" he appears to be and Othello is unwilling to confront openly his own self-doubts, Iago becomes the dominant personality—a situation which a flawless Othello would never tolerate.

HISTORY

The playwright's raw data can spring from any source. A passion play, for instance, is a dramatic adaptation of the Crucifixion as told in the gospels. A history play is a dramatic perspective of some event or series of events identified with recognized historical figures. Television docudramas are the most recent examples. Among the earliest histories were the chronicle plays which flourished during Shakespeare's time and often relied on *Chronicles* by Raphael Holinshed, first published in 1577. Holinshed's volumes and similar books by others glorified English history and were very popular throughout the Tudor period, especially following the defeat of the Spanish Armada. Similarly, Shakespeare's *Henry V* and *Henry VIII* emphasize national and religious chauvinism in their treatments of kings who, from a more objective historical perspective appear less than nobly motivated. These plays resemble romantic comedies with each one's protagonist defeating some adversary and establishing national harmony through royal marriage. *King Lear* and *Macbeth*, on the other hand, movingly demonstrate Shakespeare's skill at turning historical figures into tragic heroes.

Ever since the 16th century history plays have seldom risen above the level of patriotic whitewash and political propaganda. Of course there are notable exceptions to this trend: Robert Bolt's *A Man for All Seasons* is one. The title character, Sir Thomas More, is beheaded at the play's conclusion, following his refusal to condone Henry VIII's break from the Roman Catholic Church and the king's establishment of the Church of England with the monarch as its head. Henry wants More to condone these actions because the Pope will not grant Henry a divorce from Queen Catherine so that he can marry Anne Boleyn, who the king believes will bear him the male heir he desperately wants. The central issue for us is not whether More's theology is valid but whether any person of conscience can act freely in a world dominated by others far less principled. In Henry's only scene he arrives at Sir Thomas' house hoping his Lord Chancellor will not disappoint him:

[music in background]

HENRY: Son after son she's borne me, Thomas, all dead at birth, or dead within a month; I never saw the hand of God so clear in anything... I have a daughter, she's a good child, a well-set child—But I have no son. (He flares up) It is my bounden duty to put away the Queen, and all the Popes back to St. Peter shall not come between me and my duty! How is it that you cannot see? Everybody else does.

MORE: (Eagerly) Then why does Your Grace need my poor support?

HENRY: Because you are honest. What's more to the purpose, you're known to be honest... There are those like Norfolk who follow me because I wear the crown, and there are those like Master Cromwell who follow me because they are jackals with sharp teeth and I am their lion, and there is a mass that follow me because it follows anything that moves—and there is you.

MORE: I am sick to think how much I must displease Your Grace.

HENRY: No, Thomas, I respect your sincerity. Respect? Oh, man, it's water in the desert... How did you like our music? That air they played, it had a certain—well, tell me what you thought of it.

MORE: (Relieved at this turn; smiling) Could it have been Your Grace's own?

HENRY: (Smiles back) Discovered! Now I'll never know your true opinion. And that's irksome, Thomas, for we artists, though we love praise, yet we love truth better.

MORE: (Mildly) Then I will tell Your Grace truly what I thought of it.

HENRY: (A little disconcerted) Speak then.

MORE: To me it seemed—delightful.

HENRY: Thomas—I chose the right man for Chancellor.

MORE: I must in fairness add that my taste in music is reputably deplorable.

To what extent Henry and More discussed the king's divorce and its subsequent events nobody knows, let alone what was actually said, although we can be certain they spoke an English distinctively different from the language in the play. Bolt's imagination, funnelled through the dramatist's obligation to tell an interesting story, presides over the historical data and dictates the play's projections of More, Henry, and the other participants. Thus, we do not have "history"; instead we have a dramatic perception of history shaped, altered, and adorned by Robert Bolt, writing about 16th century figures from a 1960 vantage point. But as the scene above shows, the characters' personalities are not simple reductions of what historical giants should be. Henry struts a royal self-assurance noticeably colored by vanity and frustration; yet although he lacks More's wit and intelligence, the king clearly is no fool. Likewise, as troubled as More is by the controversy before him, he projects a formidable power of his own. *A Man for All Seasons* succeeds dramatically because Bolt provides only enough historical verisimilitude to present a context for the characters' development while he allows the resultant thematic implications to touch all times, all seasons. When we read any history play, we should search for similar implications; otherwise, the work can never become more than a theatrical precis with a narrow, didactic focus.

MODERN DRAMA

From the 1870's to the present, the theater has participated in the artistic movements reflecting accumulated theories of science, social science, and philosophy which attempt to define reality and the means we use to discern it. First caught in a pendulum of opposing views, modern drama eventually synthesized these perspectives into new forms, familiar in some ways and boldly original in others. Henrik Ibsen's plays began the modern era with their emphasis on **realism**, a seeking of truth through direct observation using the five senses. As objectively depicted, contemporary life received a closer scrutiny than ever before, showing everyday people in everyday situations. Before Ibsen, theatrical sets were limited, with rare exceptions, to castles and country estates. After Ibsen the farmhouse and city tenement were suitable for the stage. Ibsen's work influenced many others, and from realism came two main variations. The first, **naturalism**, strove to push realism towards a direct transformation of life on stage, a "slice of life" showing how the scientific principles of heredity and environment have shaped society, especially in depicting the plights of the lower classes. The second variation, **expressionism**, moved in a different direction and actually denied realism's premise that the real world could be objectively perceived; instead—influenced by Sigmund Freud's theories about human behavior's hidden, subconscious motivations and by other modernist trends in the arts, such as James Joyce's fiction and Picasso's paintings—expressionism imitated a disconnected dream-like world filled with psychological images at odds with the tangible world surrounding it. While naturalism attempts to imitate life directly, expressionism is abstract and often relies on symbols.

A modern play can employ any number of elements found in the spectrum between these extremes as well as suggest divergent philosophical views about whether humanity has the power to change its condition or whether any of its ideas about the universe are verifiable. Moreover, no work of art is necessarily confined within a particular school of thought. It is quite possible that seemingly incongruent forms can appear in the same play and work well. *The Glass Menagerie*, *A Man for All Seasons*, and *Death of a Salesman* feature characters and dialogue indicative of realistic drama, but the sets described in the stage directions are expressionistic, offering either framed outlines of places or distorted representations. Conventions from classical drama are also available to the playwright. As previously noted, Tom acts as a Greek chorus as well as an important character in his play; the same is true of the Common Man, whose identity changes from scene to scene. Playwrights Eugene Ionesco and Harold Pinter have created characters speaking and behaving in extraordinary ways while occupying sets which are typically realistic. In short, anything is possible in modern drama, a quality which is wholly compatible with the diversity and unpredictability of 20th century human experiences.

In a sense all good drama is modern. No label about a play's origin or form can adequately describe its content. Establishing the people, places, and thought within the play is crucial to our understanding. For the characters to interest us we must perceive the issues that affect their lives, and eventually we will discover why the characters' personalities and backgrounds, together with their social situations, inevitably converge with these issues and create conflicts. We must also stay aware of drama's kinship with lyric poetry's subjective mood and tone, a quality dominating all plays regardless of the form. *Death of a Salesman* challenges the classical definitions of tragedy by giving us a modern American, Willy Loman, who is indeed a "low man," a person of little social importance and limited moral fiber. His delusionary values have brought him at age sixty-four to failure and despair, yet more than ever he clings to his dreams and painted memories for solace and hope. Late one night, after Willy has returned from an aborted sales trip, his rambling conversation with his wife Linda returns to the topic which haunts him the most, his son Biff.

WILLY: Biff is a lazy bum!

LINDA: They're sleeping. Get something to eat. Go on down.

WILLY: Why did he come home? I would like to know what brought him home.

LINDA: I don't know. I think he's still lost, Willy. I think he's very lost.

WILLY: Biff Loman is lost. In the greatest country in the world a young man with such—personal attractiveness, gets lost. And such a hard worker. There's one thing about Biff—he's not lazy.

LINDA: Never.

WILLY (with pity and resolve): I'll see him in the morning; I'll have a nice talk with him. I'll get him a job selling. He could be big in no time. My God! Remember how they used to follow him around in high school? When he smiled at one of them their faces lit up. When he walked down the street... (He loses himself in reminiscences.)

LINDA (trying to bring him out of it): Willy, dear, I got a new kind of American-type cheese today. It's whipped.

WILLY: Why do you get American cheese when you know I like Swiss?

LINDA: I just thought you'd like a change—

WILLY: I don't want change! I want Swiss cheese. Why am I always being contradicted?

LINDA (with a covering laugh): I just thought it would be a surprise.

WILLY: Why don't you open a window in here, for God's sake?

LINDA (with infinite patience): They're all open dear.

WILLY: The way they boxed us in here. Bricks and windows, windows and bricks.

LINDA: We should have bought the land next door.

WILLY: The street is lined with cars. There's not a breath of fresh air in the neighborhood. The grass don't grow any more, you can't raise a carrot in the backyard. They should've had a law against apartment houses. Remember those two beautiful elms out there? When I and Biff hung the swing between them?

LINDA: Yeah, like a million miles from the city.

WILLY: They should've arrested the builder for cutting those down. They massacred the neighborhood. (Lost) More and more I think of those days, Linda. This time of year it was lilac and wisteria. And then the peonies would come out, and the daffodils. What fragrance in this room!

LINDA: Well, after all, people had to move somewhere.

WILLY: No, there's more people now.

LINDA: I don't think there's more people. I think—

WILLY: There's more people! That's what ruining this country! Population is getting out of control. The competition is maddening! Smell the stink from that apartment house! And another on the other side... How can they whip cheese?

In Arthur Miller's stage directions for *Death of a Salesman*, the Loman house is outlined by simple framing with various floors represented by short elevated platforms. Outside the house the towering shapes of the city angle inward presenting the crowded oppressiveness Willy complains about. First performed in 1949, the play continues to make a powerful commentary on modern American life. We see Willy as more desperate than angry about his condition, which he defines in ways as contradictory as his assessments of Biff. In his suffocating world so nebulously delineated, Willy gropes for peace while hiding from truth; and although his woes are uniquely American in some ways, they touch broader, more universal human problems as well.

Literature

TEST 1

Literature

TEST 1

1. (A) (B) (C) (D) (E)
2. (A) (B) (C) (D) (E)
3. (A) (B) (C) (D) (E)
4. (A) (B) (C) (D) (E)
5. (A) (B) (C) (D) (E)
6. (A) (B) (C) (D) (E)
7. (A) (B) (C) (D) (E)
8. (A) (B) (C) (D) (E)
9. (A) (B) (C) (D) (E)
10. (A) (B) (C) (D) (E)
11. (A) (B) (C) (D) (E)
12. (A) (B) (C) (D) (E)
13. (A) (B) (C) (D) (E)
14. (A) (B) (C) (D) (E)
15. (A) (B) (C) (D) (E)
16. (A) (B) (C) (D) (E)
17. (A) (B) (C) (D) (E)
18. (A) (B) (C) (D) (E)
19. (A) (B) (C) (D) (E)
20. (A) (B) (C) (D) (E)

21. (A) (B) (C) (D) (E)
22. (A) (B) (C) (D) (E)
23. (A) (B) (C) (D) (E)
24. (A) (B) (C) (D) (E)
25. (A) (B) (C) (D) (E)
26. (A) (B) (C) (D) (E)
27. (A) (B) (C) (D) (E)
28. (A) (B) (C) (D) (E)
29. (A) (B) (C) (D) (E)
30. (A) (B) (C) (D) (E)
31. (A) (B) (C) (D) (E)
32. (A) (B) (C) (D) (E)
33. (A) (B) (C) (D) (E)
34. (A) (B) (C) (D) (E)
35. (A) (B) (C) (D) (E)
36. (A) (B) (C) (D) (E)
37. (A) (B) (C) (D) (E)
38. (A) (B) (C) (D) (E)
39. (A) (B) (C) (D) (E)
40. (A) (B) (C) (D) (E)

41. (A) (B) (C) (D) (E)
42. (A) (B) (C) (D) (E)
43. (A) (B) (C) (D) (E)
44. (A) (B) (C) (D) (E)
45. (A) (B) (C) (D) (E)
46. (A) (B) (C) (D) (E)
47. (A) (B) (C) (D) (E)
48. (A) (B) (C) (D) (E)
49. (A) (B) (C) (D) (E)
50. (A) (B) (C) (D) (E)
51. (A) (B) (C) (D) (E)
52. (A) (B) (C) (D) (E)
53. (A) (B) (C) (D) (E)
54. (A) (B) (C) (D) (E)
55. (A) (B) (C) (D) (E)
56. (A) (B) (C) (D) (E)
57. (A) (B) (C) (D) (E)
58. (A) (B) (C) (D) (E)
59. (A) (B) (C) (D) (E)
60. (A) (B) (C) (D) (E)

LITERATURE

TEST 1

TIME: 60 Minutes
60 Questions

DIRECTIONS: *This test consists of selections from literary works and questions on their content, form, and style. After reading each passage or poem, choose the best answer to each question and blacken the corresponding space on the answer sheet.*

NOTE: Pay particular attention to the requirement of questions that contain the words NOT, LEAST, or EXCEPT.

QUESTIONS 1–6 are based on the following passage. Read the passage carefully before choosing your answers.

I looked at the sea of yellow faces above the garish clothes—faces all happy and excited over this bit of fun, all certain that the elephant was going to be shot. They were watching me as they would watch a conjuror about to perform a trick. They did not like me, but with the magical rifle in my hands, I was momentarily worth watching. And suddenly I realized that I would have to shoot the elephant after all. The people expected it of me and I had got to do it; I could feel their two thousand wills pressing me forward, irresistibly. And it was at this moment, as I stood there with the rifle in my hands, that I first grasped the hollowness, the futility of the white man's dominion in the East. Here was I, the white man with his gun, standing in front of an unarmed native crowd — seemingly the leading actor of the piece; but in reality I was only an absurd puppet pushed to and fro by the will of those yellow faces behind. I perceived in this moment that when the white man turns tyrant it is his own freedom he destroys. He becomes a sort of hollow posing dummy, the conventionalized figure of a sahib. For it is the condition of his rule that he shall spend his life in trying to impress the "natives", and so in every crisis he has go to do what the "natives" expect of him.

1. The controlling metaphor of the piece involves

    (A) the stage and acting

    (B) magic and mystery

    (C) the thrill of the hunt

    (D) the crowd's will

    (E) the ventriloquist's dummy

2. The narrator must shoot the elephant for the following reasons EXCEPT

    (A) he is willed by the crowd

    (B) his role of sahib demands it

    (C) he must impress the natives

    (D) his role of policeman demands it

    (E) the people expect it

3. The resolution to kill the elephant symbolizes the

    (A) power yet stupidity of the white man in the East

    (B) domination of the white man in the East

    (C) prejudice the white man has toward the natives

    (D) emptiness of the role the white man plays in the East

    (E) role of the sahib as clown

4. Which of the following best explains why the people are "happy and excited"?

    (A) They love and respect the narrator who will put on a show.

    (B) They hate but respect the role of sahib who will perform for them.

    (C) They are on a feast day of revelry to watch this show.

    (D) They scorn the narrator but anticipate his prowess in the show-down with the elephant.

    (E) They dislike the narrator and hope to see his downfall in a show of arms.

5. The narrator uses the personal pronoun frequently and the term "white man" to show his

    (A) scorn of the rabble

    (B) distancing himself from the situation

    (C) realization that he stands for many

    (D) fear of the rabble

    (E) awareness that he stands alone

6. Which word best describes the tone of the passage?

    (A) furious   (D) sardonic

    (B) philosophic   (E) disillusioned

    (C) amused

QUESTIONS 7–12 are based on the following excerpt from a longer poem. Read the poem carefully before choosing your answers.

> One speaks the glory of the British Queen,
> And one describes a charming Indian screen;
> A third interprets motions, looks, and eyes;
> At every word a reputation dies.
> 5 Snuff, or the fan, supply each pause of chat,
> With singing, laughing, ogling, and all that.

Meanwhile, declining from the noon of day,
The sun obliquely shoots his burning ray;
The hungry judges soon the sentence sign,
10   And wretches hang that jurymen may dine;

From "The Rape of the Lock" (Canto 3 lines 13–22) by Alexander Pope

7. The last two lines suggest that this society

    (A) takes pride in its justice system

    (B) speedily administers justice for humanitarian reasons

    (C) sentences the wrong people to death

    (D) sentences people for the wrong reasons

    (E) believes in the jury system

8. Lines 1–6 suggest that this society

    I.   Indulges in gossip that slanders the Queen

    II. engages in serious discussions about affairs of state

    III. engages in gossip that ruins reputations

    (A) I and III only   (D) I, II and III

    (B) III only   (E) I only

    (C) II only

9. The juxtaposition in lines 1 and 2 suggest that the people

    (A) talk of trivia

    (B) revere the monarchy and Indian screens equally

    (C) are Imperialists

    (D) are Royalists

    (E) talk of serious matters

10. The word "obliquely" (line 8) in this context could mean all of the following EXCEPT

    (A) perpendicularly

(B)   at a steep angle

(C)   a pun on hidden meanings

(D)   a pun on stealth

(E)   a suggestion of the amoral standing of this society

11.   The rhyming couplets reflect that the poet is

(A)   poking gentle fun at the society

(B)   lampooning the society

(C)   savagely satirizing the society

(D)   amusingly parodying Homer

(E)   using doggerel

12.   The change in voice from the first half of the excerpt into the second is best described as one from

(A)   light to dark   (D)   criticism to acceptance

(B)   amused to critical   (E)   amused to sadness

(C)   light-hearted to sarcastic

QUESTIONS 13–20 are based on the following passage. Read the passage carefully before choosing your answers.

We know that there was an older play by Thomas Kyd, that extraordinary dramatic (if not poetic) genius who was in all probability the author of two plays so dissimilar as *The Spanish Tragedy* and *The Arden of Feversham*; and what this play was like we can guess from three clues: from *The Spanish Tragedy* itself, from the tale of Belleforest upon which Kyd's *Hamlet* must have been based, and from a version acted in Germany in Shakespeare's lifetime which bears strong evidence of having been adapted from the earlier, not the later, play. From these three sources it is clear that in the earlier play the motive was a revenge motive simply; that the action or delay is caused, as in *The Spanish Tragedy*, solely by the difficulty of assassinating a monarch surrounded by guards; and that the 'madness' of Hamlet was feigned in order to escape suspicion, and successfully. In the final play of Shakespeare, on the other hand, there is a motive which is more important than that of revenge, and which explicitly 'blunts' the latter; the delay is unexplained on grounds of necessity or expediency; and the effect of 'madness' is not to lull but arouse the king's suspicion. The alteration is not complete enough, however, to be convincing. Furthermore, there are verbal parallels so close to *The Spanish Tragedy* as to leave no doubt that in places Shakespeare was merely *revising* the text of Kyd. And finally there are unexplained scenes — the Polonius-Reynaldo scenes — for which there is little excuse; these scenes are not in the verse style of Kyd and not beyond doubt in the style of Shakespeare. These Mr. Robertson believes to be scenes in the original play of Kyd reworked by a third hand, perhaps Chapman, before Shakespeare touched the play.

Excerpt from "Hamlet and His Problems" in Selected Essays *by T. S. Eliot, copyright 1950 by Harcourt Brace Jovanovich, Inc. and renewed 1978 by Esme Valerie Eliot, reprinted by permission of the publisher.*

13. The author suggests that Kyd's older play was called

    (A) *The Spanish Tragedy*   (D) *A German Tragedy*

    (B) *Belleforest*   (E) *Hamlet*

    (C) *The Arden of Feversham*

14. The author suggests that Shakespeare's play is a revision of

    (A) a German version of Kyd's

    (B) *The Arden of Fersham*

    (C) *The Spanish Tragedy*

    (D) the tale of Belleforest

    (E) his own earlier play

15. Mr. Robertson suggests that Chapman reworked

    (A) *The Spanish Tragedy*

    (B) Kyd's older play

    (C) *The Arden of Feversham*

(D) Kyd's Polonius-Reynaldo scenes

(E) Shakespeare's Polonius-Reynaldo scenes

16. We can guess what the Kyd play was like through clues in

I.   *The Arden of Feversham*

II. a German version in Shakespeare's time

III. *The Spanish Tragedy* and the tale of Belleforest

(A) I and III   (D) III only

(B) I only   (E) II and III

(C) II only

17. Kyd's earlier play was a(n)

(A) historical saga   (D) chronicle

(B) miracle play   (E) morality play

(C) revenge play

18. The author explains the motive of Shakespeare's Hamlet as

(A) revenge for his mother and suspicion of the monarch

(B) revenge for his mother to blunt the suspicion of the monarch

(C) revenge on Polonius to expedite the revenge on the monarch

(D) an oedipal love of his mother

(E) none of the above

19. The author explains the action in *The Spanish Tragedy* is caused by the

(A) hero feigning madness

(B) monarch's madness

(C) monarch's love from his guards

(D) monarch being constantly guarded

(E) hero's procrastination

20. Which of the following words best describe the author's tone?

   (A) calm and objective   (D) condescending and lecturing

   (B) erudite and pompous   (E) learned and high-brow

   (C) pedagogical and dull

<u>QUESTIONS 21–28</u> are based on the following passage. Read the passage carefully before choosing your answers.

Two paper tendrils, also accordian-pleated, hung down from the clapper of the bell. Miss Faust pulled one. It unfolded stickily and became a long banner with a message written on it. "Here," said Miss Faust, handing the free end to Dr. Breed, "pull it the rest of the way and tack the end to the bulletin board."

Dr. Breed obeyed, stepping back to read the banner's message. "Peace on Earth!" he read out loud heartily.

Miss Faust stepped down from her desk with the other tendril, unfolding it, "Good Will Toward Men!" the other tendril said.

"By golly," chuckled Dr. Breed, "they've dehydrated Christmas! The place looks festive, very festive."

"And I remembered the chocolate bars for the Girl Pool, too," she said. "Aren't you proud of me?"

Dr. Breed touched his forehead, dismayed by his forgetfulness. "Thank God for that! It slipped my mind."

"We musn't ever forget that," said Miss Faust. "It's tradition now—Dr. Breed and his chocolate bars for the Girl Pool at Christmas." She explained to me that the Girl Pool was the typing bureau in the Laboratory's basement. "The girls belong to anybody with access to a dictaphone."

All year long, she said, the girls of the Girl Pool listened to the faceless voices of scientists on dictaphone records—records brought in by the mail girls. Once a year the girls left their cloister of cement block to go a-caroling—to get their chocolate bars from Dr. Asa Breed.

"They serve science too," Dr. Breed testified, "even though they may not understand a word of it. God bless them everyone!"

From <u>Cat's Cradle</u> *by Kurt Vonnegut, Jr. Reprinted by permission of Delacourte Press/Seymour Lawrence, a division of Bantam, Doubleday, Dell Publishing Broup, Inc.*

21. "they've dehydrated Christmas" means all of the following EXCEPT

    (A) they've fossilized it

    (B) they've concentrated it

    (C) they've decimated it

    (D) they've dessicated it

    (E) they've condensed it

22. Dr. Breed is a nuclear warfare scientist. What is the closest explanation for this name?

    (A) an oxymoron, because of his job

    (B) a pun on his job

    (C) pathetic fallacy, because he destroys nature

    (D) ironic, because of his potential for destroying life

    (E) a paradox on what his job entails

23. Miss Faust is his secretary. What is the closest explanation for her name?

    (A) She has overstepped the bounds of learning.

    (B) She dabbles in black magic.

    (C) She serves a Mephistopheles.

    (D) She practices devil worship.

    (E) She is doomed to hell.

24. When Dr. Breed reads the banner's messages, what literary technique is at work?

    (A) homile   (D) symbolism

    (B) irony   (E) parable

    (C) emblemism

25. What best captures the meaning behind the words: "The girls belong to anybody with access to a dictaphone."

(A) The girls have sold themselves to the scientists in the way society has prostituted itself to technology.

(B) The Girl Pool represents the robotised way of modern technology.

(C) The girls' demeaning and sterile job represents the way women were treated in the work force.

(D) The girls have become as mechanized as the dictaphones they use.

(E) The girls must recognize the superior intelligence of the machines and their masters.

26. The use of the words "cloister of cement block" suggests the girls are like

(A) nuns trained to work silently in modern surroundings

(B) nuns sequestered in peaceful surroundings

(C) prisoners in a modern efficient facility

(D) prisoners who prefer austere surroundings

(E) nuns immured in modern-day harshness

27. Miss Faust is talking to

I.   Herself and Dr. Breed

II.   The Girl Pool and the scientists

III. Dr. Breed and the narrator

(A) I and II   (D) III only

(B) I only   (E) II only

(C) II and III

28. The parody of Tiny Tim's blessing from Dickens's *Christmas Carol* functions to

(A) highlight the sterility of this Christmas image as opposed to Dickens's

(B) show Dr. Breed's love for the Girl Pool: his chocolate gift

(C) show Dr. Breed's Scrooge-like attitude — he forgets the chocolate for the Girl Pool

(D) contrast the warmth of this Christmas image as opposed to Dickens's

(E) underline the old-fashioned atmosphere of the office at Christmas

QUESTIONS 29–35 are based on the following excerpt from a longer poem. Read the poem carefully before choosing your answers.

In Breughel's *Icarus*, for instance: how everything turns away
Quite leisurely from the disaster; the plowman may
Have heard the splash, the forsaken cry,
But for him it was not an important failure; the sun shone
5   As it had to on the white legs disappearing into the green
Water; and the expensive delicate ship that must have seen
Something amazing, a boy falling out of the sky,
Had somewhere to get to and sailed calmly on.

"Musee des Beaux Arts," by W.H. Auden. Copyright 1940 and renewed 1968 by W.H. Auden. Reprinted from W.H. AUDEN: COLLECTED POEMS, edited by Edward Mendelson, by permission of Random House, Inc.

29. The technique used between lines 1–2 is

(A) alliteration   (D) personification

(B) enjambment   (E) bathos

(C) onomatopoeia

30. What examples are given for "everything turns away"?

I.   The boy

II. The plowman and the ship

III. The plowman and the painter

(A) I only   (D) II only

(B) I and III   (E) I and II

(C) III only

31. Who is the "boy falling from the sky"?

   (A) a symbol for the painter

   (B) a symbol for the poet

   (C) Icarus

   (D) Daedalus

   (E) Minos

32. What best expresses why "it was not an important failure" to the plowman?

   (A) He perhaps just hears the splash and is too preoccupied with his own life to stop.

   (B) He sees the immediate failure not the myth created of the son's disobedience.

   (C) He sees only the father's failure and, in contrast to his life, that is unimportant.

   (D) He understands how an inventor's skill can create a myth but his own skill of plowing is more important.

   (E) He sees only that a stranger falls out of the sky and he does not care about others.

33. All of the following are in Breughel's *Icarus* EXCEPT

   (A) the sea   (D) a ship

   (B) the sun   (E) the plowman

   (C) a body

34. Which of the following most clearly expresses the poem's meaning?

   (A) society's blatant disregard for life

   (B) people's inhumanity toward others

   (C) society's indifference to suffering

   (D) a courageous attempt to escape the bounds of society

   (E) society's contempt for the weak and failure

35. The words "for instance" give the poem a(n)

(A) didactic tone   (D) conversational tone

(B) ironic tone   (E) regular rhythm

(C) irregular scansion

QUESTIONS 36–47 are based on the following excerpt from a play. Read the excerpt carefully before choosing your answers.

Sir Anthony.   Madam, a circulating library in a town is as an evergreen tree of diabolical knowledge! It blossoms through the year! — And depend on it. Mrs. ——, that they who are so fond of handling the leaves, will long for the fruit at last.

Mrs. ——   Fie, Fie, Sir Anthony! you surely speak laconically.

Sir Anthony.   Why, Mrs. ——, in moderation now, what would you have a woman know?

Mrs. ——   Observe me, Sir Anthony. I would by no means wish a daughter of mine to be a progeny of learning; I don't think so much learning becomes a young woman; for instance, I would never let her meddle with Greek or Hebrew, or algebra, or simony, or fluxions, or paradoxes, or such inflammatory branches of learning— neither would it be necessary for her to handle any of your mathematical, astronomical, diabolical instruments. —But, Sir Anthony, I would send her, at nine years old, to a boarding school, in order to learn a little ingenuity, and artifice. Then, sir, she should have a supercilious knowledge in accounts;—and as she grew up, I would have her instructed in geometry, that she might know something of the contagious countries; but above all, Sir Anthony, she should be mistress of orthodoxy, that she might not mis-spell, and mispronounce words so shamefully as girls usually do; and likewise that she might reprehend the true meaning of what she is saying. This, Sir Anthony, is what I would have a woman know; and I don't think there is a superstitious article in it.

Sir Anthony.   Well, well, Mrs. ——, I will dispute the point no further with you; though I must confess, that you are a truly moderate and polite arguer, for almost every third word you say is on my side of the question....

From The Rivals, *Act I Sc. ii, by Richard Sheridan.*

36. Mrs. ———'s last name gave rise to which of the following dictonary terms?

    (A) homonym

    (D) synonym

    (B) altruism

    (E) synecdoche

    (C) malapropism

37. Which best describes what Mrs. — does to words?

    (A) She changes the meaning to something outrageous.

    (B) She chooses the wrong meaning.

    (C) She gives a word close in meaning that sounds the same.

    (D) She gives a word close in sound that gives a ridiculous meaning.

    (E) She gives a word close in sound but often wrong in meaning.

38. All of the following words Mrs. ——— uses wrongly EXCEPT

    (A) fluxions

    (D) contagious

    (B) laconically

    (E) orthodoxy

    (C) ingenuity

39. Which of the following best demonstrate the pattern behind Mrs. —'s errors?

    I.   progeny / prodigy

    II. superstitious / suspicious

    III. reprehend / apprehend

    (A) I and III

    (D) II and III

    (B) II only

    (E) I, II, and III

    (C) III only

40. What device does Sir Anthony use to describe a circulating library?

    (A) a mixed metaphor

    (D) an extended metaphor

    (B) personification

    (E) pathetic fallacy

    (C) an extended simile

41. What best describes Sir Anthony's meaning behind the notion of the "leaves" and the "fruit"?

   (A) Those who leaf quickly through books will never learn from the tree of knowledge.

   (B) Those who read evil books will become evil.

   (C) Those who read books about exciting adventures will want to experience the same.

   (D) Those who read novels that look exciting will want to read more and more.

   (E) Those who choose a book by its cover will be disappointed at length.

42. All the subjects Mrs. —— does *not* want women to know are

   (A) traditionally feminine subjects

   (B) radically feminine subjects

   (C) radical university subjects

   (D) traditionally gentleman subjects

   (E) traditionally difficult subjects

43. All the subjects Mrs. —— *does* want women to know would equip a woman for the role of

   (A) submissive but knowledgeable homemaker

   (B) docile but suitably knowledgeable wife

   (C) docile wife

   (D) artificial flirt

   (E) knowledgeable mistress

44. When Mrs. —— hopes that a woman should "not mis-spell, and mispronounce words," what dramatic technique is at work?

   (A) soliloquy   (D) dramatic irony

   (B) irony   (E) dramatic license

   (C) satire

45. What best describes the meaning behind Sir Anthony's concluding speech?

   (A) Mrs. —— has in fact agreed with everything he has said so he has enjoyed the argument.

   (B) Because Mrs. —— does not understand him there has been no argument.

   (C) He loves this type of argument because he wins.

   (D) He admires Mrs. ——'s powers of debating in an argument.

   (E) He knows Mrs. —— has not understood him and gone against most of her own argument.

46. If you were playing the role of Mrs. —— how would you facially receive Sir Anthony's concluding speech?

   (A) smiling and proud because you think you have impressed him

   (B) enraged because he has made a fool of you

   (C) with a puzzled frown because you cannot understand him

   (D) with a blank look because you think you have upset him

   (E) disappointed because you would like to continue the argument

47. What words best describe Sir Anthony's tone in his concluding speech?

   (A) droll and dry   (D) whimsical and weary

   (B) amused but angry   (E) laconic and sardonic

   (C) sarcastic but amused

QUESTIONS 48–54 are based on the following poem. Read carefully before choosing your answers.

> Oh, to vex me, contraryes meet in one:
> Inconstancy unnaturally hath begott
> A dangerous habit; that when I would not
> I change in vowes, and in devotione.
> 5 As humourous is my contritione

As my prophane Love, and as soone forgott:
As ridlingly distemper'd, cold and hott,
As praying as mute; as infinite, as none.
I durst not view heaven yesterday; and today
10 In prayers and flattering speaches I court God:
Tomorrow I quake with true feare of his rod.
So my devout fitts come and go away
Like a fantastique Ague: save that here
Those are my best dayes, when I shake with feare.

"19," by John Donne

48. The poem is written as a(n)

(A) sestina   (D) dramatic monologue

(B) sonnet   (E) aubade

(C) hymn

49. What best explains lines 3–4?

(A) I want to change my vows and truly love God.

(B) Just when I want to love God, I change my mind.

(C) Just when I least want to, I become inconsistent in my love of
     God.

(D) I do not want to love God and fight against constancy.

(E) Just when I want to love God, he changes the vows.

50. Which word best replaces "humorous" in this context?

(A) hilarious   (D) fickle

(B) capricious   (E) ridiculous

(C) amusing

51. The word "Love" is capitalized because it

(A) refers to the poet's mistress.

(B) refers to the love of the devil.

(C) personifies any love that is not the love of God.

(D) personifies the poet's secular love which takes him away from God.

(E) refers to all the loves the poet has experienced.

52. What best explains the description of the "prophane Love"?

(A) The poet is laughing at the inconstancy of women.

(B) The poet is criticizing the fickle nature of women.

(C) The poet sets up a contrast between the love of women and the love of God.

(D) The poet sets up a paradox between how he feels about women and how he feels about God.

(E) The poet sets up a paradigm of how he feels today about women and God.

53. The "Oh" in the first line expresses a cry of

(A) anger   (D) ecstasy

(B) bewilderment   (E) misery

(C) anguish

54. All of the following describe the poet's voice EXCEPT

(A) contrite   (D) meditative

(B) haughty   (E) perplexed

(C) God fearing

QUESTIONS 55–60 are based on the following excerpt from a letter. Read carefully before choosing your answers.

But the Divell as hee affecteth Deitie, and seeketh to have all the complements of Divine honor applied to his service, so hath he among the rest possessed also most Poets with his idle fansies. For in lieu of solemne and devout matter, to which in duety they owe their abilities, they now busy themselves in expressing such passions, as onely serve for testimonies to how unwoorthy affections they have wedded their wils. And because the best course to let them see the

78

errour of their workes, is to weave a new webbe in their owne loom; I have heere layd a few course threds together, to invite some skillfuller wits to goe forward in the same, or to begin some finer peece, wherin it may be seene, how well verse and vertue sute together. Blame me not (good Cosen) though I send you a blameworthy present, in which the most that can commend it, is the good will of the writer, neither Arte nor invention, giving it any credite. If in mee this be a fault, you cannot be faultless that did importune mee to committe it, and therefore you must bear part of the penance, when it shall please sharpe censures to impose it. In the meane time with many good wishes I send you these few ditties, add you the Tunes, and let the Meane, I pray you, be still a part in all your Musicke.

From "The Author to his Loving Cosen," by Robert Southwell

55. In the author's view, poets should write about

   (A) the devil putting on Godly attributes

   (B) the honor and duty due to God

   (C) fantasies that help the reader to relax

   (D) love and passion pertaining to women

   (E) serious matters pertaining to God

56. The author criticizes poets because

   I. They waste their abilities on poems that deal with loving women instead of loving God

   II. They write about love in such a way that shows they disdain marriage

   III. Their love poems show that worldly passion has got the better of them

   (A) I only   (D) I and II

   (B) I and III   (E) I, II, and III

   (C) II only

57. What best describes the role of the author in the figure of speech used to describe his purpose?

   (A) He personifies the writer struggling to put across his web of ideas.

   (B) He plays the weaver in the extended metaphor about the loom and weaving, trying to encourage better poetry.

   (C) He plays the role of the new poet weaving new ideas for the old poets to copy.

   (D) He plays the role of the weaver trying to put back old techniques such as alliteration into the poetry of his days.

   (E) He personifies the role of the old jaded writer trying to encourage younger poets to write better rhyming poetry.

58. Why does the author send the book to his "cosen"?

   (A) He wants him to share in the praise if it is good.

   (B) He wants him to share in the blame if it is criticized.

   (C) The cousin asked him to write it.

   (D) He wants the cousin to learn from the book of poems.

   (E) The cousin is a patron who will promote the book.

59. The author's voice changes from

   (A) lecturing to praising

   (B) didactic to pedantic

   (C) critical to encouraging

   (D) harsh to gentle

   (E) arrogant to pleasant

60. What best describes the last sentence?

   (A) The author is punning on the idea of music and moderation.

   (B) The author is using a pun on the mean in music and the "Golden mean" in life.

   (C) The author is encouraging the cousin to set the poems to music, but to do it in moderation.

(D)　The author is encouraging the cousin to write his own poems, but in a moderate way, not the passionate way of the contemporary poets.

(E)　The author is warning the cousin to lead a moderate life despite loving to read poetry, because poetry could be the devil's way.

TEST 1

ANSWER KEY

1.	(A)	16.	(E)	31.	(C)	46.	(A)
2.	(D)	17.	(C)	32.	(A)	47.	(A)
3.	(D)	18.	(E)	33.	(C)	48.	(B)
4.	(D)	19.	(D)	34.	(C)	49.	(C)
5.	(C)	20.	(A)	35.	(D)	50.	(B)
6.	(E)	21.	(C)	36.	(C)	51.	(D)
7.	(D)	22.	(D)	37.	(D)	52.	(C)
8.	(B)	23.	(C)	38.	(A)	53.	(C)
9.	(B)	24.	(B)	39.	(A)	54.	(B)
10.	(A)	25.	(B)	40.	(D)	55.	(E)
11.	(A)	26.	(E)	41.	(C)	56.	(B)
12.	(E)	27.	(D)	42.	(D)	57.	(B)
13.	(E)	28.	(A)	43.	(B)	58.	(C)
14.	(C)	29.	(B)	44.	(D)	59.	(D)
15.	(D)	30.	(D)	45.	(D)	60.	(B)

DETAILED EXPLANATIONS OF ANSWERS

TEST 1

1.　**(A)**　Although magic and mystery are mentioned as is the will of the crowd the controlling metaphor hinges on the stage and acting (A) when the audience wills the leading actor of the piece. There is no mention of the hunt itself nor a ventriloquist's dummy, simply an absurd puppet and a dummy not necessarily a ventriloquist's.

2.　**(D)**　Nowhere in this excerpt is the writer referred to as a policeman (D). You may know this from your reading but do not let knowledge outside the passage sway you. All the other reasons are clearly expressed in the passage.

3.　**(D)**　The whole meaning of the piece suggests that the white man must not make a fool of himself in front of the crowd. He does not see the stupidity in his role but the emptiness of it (D). The tone of the piece here does not suggest a wish to play the fool nor any prejudice toward the natives.

4.　**(D)**　This is a fun show for the rabble. At this point the reader knows the people do not like the narrator but has not yet learned the deeper meaning of the role of sahib not wanting to make a fool of himself, nor the fact that the people are waiting for that result. The closest answer is (D) — the people are not on a feast day but have turned it into a celebration of sorts by wanting to see the elephant killed, even by someone they dislike.

5.　**(C)**　There is no scorn for the rabble but a personal analysis of what must be done. Hence the "I" pronoun. But at the same time the narrator realizes he is engaged in a much larger situation, that he is a symbol or represents "the white man" the many in the colonial set-up (C). He stands alone in the sense that he must kill the animal alone but the killing represents something much bigger than just one man versus an animal. The personal pronoun use is not a distancing device but a personal involvement.

6. **(E)** The tone of the passage involves elements of anger but furious is too strong. There is no amusement in the serious tone. There is a certain sad sarcasm in the passage, but again sardonic is too strong, and although the narrator is expressing a philosophy of sorts, philosophic suggests a depth that is not present. The best word is one that shows he has faced an awakening here and all illusions of his role disappear (E).

7. **(D)** The prisoners are speedily sentenced because the judges and the jurymen are hungry and want to go home for supper as the day ends — the prisoners may be guilty, but the wrong reasons determine their sentences (D). No doubt the people do believe in the system, but the sarcasm of the piece suggests that this society uses the system for personal selfish benefits — certainly not a humanitarian society.

8. **(B)** The society depicted is shallow and trivial, engaging in chatty conversations that everyone takes seriously. Serious as the discussions may be, they possibly involve extramarital affairs rather than affairs of state — such gossip ruins reputations (B). The gossiping involves the Queen but it is not revealed that she is slandered.

9. **(B)** The question wants you to analyze the clash or conflict of two very different concepts in conversation: the glory of the Queen in one breath and a fire screen (or room divider) in another. The juxtaposition is not so much to suggest trivia or seriousness (the Queen's glory is serious but the furniture is not), but that this society holds both in equal reverence (B). No real evidence is given that the people are Royalists or Imperialists.

10. **(A)** There is a clever use of the language in this one adverb. It stands for the angle of the sun as it declines at a steep angle but also for the hidden meanings behind the word as it refers to this society: the deceit, the amorality. It certainly does not mean that the sun is at a perpendicular angle (A).

11. **(A)** You need to know the meanings of words like doggerel: crude irregular couplets of a burlesque nature; lampoon: sharp, often virulent attack on a person or society; neither of these definitions fit these highly stylized couplets which are gentle, certainly not savage, in their satire and criticism (A). There is a parody of Homer in the poem which is a mock epic, but not in the couplets employed.

12. **(E)** The move is light to dark in the physical movement of the day but not specifically in the voice. On analysis you will find the "coming down" of mood from amusement at the chat of the day — the trivia — to a sadness of the effect of the hunger of the court officials, a hunger which sends men to the gallows. The answer is (E).

13. **(E)** The key word here is "suggests." The author does not clearly say that Kyd's play was called *Hamlet* but refers to it as Kyd's *Hamlet* from the tale of Belleforest (E). Do not be confused by the many plays mentioned nor by the terms "earlier" and "older." Work your way systematically through the passage and the meaning is clear.

14. **(C)** The answer comes toward the end of the passage. The author clearly states that there are close "verbal parallels" to Kyd's *Spanish Tragedy* (C). Again, systematically eradicate the other options by close reading of the text.

15. **(D)** You need to analyze what Chapman did indeed rework — not entire plays but certain scenes. The author clearly states what is done before Shakespeare supposedly touched the play which then became the *Hamlet* we know today, so obviously (E) is not correct. The scenes reworked must be Kyd's Polonius-Reynoldo scenes (D).

16. **(E)** In the opening sentence, the author's vague "this play" with the antecedent in the previous clause refers to the older play by Kyd. He then suggests that clues to this play lie in *The Spanish Tragedy*, the tale of Belleforest, and a version acted in Germany (E).

17. **(C)** The author does not directly refer to the play as a revenge play but clearly states that the motive was simply revenge (C). To back up your choice eliminate the other options by learning what they entail: a historical saga would be longer and entrenched in historical fact (Shakespeare's *Henry* plays for example); a miracle play is a medieval religious drama based on the life of Christ; a chronicle would again be more historical and chronologically based; a morality play is again medieval, showing the vices opposed to good virtues, as in *Everyman*.

18. **(E)** Because *Hamlet* is so well known you may interpret the motive from what you have read or seen in the play. Here the author never states the

motive (E), but simply refers to it as "more important than revenge."

19. **(D)**   The earlier play obviously has much less psychological depth to it than Shakespeare's play. *The Spanish Tragedy* develops from that play, and the author clearly states that the action or delay in the play comes about simply from "the difficulty of assassinating a monarch surrounded by guards" (not the procrastination of the Renaissance man nor his feigned madness nor the king's madness). The answer then is (D).

20. **(A)**   The author's tone throughout is consistent in its calm objectivity (A), even when he is criticizing Shakespeare's play for incompleteness. The tone is erudite in that what is being said is learned and well researched, but the tone is professional rather than pompous, for the educated reader rather than for the highbrow.

21. **(C)**   The point of the banner is that it has compressed, preserved the meaning of Christmas into two sides of paper, so all the words that have to do with shrinking or drying are appropriate. Decimated means destroyed in great numbers; this is the odd one out (C).

22. **(D)**   The name is ironic because of the lack of potential for breeding that such a scientist brings to the world (D). To check on the validity of your answer make sure that you know the other terms: oxymoron is usually used in poetry for two paradoxical words in close proximity: "pleasant pain" for example; a pun is a play on words which is what Vonnegut is doing but the answer is not full enough to show how the pun operates; pathetic fallacy is a term used for the empathy often shown for the human race from nature and human characteristics given to nature; paradox is a seemingly self-contradictory phrase which turns out to be true.

23. **(C)**   Faust was of course the learned philosopher and dabbler in "magic" that sold his soul to the devil. Vonnegut plays on the name to suggest that as Breed's secretary doing all his bidding (even remembering the chocolate bars) she is serving the devil in the same way the original Faust did (C).

24. **(B)**   The fact that a nuclear warfare scientist reads out the message of peace and love is irony, because it reverses the truth in an amusing yet sobering way (B). Homile is a simple story used to illustrate a point using

folk or country images, similar to a parable which has now taken on more religious connotations. Emblemism was used to give an image a "concrete" reality: a gold-edged love poem for example—whereas symbolism endows the image with greater hidden meanings beyond reality.

25. **(B)** All the answers have a measure of truth to them, but range from the exaggerated (A) which goes too far, to (C) which is perhaps a feminist approach to the interpretation. The words themselves suggest more of the robotizing of industry where machines "belong" to anyone who can work them (B) rather than any idea of prostitution or demeaning work, or that the girls are mechanized — it is the "belonging" that is the key idea here.

26. **(E)** The words need to be clearly analyzed to interpret the meaning — "cloister" connotes "nunnery"; "cement block" conjures up the modern prison. You need to know the word "immured" as imprisoned and imagine the harshness of the Girl Pool environment. The answer then is (E).

27. **(D)** In amongst all the banter, the narrator does in fact use the "me" pronoun. The answer is (D). You know that the Girl Pool is not there as they leave their cloisters only once a year. The scientists remain "faceless," certainly not there in the office.

28. **(A)** Everyone knows the Tiny Tim blessing; the echo of the words should conjure up for the reader the hope and forgiveness of the Dickens story at the end. This "Christmas story," in contrast, is harsh and banal so the blessing highlights the sterility (A).

29. **(B)** If you do not know the word "enjambment" — the running of one line of poetry into the next without a break for the rhyme or syntax — eliminate the options from words you do know. Alliteration is the repeat of the consonants; in onomatopoeia the words sounds like the action; personification is describing an inanimate object or season or virtue as a person, usually capitalized; bathos extreme anticlimax. None of these applies here, so (B) must be the answer.

30. **(D)** Even without seeing the painting you should see the characters and things through the poem. The boy falls from the sky, the sun goes on shining but the ship and the plowman turn away (D). The painter of course is not in the painting.

31. **(C)**   You should have a background on the most important Greek myths. Icarus, warned by his father Daedulus not to fly too near to the sun because his wings made of wax would melt, defies his father and falls into the sea. The answer is (C).

32. **(A)**   The poem deals with the indifference of the world to suffering. The plowman may have heard a splash and a cry, but his plowing is more important so he continues his life (A).

33. **(C)**   All the elements of the picture are here except a body (C). The sun shines on "white legs" disappearing into the sea. The painting is very interesting in that at first glance you do not see the "white legs" — a very significant part of the painting — which exemplifies the poet's point about indifference to suffering.

34. **(C)**   All of the options are too strong except (C). The poet does not extol courage, the style alone reveals that, nor agonize over suffering. He calmly states and accepts that society could not care less about the suffering of others.

35. **(D)**   The tone throughout is distanced, calm and objective. What sets the scene is the conversational "for instance" at the beginning of this, the second verse, as if the poet is holding a pleasant after-dinner conversation with you, the reader (D). If this is not immediately apparent, work you way through the options: didactic – too strong, no lecturing voice here; ironic – straightforward "truths" here; irregular scansion – the free verse form cannot be analyzed for scansion, nor does it have regular rhythm.

36. **(C)**   Mrs. Malaprop is a famous character in English Literature, giving rise to the term "malapropism" (C). First analyze what she does to the language, then, if you are not familiar with the word, analyze the options: homonym – words that sound the same but are spelled differently (there, their, they're); altruism – doing good for the poor; synonym – word that has the same meaning (joyful, glad); synechdoche – part is used for the whole or vice verse (ten sail – ten ships).

37. **(D)**   The key here is to find out exactly what Mrs. Malaprop does. It is not just that she uses the wrong word but the one she uses is so close in sound but so ridiculous in meaning (D).

38. **(A)**   You need not only to analyze what Mrs. Malaprop is doing to the language but also to appreciate the fact that some words that may sound wrong are in fact in their true use. (A) fluxions here is correct — a mathematical term to do with time. If you do not know the word, work through the others which do tend to stand out in their misuse as long as your vocabulary can substitute the right meaning: (B) ironically; (C) ingenuousness; (D) contiguous; (E) orthography.

39. **(A)**   The pattern is interesting in that Mrs. Malaprop is very close in sound but she twists the meaning which makes for humor. Thus in II suspicious almost fits the pattern except the meaning is too close. The answer then is I and III (A).

40. **(D)**   Sir Anthony gives the metaphor of the circulating libraries being "evergreen trees of diabolical knowledge" (with a hint of the biblical tree of Knowledge in the Garden of Eden), not a simile because the words "like" or "as if" are not employed, but then Sir Anthony cannot seem to give the metaphor up and extends it (not mixes it — he still keeps to the tree with blossoms and fruit and leaves). The answer is (D).

41. **(C)**   All of the options have something of truth in them except (E) which plays with another notion of books and their covers. Sir Anthony believes books should be for learned subjects. The books he condemns are the "new" novels full of fantasies and exciting adventures — very tempting to young women who had very little to do in those days. The answer is then (C).

42. **(D)**   The young women of those days learned the art of being ladies in school — drawing, music, deportment. They were not encouraged, in fact often forbidden, to learn the subjects their brothers were learning — Math, the Classics, Astronomy — gentlemanly subjects (D).

43. **(B)**   All young ladies were expected to be good wives — not homemakers because they would have people to run their homes for them. A good wife would be *suitably* knowledgeable in that she would know how to draw, play the piano, sing, and behave in company; she would also be docile to her husband. The answer is (B).

44. **(D)** Obviously irony is at play here because Mrs. Malaprop epitomizes a woman mis-spelling and mispronouncing, but an added dimension in this scene is that she is blissfully unaware of the situation while the characters around her and the audience understand what is happening in the "argument." The added dimension to the irony makes it then dramatic irony (D). A soliloquy – a speech delivered alone on the stage as if the character is thinking aloud; satire – often a harsh criticism of a society's or person's values couched in such terms it is difficult initially to see the criticism; dramatic license – akin to poetic license when the writer "plays" with the truth for the sake of the art.

45. **(D)** Sir Anthony obviously does enjoy an argument and knows what it should entail, but he realizes there that he has not in fact had one. Mrs. Malaprop is too kind an arguer because she has agreed with him on most points. (E) is the closest explanation of the man's polite but ironic statement.

46. **(A)** Reading carefully you should pick up the humor that Mrs. Malaprop has not understood a word of Sir Anthony's criticism and in fact has mainly agreed with the man, all the while believing she is in dispute with him. The actress would try to convey the point that she is immensely pleased with her verbal skills (A).

47. **(A)** Droll (amusing in an odd way) and dry (an edge to what he says) sum up the tone (A). The man is amused but he is not angry, nor sarcastic. He is whimsical (a tinge of fanciful humor to his words) but certainly not weary. He is accused of being laconic (expressing much in a few words but Mrs. Malaprop has the wrong word), and sardonic (akin to sarcastic) is too harsh.

48. **(B)** A sonnet is easy to recognize because it always has 14 lines — as this does (B). A sestina has six stanzas of six lines each. A hymn extols religious faith; a dramatic monologue gives the impression someone is there giving replies we do not "hear"; an aubade is a poem or song to the dawn.

49. **(C)** The word "would" here means to like to, or to wish, or desire to; realizing that the negative comes after this verb you should then consider each meaning, sliding the verb sequence into the lines. (C) then reads as the best explanation.

50. **(B)** The poem deals with the serious subject of a battle of faith: secular love versus religious. Humorous in this context does not have the modern connotation but more that of changing on a whim. The answer then is (B). Fickle is close but holds more the connotation of a deliberate vacillation — here the poet cannot help himself.

51. **(D)** The poet is agonizing over the fact that secular love is not as constant as the love of God. The capital does not suggest one mistress, nor does the word prophane, but a personification of any secular love that takes him away from God (D). Love of the devil is too strong and "all loves" is too general.

52. **(C)** All the terms used for the "prophane Love" could be reversed and there you have the poet's interpretation of the love of God: never capricious, never forgotten, always constant, etc. (C) is the best answer.

53. **(C)** The extremes of emotion can be ruled out here as the poem does not support anger or ecstasy. Misery is also too strong as the poet works his way to the acceptance of the love/fear of God. The choice between bewilderment and anguish depends upon the development of the poem — the poet expresses clearly the state of his predicament. The first cry then is one of sorrow and pain, of anguish (C).

54. **(B)** The word haughty should connote high and mighty, pompous, above it all, on high. These synonyms do not capture the tone of the poem at all. If anything, the poet is humble; a supplicant. The answer then is the odd word out: (B).

55. **(E)** The language is at first off-putting, but reading carefully through the passage's first few lines reveals clearly the author's viewpoint. He blames the devil but does not say poets write about him. He does not want poets to write about passion of loving women, nor fantasies of any kind. In "lieu of" simply means "instead of"; "solemn and devout" can easily translate to serious matters pertaining to God — the answer is (E).

56. **(B)** Although the word "wedded" is in the area of criticism, the author does not criticize poets for their views on marriage; he does criticize that poets have wedded their wills to expressing themselves on "unworthy affections." Because he sets these up in direct contrast to the love of God,

one translates such affections as passion for women. He suggests also through the association with the "Divell," that such affections are beyond the poets' control. The answer then is a combination of I and III: (B).

57. **(B)** You need to find the figure of speech (an extended metaphor of the weaver and weaving) and determine what it means in the context of the whole piece. He is not personifying, nor jaded, nor encouraging alliteration. He makes a plea that his poetry "a few coarse threads" will weave "a new webbe in their loom," so that better poets will carry on what he has started or begin an even better strain of poetry, "a finer peece," which will combine verse and goodness together in the implied sense of woven together. The answer is (B).

58. **(C)** You need to sort out all the mannered flattery of the concluding lines and understand the word "importune." The cousin in fact asked the author to write the book (C).

59. **(D)** The author's tone is lecturing to begin with, but does not change to praise. It is didatic but moves from that. He is not encouraging the cousin at the end but humbly setting out his reasons for writing poetry. Arrogant does not fully capture the tone at the beginning. It is too sincere for arrogance. The best couple is the simplest — harsh to gentle (D).

60. **(B)** The mean in music means the middle part. The author puns on this and the (Golden) Meane in life, i.e., take the middle way, the way of moderation in the "music of life." The answer is (B), the most complete explanation of the lines.

Literature

TEST 2

Literature

TEST 2

1. Ⓐ Ⓑ Ⓒ Ⓓ Ⓔ
2. Ⓐ Ⓑ Ⓒ Ⓓ Ⓔ
3. Ⓐ Ⓑ Ⓒ Ⓓ Ⓔ
4. Ⓐ Ⓑ Ⓒ Ⓓ Ⓔ
5. Ⓐ Ⓑ Ⓒ Ⓓ Ⓔ
6. Ⓐ Ⓑ Ⓒ Ⓓ Ⓔ
7. Ⓐ Ⓑ Ⓒ Ⓓ Ⓔ
8. Ⓐ Ⓑ Ⓒ Ⓓ Ⓔ
9. Ⓐ Ⓑ Ⓒ Ⓓ Ⓔ
10. Ⓐ Ⓑ Ⓒ Ⓓ Ⓔ
11. Ⓐ Ⓑ Ⓒ Ⓓ Ⓔ
12. Ⓐ Ⓑ Ⓒ Ⓓ Ⓔ
13. Ⓐ Ⓑ Ⓒ Ⓓ Ⓔ
14. Ⓐ Ⓑ Ⓒ Ⓓ Ⓔ
15. Ⓐ Ⓑ Ⓒ Ⓓ Ⓔ
16. Ⓐ Ⓑ Ⓒ Ⓓ Ⓔ
17. Ⓐ Ⓑ Ⓒ Ⓓ Ⓔ
18. Ⓐ Ⓑ Ⓒ Ⓓ Ⓔ
19. Ⓐ Ⓑ Ⓒ Ⓓ Ⓔ
20. Ⓐ Ⓑ Ⓒ Ⓓ Ⓔ

21. Ⓐ Ⓑ Ⓒ Ⓓ Ⓔ
22. Ⓐ Ⓑ Ⓒ Ⓓ Ⓔ
23. Ⓐ Ⓑ Ⓒ Ⓓ Ⓔ
24. Ⓐ Ⓑ Ⓒ Ⓓ Ⓔ
25. Ⓐ Ⓑ Ⓒ Ⓓ Ⓔ
26. Ⓐ Ⓑ Ⓒ Ⓓ Ⓔ
27. Ⓐ Ⓑ Ⓒ Ⓓ Ⓔ
28. Ⓐ Ⓑ Ⓒ Ⓓ Ⓔ
29. Ⓐ Ⓑ Ⓒ Ⓓ Ⓔ
30. Ⓐ Ⓑ Ⓒ Ⓓ Ⓔ
31. Ⓐ Ⓑ Ⓒ Ⓓ Ⓔ
32. Ⓐ Ⓑ Ⓒ Ⓓ Ⓔ
33. Ⓐ Ⓑ Ⓒ Ⓓ Ⓔ
34. Ⓐ Ⓑ Ⓒ Ⓓ Ⓔ
35. Ⓐ Ⓑ Ⓒ Ⓓ Ⓔ
36. Ⓐ Ⓑ Ⓒ Ⓓ Ⓔ
37. Ⓐ Ⓑ Ⓒ Ⓓ Ⓔ
38. Ⓐ Ⓑ Ⓒ Ⓓ Ⓔ
39. Ⓐ Ⓑ Ⓒ Ⓓ Ⓔ
40. Ⓐ Ⓑ Ⓒ Ⓓ Ⓔ

41. Ⓐ Ⓑ Ⓒ Ⓓ Ⓔ
42. Ⓐ Ⓑ Ⓒ Ⓓ Ⓔ
43. Ⓐ Ⓑ Ⓒ Ⓓ Ⓔ
44. Ⓐ Ⓑ Ⓒ Ⓓ Ⓔ
45. Ⓐ Ⓑ Ⓒ Ⓓ Ⓔ
46. Ⓐ Ⓑ Ⓒ Ⓓ Ⓔ
47. Ⓐ Ⓑ Ⓒ Ⓓ Ⓔ
48. Ⓐ Ⓑ Ⓒ Ⓓ Ⓔ
49. Ⓐ Ⓑ Ⓒ Ⓓ Ⓔ
50. Ⓐ Ⓑ Ⓒ Ⓓ Ⓔ
51. Ⓐ Ⓑ Ⓒ Ⓓ Ⓔ
52. Ⓐ Ⓑ Ⓒ Ⓓ Ⓔ
53. Ⓐ Ⓑ Ⓒ Ⓓ Ⓔ
54. Ⓐ Ⓑ Ⓒ Ⓓ Ⓔ
55. Ⓐ Ⓑ Ⓒ Ⓓ Ⓔ
56. Ⓐ Ⓑ Ⓒ Ⓓ Ⓔ
57. Ⓐ Ⓑ Ⓒ Ⓓ Ⓔ
58. Ⓐ Ⓑ Ⓒ Ⓓ Ⓔ
59. Ⓐ Ⓑ Ⓒ Ⓓ Ⓔ
60. Ⓐ Ⓑ Ⓒ Ⓓ Ⓔ

LITERATURE

TEST 2

TIME: 60 Minutes
60 Questions

DIRECTIONS: *This test consists of selections from literary works and questions on their content, form, and style. After reading each passage or poem, choose the best answer to each question and blacken the corresponding space on the answer sheet.*

NOTE: Pay particular attention to the requirement of questions that contain the words NOT, LEAST, or EXCEPT.

QUESTIONS 1–10 are based on the following passage. Read the passage carefully before choosing your answers.

By the door of the station-keeper's den, outside, was a tin washbasin, on the ground. Near it was a pail and a piece of yellow bar soap, and from the eaves hung a hoary blue woolen shirt, significantly — but this latter was the station-keeper's private towel,
5 and only two persons in all the party might venture to use it — the stage-driver and the conductor. The latter would not, from a sense of decency; the former would not, because he did not choose to encourage the advances of the station-keeper. We had towels — in the valise; they might as well have been in Sodom and Gomorrah. We
10 (and the conductor) used our handkercheifs, and the driver his pantaloons and sleeves. By the door, inside, was fastened a small old-fashioned looking-glass frame, with two little fragments of the

original mirror lodged down in one corner of it. This arrangement
afforded a pleasant double-barreled portrait of you when you looked
15 into it, with one half of your head set up a couple of inches above the
other half. From the glass frame hung the half of a comb by a string
— but if I had to describe the partiarch or die, I believe I would order
some sample coffins. It had come down from Esau and Samson, and
has been accumulating hair ever since — along with certain impuri-
20 ties …. The table was a greasy board on stilts, and the tablecloth and
napkins had not come — and they are not looking for them, either. A
battered tin platter, a knife and fork, and a pint tin cup, were at each
man's place, and the driver had a queen's-ware saucer that had seen
better days. Of course, this duke sat at the head of the table. There
25 was one isolated piece of table furniture that bore about it a touching
air of grandeur in misfortune. This was the caster. It was German
silver, and crippled and rusty, but it was so preposterously out of
place that it was suggestive of a tattered exile king among barbarians, and the majesty of its native position compelled respect even in
30 its degradation. There was only one cruet left, and that was a
stopperless, fly-specked, broken-necked thing, with two inches of
vinegar in it, and a dozen preserved flies with their heels up and
looking sorry they had invested there.

"Roughing It" by Mark Twain

1. The attitude of the author toward the place he describes is one of

(A) disgust   (D) deference

(B) condescension   (E) sympathy

(C) amusement

2. The author expects the members of his audience to be

(A) bored with the usual recitation of a country they have grown up
in

(B) shocked but interested in a place they will never visit for themselves

(C) amused at the unlikely exaggeration found in the descriptions

(D) alarmed by the unsanitary living conditions of people in their
own country

(E)   comfortable in the knowledge that they will never have to live in such a place

3.   The humor of the description of the "towel" in lines 3–8 depends primarily on the fact that

(A)   the shirt had once been blue but has become bleached with time

(B)   the woolen fabric will not absorb water well enough to make a good towel

(C)   the shirt is so old that is is probably full of holes

(D)   the driver and the conductor do not want to soil the only towel available

(E)   the shirt is probably so filthy that it would get clean hands dirty again

4.   The stage-driver will not use the station-keeper's towel because he is afraid

(A)   the station-keeper will consider it a sign of special friendship, and the driver hates the station-keeper

(B)   he will have to share his own personal toilet articles with the station-keeper

(C)   not to follow the good example of the stage conductor

(D)   the station-keeper will strike him for being so presumptuous as to use that personal an object

(E)   it will make the station-keeper think he has to offer unusual courtesies to all the travelers

5.   Which of the following does NOT contribute to the description of the age of the comb?

(A)   "the half of a comb" (line 16)

(B)   "patriarch" (line 17)

(C)   "sample coffins" (line 18)

(D)   "Esau and Samson" (line 18)

(E)   "accumulating hair" (line 19)

6. Which of the following creates humor through the greatest contrast of elegant language used to describe something quite disgusting?

   (A) "the driver his pantaloons and sleeves" (lines 10–11)

   (B) "pleasant double-barreled portrait of you" (line 14)

   (C) "along with certain impurities" (lines 19–20)

   (D) "a greasy board on stilts" (line 20)

   (E) "the tablecloth and napkins had not come" (lines 20–21)

7. As it is used in the passage (last line), "invested" can be understood in all of the following senses EXCEPT

   (A) to search into systematically and carefully

   (B) to spend time or effort with the expectation of receiving pleasure or satisfaction

   (C) to install in office with ceremony

   (D) to cover

   (E) to hem in or besiege

8. The device the author uses to create humor in such phrases as "in the valise" (lines 8–9), "along with certain impurities" (lines 19–20), and "they were not looking for them, either" (line 21) is

   (A) exaggeration   (D) imagery

   (B) afterthought   (E) anticipation

   (C) simile

9. All of the following are elements of contrast in the last 11 lines EXCEPT

   (A) "queen's-ware saucer" (line 23) and "had seen better days" (lines 23–24)

   (B) "this duke" (line 24) and "head of the table" (line 24)

   (C) "grandeur" (line 26) and "misfortune" (line 26)

   (D) "exile king" (line 28) and "among barbarians" (lines 28–29)

(E)   "majesty" (line 29) and "in its degradation" (lines 29-30)

10.   What is the effect of the personification of flies "with their heels up and looking sorry" (line 32-33)?

(A)   The essentially human qualities of flies are presented in a sympathetic light.

(B)   The reader is expected to draw the connection between the dead flies and the humans who wish they were dead.

(C)   It is the culmination of filthy, unsanitary conditions that will inevitably result in sickness of the human inhabitants.

(D)   The author destroys the effect of this descriptive passage by ending with such an impossible exaggeration.

(E)   It creates a vivid, humorous caricature because flies have no heels or facial expressions.

QUESTIONS 11–15 are based on the following poem. Read the poem carefully before choosing your answers.

Me Deare Deare Lord, I know not what to say:
    Speech is too Course a web for me to cloath
My Love to thee in or it to array,
    Or make a mantle. Wouldst thou not such loath?
5   Thy Love to mee's too great, for mee to shape
    A Vesture for the Same at any rate.

When as thy Love doth Touch my Heart down tost
    It tremblingly runs, seeking thee its all,
And as a Child when it his nurse hath lost
10   Runs seeking her, and after her doth Call.
    So when thou hidst from me, I seek and sigh.
    Thou saist return return Oh Shulamite.

Rent out on Use thy Love thy Love I pray.
    My Love to thee shall be thy Rent and I
15 Thee Use on Use, Intrest on intrest pay.
    There's none Extortion in such Usury.

I'le pay thee Use on Use for't and therefore
    Thou shalt become the greatest Usurer.
But yet the principall I'le neer restore.
20   The Same is thine and mine. We shall not Jar.
    And so this blessed Usury shall be
    Most profitable both to thee and mee.

And shouldst thou hide thy shining face most fair
    Away from me. And in a sinking wise
25 My trembling beating heart brought nigh t'dispare
    Should cry to thee and in a trembling guise
    Lord quicken it. Drop in its Eares delight
    Saying Return, Return my Shulamite.

"Meditation 146, Second Series," by Cotton Mather

11.   The poem as a whole expresses

    (A) man's distress over his search for God

    (B) man's inability to communicate effectively with God

    (C) God's great love for mankind

    (D) the patience God exhibits when dealing with mankind

    (E) the speaker's sorrow at man's inability to love God

12.   In stanza one the speaker

    (A) complains about God's distance from man

    (B) expresses that God's love for him is too great and too demanding

    (C) says that his words are inadequate to express his feelings

    (D) feels wrapped in a coarse web of sin and deceit

    (E) fears that he will never love God as God loves him

13.   Which of the following words does NOT support the metaphor of the speaker's words being mere wrapping for his love to God?

    (A) "web" (line 2)   (D) "loath" (line 4)

    (B) "array" (line 3)   (E) "Vesture" (line 6)

    (C) "mantle" (line 4)

14. In stanza 2 and stanza 5, which of the following represents man's despair when he does not feel God's presence?

    I.   Child

    II. Heart

    III. Face

    (A) I only

    (B) II only

    (C) III only

    (D) I and II only

    (E) I, II, and III

15. Which of the following is the BEST statement of meaning in stanzas 3 and 4?

    (A) The narrator is accusing God of being parsimonious with his love.

    (B) The narrator is thanking God for showing man how to earn enough money to have a good life.

    (C) The narrator knows that his term on this planet is but "rented" space and time.

    (D) The narrator expresses his belief that too much concentration on money will "Jar" the relationship between man and God.

    (E) The narrator hopes that this kind of "Usury" will be profitable to both man and God.

QUESTIONS 16–24 are based on the following passage. Read the passage carefully before choosing your answers.

At the Everglades Club after dark Paula and Lowell Thayer and Anson and a casual fourth played bridge with hot cards. It seemed to Anson that her kind, serious face was wan and tired—she had been around now for four, five, years. He had known her for three.

"Two spades."

"Cigarette? ... Oh, I beg your pardon, By me."

"By."

"I'll double three spaces."

There were a dozen tables of bridge in the room, which was filling up with smoke. Anson's eyes met Paula's, held them persistently even when Thayer's glance fell between them....

"What was bid?" he asked abstractedly.

        "Rose of Washington Square"

sang the young people in the corners:

        "I'm withering there
        In basement air——"

The smoke banked like fog, and the opening of a door filled the room with blown swirls of ectoplasm. Little Bright Eyes streaked past the tables seeking Mr. Conan Doyle among the Englishmen who were posing as Englishmen about the lobby.

"You could cut it with a knife."

"...cut it with a knife."

"...a knife."

At the end of the rubber Paula suddenly got up and spoke to Anson in a tense, low voice. With scarcely a glance at Lowell Thayer, they walked out the door and descended a long flight of stone steps — in a moment they were walking hand in hand along the moonlit beach.

16.   What is significant about the length of time Anson has known Paula?

    (A) He is so infatuated with her that he cannot keep track of time.

    (B) She has been around in his social circles for a few years before he met her.

    (C) His relationship with her has become routine and a bit boring for him.

    (D) Although he met her before, he has only been serious about her for three years.

    (E) His friendship with Lowell Thayer is more important than his feelings for Paula.

17. Paula's face is "wan and tired" because

    (A) she has been playing cards for several hours

    (B) the smoke in the room has become annoying to her

    (C) she is under an emotional strain caused by love

    (D) there have been some arguments at the table

    (E) she does not like to play bridge

18. All of the following are signs of intense passion in the passage EXCEPT the

    (A) cards

    (B) smoke filling up the room

    (C) players' glances

    (D) tone in Paula's voice

    (E) fourth player at the bridge table

19. Which of these is the best explanation for "Thayer's glance fell between them"?

    (A) Thayer disapproves of the fact that Paula and Anson are smoking cigarettes.

    (B) Thayer has been courting Paul behind Anson's back and trying to win her love.

    (C) Thayer suspects that Paula has been having a secret affair with Anson.

    (D) Thayer is the only one who notices that Paula and Anson are in love.

    (E) Thayer is hoping to cue his bridge partner across the table.

20. How does the song the young people are singing reflect the action at the table?

    I.   Paula is suffering because Anson does not love her enough.

    II. Anson is suffering because Paula cannot decide between the two men.

III. Lowell is suffering because Paula obviously prefers Anson.

(A) I only   (D) I and II

(B) II only   (E) I and III

(C) III only

21. What is "it" in the sentence "You could cut it with a knife"?

I. The tension created by strong emotions

II. The blown swirls of ectoplasm

III. The posturing of the Englishmen in the lobby

(A) I only   (D) I and III

(B) II only   (E) I and II

(C) III only

22. The references to "blown swirls of ectoplasm" and "who were posing as Englishmen" are indicative of

(A) local color of the seaside resort club

(B) obstacles of society that Paula must overcome

(C) the lack of clarity and honesty

(D) the easy acceptance of wealthy foreigners into society

(E) objects of amusement to the members of the club

23. By the end of the passage it can be inferred that

(A) Lowell has proposed marriage to Paula several times

(B) Paula would like for Anson to propose marriage to her

(C) Paula is tired of the animosity Lowell feels for Anson

(D) Anson is unaware of the problem Lowell creates

(E) The friendship between Lowell and Anson is over

24. All of the following is evidence that Anson cares for Paula EXCEPT

(A) his ignoring the fourth person at the bridge table

(B)   his observation of her "kind, serious face"

(C)   their eyes meeting as they play cards

(D)   Anson's abstracted attention to the bid

(E)   walking hand in hand along the moonlit beach

QUESTIONS 25–33 are based on the following poem. Read the poem carefully before choosing your answers.

Of the Last Verses in the Book

When we for age could neither read nor write,
The subject made us able to indite;
The soul, with nobler resolutions decked,
The body stooping, does herself erect.
5   No mortal parts are requisite to raise
Her that, unbodied, can her Maker praise.
The seas are quiet when the winds give o'er;
So calm are we when passions are no more!
For then we know how vain it was to boast
10   Of fleeting things, so certain to be lost.
Clouds of affection from our younger eyes
Conceal that emptiness which age descries.
The soul's dark cottage, battered and decayed,
Lets in new light through chinks that time has made;
15   Stronger by weakness, wiser men become,
As they draw near to their eternal home.
Leaving the old, both worlds at once they view,
That stand upon the threshold of the new.

by Edmund Waller.

25.   All of the following are elements of opposition in the development of the poem EXCEPT

(A)   "we for age" (line 1) and "nobler resolutions" (line 3)

(B)   "soul" (line 3) and "body" (line 4)

(C)   "mortal parts" (line 5) and "Her" (line 6)

(D) "calm" (line 8) and "passions" (line 8)

(E) "dark cottage" (line 13) and "new light" (line 14)

26. The word "Her" (line 6) refers to

(A) an aged body

(B) "subject" (line 2)

(C) something the author has read or written

(D) the soul

(E) one of the resolutions mentioned in line 3

27. What is the literary device used by the author in line 15, "stronger by weakness"?

(A) irony   (D) paradox

(B) allusion   (E) metaphor

(C) comparison

28. What is the best interpretation of line 15?

(A) A strong man cannot be wise.

(B) Young people do not appreciate the advice of older men.

(C) People become wiser as they grow older and weaker.

(D) People become weaker as they grow older.

(E) Physical weakness makes a person appreciate his youth.

29. Which of the following best represents the author's attitude toward old age?

(A) resentment at not being able to read and write

(B) looking forward to new vistas

(C) suffering caused by physical infirmities

(D) confusion about where he is going

(E)   nostalgia for times past

30.   According to the context of the poem, what is the best meaning of "indite" (line 2)?

(A)   stand erect

(B)   give thanks to the Maker

(C)   write these last verses of this poem

(D)   look through the chinks of the dark cottage

(E)   find ourselves after we have been lost

31.   What concept is NOT connected with youth in this poem?

(A)   blowing winds   (D)   clouds

(B)   transience   (E)   new beginning

(C)   emptiness

32.   According to the context of the poem, what is the probable meaning of "descries" (line 12)?

(A)   resents   (D)   avoids

(B)   sees   (E)   looks forward to

(C)   sings about

33.   The last two lines convey which of the following ideas?

I.   Humanity able to see both mortal and immortal existence

II.   Humanity blinded by the immortal light after being in the dark for so long

III. Humanity, although wise, too weak to move forward

(A)   I only   (D)   I and II only

(B)   II only   (E)   I and III only

(C)   III only

QUESTIONS 34–41 are based on the following passage. Read the passage carefully before choosing your answers.

"What is he, then?"

"Why, I'll tell you what he is," said Mr. Jonas, apart to the young ladies, "he's precious old, for one thing; and I an't best pleased with him for that, for I think my father must have caught it of him. He's a strange old chap, for another," he added in a louder voice, "and don't understand any one hardly, but him!" He pointed to his honoured parent with the carving-fork, in order that they might know whom he meant.

"How very strange!" cried the sisters.

"Why, you see," said Mr. Jonas, "he's been addling his old brains with figures and book-keeping all his life; and twenty years ago or so he went and took a fever. All the time he was out of his head (which was three weeks) he never left off casting up; and he got to so many million at last that I don't believe he's ever been quite right since. We don't do much business now though, and he an't a bad clerk."

"A very good one," said Anthony.

"Well! He an't a dear one at all events," observed Jonas; "and he earns his salt, which is enough for our look-out. I was telling you that he hardly understands any one except my father; he always understands him, though, and wakes up quite wonderful. He's been used to his ways so long, you see! Why, I've seen him play whist, with my father for a partner; and a good rubber too; when he had no more notion what sort of people he was playing against, than you have."

Martin Chuzzlewit, by Charles Dickens.

34. From this passage it can be inferred that Mr. Jonas is all of the following EXCEPT

    (A) irritated that the old clerk understands hardly anyone except the father

    (B) unconcerned about hurting the old clerk's feelings

    (C) worried that the old clerk might make a serious error

    (D) intent upon impressing the sisters

(E) terribly rude for saying the things he does about his father and the clerk

35. If the old clerk is not "quite right" in the head, then why is he kept on as an employee?

(A) Mr. Jonas will not go against his father's wishes.

(B) Mr. Jonas does not want to offend the ladies.

(C) Mr. Jonas reveres people of the older generation.

(D) Mr. Jonas is somewhat afraid of the "strange old chap."

(E) Mr. Jonas knows the clerk is the best one in the business.

36. As used in the passage, the word "precious" means

(A) expensive

(B) of high value

(C) beloved

(D) very overrefined in behavior

(E) very great

37. What has made the old clerk not "quite right" in the head?

(A) going a bit deaf in his old age

(B) working with numbers and bookkeeping all his life

(C) working sums and figures in his fever

(D) having to put up with Mr. Jonas' abuse

(E) having too much to do in the business now

38. The sentence "He an't a dear one at all events." can best be interpreted to mean which of the following?

(A) Mr. Jonas does not like the old clerk.

(B) The customers of the business do not like the old clerk.

(C) Sometimes the clerk creates serious problems.

(D) He is only a good clerk with some things in the business.

(E) His wages do not cost the company very much money.

39. All of the following are things Mr. Jonas dislikes about the clerk EXCEPT that he is

(A) old

(B) a bit strange

(C) a good whist player

(D) not always aware of who is around him

(E) not able to hear well

40. What is the meaning of "he got to so many million at last"?

(A) He irritated countless customers.

(B) He had trouble keeping up with the high figures.

(C) He became quite advanced in years.

(D) He thought the three weeks was a million days.

(E) He lost the company too much money in revenues.

41. A reasonable description of the old man is that he

(A) knows what he is doing when it is something he has been accustomed to doing

(B) only pretends to be deaf and addled in order to irritate Mr. Jonas

(C) can do only the simplest of tasks, although he would like to be able to do more

(D) can do anything he wants to do, but only chooses to do what pleases him

(E) will only perform such tasks as please Mr. Jonas' father

QUESTIONS 42–48 are based on the following poem. Read the poem carefully before choosing your answers.

Vergissmeinnicht[1]

Three weeks gone and the combatants gone
returning over the nightmare ground
we found the place again, and found
the soldier sprawling in the sun.

5   The frowning barrel of his gun
overshadowing. As we came on
that day, he hit my tank with one
like the entry of a demon.

Look. Here in the gunpit spoil
10 the dishonoured picture of his girl
who has put: *Steffi. Vergissmeinnicht*
in a copybook gothic script.

We see him almost with content,
abased, and seeming to have paid
15 and mocked at by his own equipment
that's hard and good when he's decayed.
But she would weep to see today
how on his skin the swart flies move;
the dust upon the paper eye
20 and the burst stomach like a cave.

For here the lover and killer are mingled
who had one body and one heart.
And death who had the soldier singled
has done the lover mortal hurt.

"Vergissmeinnicht," by Keith Douglas. Chilmark Press, Washington, D.C.

42. The soldier has come to "the place" with his companions so he can

   (A) gloat in his victory

   (B) overcome his fear of death

_____
1. Forget me not (German).

    (C)   retrieve the picture of Steffi to send to her

    (D)   return to the place where he was almost killed

    (E)   see if there are salvageable spoils of war

43.   What literary device is "The frowning barrel of his gun"?

    (A)   simile   (D)   paradox

    (B)   personification   (E)   contrast

    (C)   allusion

44.   The effect of "The frowning barrel of his gun/overshadowing" is best expressed by which of the following?

    I.   Upset of defeat

    II.   Threat of destruction

    III.   Fear of dying

    (A)   I only   (D)   II and III

    (B)   I and II   (E)   III only

    (C)   II only

45.   As used in line 9, the word "spoil" can be taken to mean all of the following EXCEPT

    (A)   eager for a fight

    (B)   damaged in such a way as to be rendered useless

    (C)   territory taken in war by the conqueror

    (D)   waste material

    (E)   stripped of goods by force

46.   Given the context of the poem, what is the best interpretation of line 13?

    I.   The soldier is now content.

    II.   The victors are now content.

    III.   The soldier's girlfriend is now content.

(A) I only   (D) I and II

(B) II only   (E) II and III

(C) III only

47. What is the irony of lines 14–16?

    I.   The equipment to protect him has brought him down.

    II. The equipment is ruined before it was paid for.

    III. The equipment lasted longer than the man who used it.

    (A) I only   (D) I and II

    (B) II only   (E) I and III

    (C) III only

48. What is the tone of the poem?

    (A) mocking   (D) beneficent

    (B) sadistic   (E) indifferent

    (C) pragmatic

QUESTIONS 49–55 are based on the following passage. Read the passage carefully before choosing your answers.

    —Is this Johannesburg? he asks.
    But they laugh confidently. Old hands some of them are.
    —That is nothing, they say. In Johannesburg there are buildings, so high—but they cannot describe them.
    —My brother, says one, you know the hill that stands so straight up, behind my father's kraal. So high as that.
    The other man nods, but Kumalo does not know that hill.
    And now the buildings are endless, the buildings, and the white hills, and the great wheels, and streets without number, and cars and lorries and buses.
    —This surely is Johannesburg, he says.
    But they laugh again. They are growing a little tired. This is nothing, they say.
    Railway-lines, railway-lines, it is a wonder. To the left, to the

right, so many that he cannot count. A train rushes past them, with a sudden roaring of sound that makes him jump in his seat. And on the other side of them, another races beside them, but drops slowly behind. Stations, stations, more than he has ever imagined. People are waiting there in hundreds, but the train rushes past, leaving them disappointed.

The buildings get higher, the streets more uncountable. How does one find one's way in such a confusion? It is dusk, and the lights are coming on in the streets.

One of the men points for him.

—Johannesburg, umfundisi.

He sees great high buildings, there are red and green lights on them, almost as tall as the buildings. They go on and off. Water comes out of a bottle, till the glass is full. Then the lights go out. And when they come on again, lo the bottle is full and upright, and the glass empty. And there goes the bottle over again. Black and white, it says, black and white, though it is red and green. It is too much to understand.

He is silent, his head aches, he is afraid. There is this railway station to come, this great place with all its tunnels under the ground. The train stops, under a great roof, and there are thousands of people. Steps go down into the earth, and here is the tunnel under the ground. Black people, white people, some going, some coming, so many that the tunnel is full. He goes carefully that he may not bump anybody, holding tightly on to his bag. He comes out into a great hall, and the stream goes up the steps, and here he is out in the street. The noise is immense. Cars and buses one behind the other, more than he has ever imagined. The stream goes over the street, but remembering Mpanza's son, he is afraid to follow. Lights change from green to red and back again to green. He has heard that. When it is green, you may go. But when he starts across, a great bus swings across the path. There is some law of it that he does not understand, and he retreats again. He finds himself a place against the wall, he will look as though he is waiting for some purpose. His heart beats like that of a child, there is nothing to do or think to stop it. *Tixo*, watch over me, he says to himself. *Tixo*, watch over me.

49. All of these things contribute to Kumalo's confusion and fear EX-
CEPT

    (A) the hill behind the father's kraal

    (B) the lights on the buildings

    (C) the underground station

    (D) the noise

    (E) the cars and buses on the street

50. Why does Kumalo ask the men two times if they have arrived at
Johannesburg?

    (A) He is eagerly looking forward to his visit in Johannesburg.

    (B) He is afraid he will offend the men if he does not carry on some
        form of polite conversation.

    (C) He comes from the country and mistakes all towns as the great
        city.

    (D) He thinks the men, being tired, might go to sleep and not tell him
        where to get off.

    (E) He is a visitor from another country and is careful to ask direc-
        tions of seasoned travelers.

51. Why do Kumalo's fellow travelers grow tired?

    (A) They have been working long hours in the city.

    (B) The long train ride has tired them.

    (C) Country people are easily tired by all the confusion.

    (D) Kumalo's many questions are becoming tiresome.

    (E) No one has any patience with the train's delays.

52. Which of the following are indications of Kumalo's inexperience with
train travel?

    I.   The number of railway lines and stations

    II. The disappointment of the people at the station

    III. His not knowing where to get off the train

(A) I only

(D) II and III only

(B) II only

(E) I, II, and III

(C) I and II only

53. According to the context, what is probably the tone used by the man who addresses Kumalo as *umfundisi*?

(A) derisive

(D) indifferent

(B) irritated

(E) obsequious

(C) respectful

54. Which of the following describes Kumalo?

I.   He has difficulty dealing with things in the city because he is illiterate.

II. He has grown up in the country and is therefore unused to so much activity,

III. He is so overwhelmed by the newness of the city sights and sounds that he is frozen in fear.

(A) I only

(D) II and III only

(B) II only

(E) I, II, and III

(C) I and II only

55. All of the following are indications of Kumalo's fear EXCEPT

(A) the stream of people crossing the street

(B) remembering what happened to Mpanza's son

(C) some law of light-changing that he does not understand

(D) looking as though he is waiting for some purpose

(E) calling upon *Tixo* to watch over him

QUESTIONS 56–60 are based on the following passage. Read the passage carefully before choosing your answers.

MRS. PINCHWIFE

O my dear, dear bud, welcome home! Why dost thou look so fropish? Who has nangered thee?

PINCHWIFE.

You're a fool.

(Mrs. Pinchwife *goes aside and cries*)

ALITHEA.

Faith, so she is, for crying for no fault, poor tender creature!

PINCHWIFE.

What, you would have her as impudent as yourself, as arrant a jill-flirt, a gadder, a magpie, and to say all, a mere, notorious town-woman?

ALITHEA.

Brother, you are my only censurer; and the honor of your family shall sooner suffer in your wife there than in me, though I take the innocent liberty of the town.

PINCHWIFE.

Hark you, mistress, do not talk so before my wife. The innocent liberty of the town!

ALITHEA.

Why, pray, who boasts of any intrigue with me? What lampoon has made my name notorious? What ill women frequent my lodgings? I keep no company with any women of scandalous reputations.

PINCHWIFE.

No, you keep the men of scandalous reputations company.

ALITHEA.

Where? Would you not have me civil? answer 'em in a box at the plays, in the drawing room at Whitehall, in St. James's Park, Mulberry Garden, or—

PINCHWIFE.

Hold, hold! Do not teach my wife where the men are to be found! I believe she's the worse for your town documents already. I bid you keep her in ignorance, as I do.

MRS. PINCHWIFE.

Indeed, be not angry with her, bud; she will tell me nothing of the town, though I ask her a thousand times a day.

PINCHWIFE.

Then you are very inquisitive to know, I find!

MRS. PINCHWIFE.

Not I, indeed dear; I hate London. Our place-house in the country is worth a thousand of 't; would I were there again!

PINCHWIFE.

So you shall, I warrant, But were you not talking of plays and players when I came in? — [*To* Alithea.] You are her encourager in such discourses.

MRS. PINCHWIFE.

No, indeed, dear; she chid me just now for liking the playermen.

PINCHWIFE (*aside*).

Nay, if she be so innocent as to own to me her liking them, there is no hurt in't. —Come, my poor rogue, but thou lik'st none better than me?

MRS. PINCHWIFE.

Yes, indeed, but I do; the playermen are finer folks.

PINCHWIFE.

But you love none better than me?

MRS. PINCHWIFE.

You are mine own dear bud, and I know you; I hate a stranger.

PINCHWIFE.

Ay, my dear, you must love me only, and not be like the naughty town-women, who only hate their husbands and love every man else, love plays, visits, fine coaches, fine clothes, fiddles, balls, treats, and so lead a wicked town-life.

MRS. PINCHWIFE.

Nay, if to enjoy all these things be a town-life, London is not so bad a place, dear.

PINCHWIFE.

How! If you love me, you must hate London.

From "The Country Wife," by William Wycherty.

56. In its context, "why dost thou look so fropish" suggests that the husband

   (A)   is concerned for his wife's health

   (B)   enters the house in a bad mood

   (C)   has heard people gossip about his sister

(D) wants nothing more than to be left alone

(E) frequents bars and play-houses

57. It can be inferred from her lines that Mrs. Pinchwife is a(n)

(A) totally arrogant snob

(B) somewhat naive young woman

(C) immoral, adulterous wife

(D) victim of idle social gossip

(E) envied, beautiful socialite

58. Because Alithea defends her honor so quickly, it can be inferred that

(A) she has actually been keeping company with men of dubious reputation

(B) her female friends have questionable reputations

(C) many wives suspect her of having an affair with their husbands

(D) this is a conversation she has had many times with her brother

(E) she is afraid her sister-in-law will get the wrong impression of her

59. The humor in this conversation is created by which of the following?

I. Alithea has already shown her sister-in-law some of the pleasures of town life.

II. The husband, while trying to explain what his wife should avoid, shows her what to look for.

III. It is obvious the wife does not want to be kept ignorant by her husband.

(A) I only   (D) I and II only

(B) II only   (E) I, II, and III

(C) III only

60. Mr. Pinchwife does not want his wife to attend plays because he is afraid she will

    (A) become used to spending too much of her time away from home

    (B) refuse to return to their home in the country

    (C) have an affair with one of the actors

    (D) spend more money than he can afford

    (E) catch him having an affair with one of the actresses

TEST 2

ANSWER KEY

1. (C)	16. (C)	31. (E)	46. (D)
2. (B)	17. (C)	32. (B)	47. (E)
3. (E)	18. (E)	33. (A)	48. (C)
4. (D)	19. (B)	34. (C)	49. (A)
5. (C)	20. (E)	35. (A)	50. (C)
6. (C)	21. (E)	36. (E)	51. (D)
7. (A)	22. (C)	37. (C)	52. (E)
8. (B)	23. (B)	38. (E)	53. (C)
9. (B)	24. (A)	39. (C)	54. (D)
10. (E)	25. (A)	40. (B)	55. (A)
11. (A)	26. (D)	41. (A)	56. (B)
12. (C)	27. (D)	42. (D)	57. (B)
13. (D)	28. (C)	43. (B)	58. (A)
14. (E)	29. (B)	44. (B)	59. (E)
15. (E)	30. (C)	45. (A)	60. (C)

DETAILED EXPLANATIONS
OF ANSWERS

TEST 2

1. **(C)** The author is deliberately trying to create a humorous scene. This effect is accomplished through exaggeration of the filth and rusticity of the stagecoach station. Although certain aspects of the place are disgusting — the "private towel," the comb, and the vinegar cruet — the author's tone is gentle. A sly humor is evidenced in such phrases as "sense of decency" (lines 6–7) and "encourage the advances" (lines 7–8), and it is apparent through these that the author has a keen eye in observing human nature. There is no evidence that the author is deferential, condescending, or sympathetic.

2. **(B)** It is unlikely that most people will visit such a place, but the description is certainly interesting. As "local color," a description of something in the West, the audience is probably Easterners who would be a bit shocked but curious. Anyone reading this selection would be uncertain if the descriptions were too exaggerated. "Alarmed" by (D) is too strong a reaction, and (E) would, at best, be only a part of the audience's reaction. People who would live in such an atmosphere would be unlikely to read this description, so (A) can be eliminated.

3. **(E)** The word "hoary" means "white" and "old." Choice (A) might be a possibility, therefore, but given the conditions in the rest of the station-house, the towel is probably as filthy as everything else. The conductor and the narrator obviously think their handkerchiefs are cleaner than the towel. Choice (B) is illogical. Choice (C) may be true but there is no evidence in the passage to support it, and the shirt's being full of holes would not prevent it from absorbing what little water would be on the men's hands or faces.

4. **(D)** "Advances" is this context is certainly meant to refer to physical violence. This is a rustic location, and it is implied that the only person

familiar enough with the station-keeper to use his towel is the conductor. The conductor refuses to use the shirt because of sanitary reasons, so (C) is not correct. There is no sign of friendship or animosity between the station-keeper and the driver. No indication is offered that the station-keeper feels moved to offer special considerations to anyone or expect special sharing from anyone.

5. **(C)** "Sample coffins" is a phrase the narrator uses to refer to his preference for death over describing the comb in more detail. Since the comb is old, it is broken (as the mirror is) and has "accumulated hair" because it has been used much. "Patriarch" indicates an aged object or person, and Esau and Samson are two people who lived during the times of Old Testament history.

6. **(C)** The "certain impurities" are almost certainly lice, among other equally noxious possibilities. As the phrase "certain impurities" is a delicate euphemism for the possibilities, humor is created. The language in (A) is ordinary. Choice (B) does create humor through the contrast of "pleasant" and "double-barreled," but the contrast is not as exaggerated as in choice (C). Ordinary word choice in (D) describe the filthy table, and although choice (E) contains humorous phrasing, there is nothing disgusting about it.

7. **(A)** Choice (A) is the definition for "to investigate." Although the flies obviously did investigate the cruet before they died there, all of the remaining choices are proper definitions of the word "invested." Each of the definitions can be used to describe the flies at various stages of their landing upon and entering the bottle. Choice (C) humorously echoes the pattern of royalty come to a fallen state, and the irony of (B) is particularly effective.

8. **(B)** All of these phrases come at the end of sentences in which the author has built in an expectation of a surprise or exaggeration at the end. This surprise or exaggeration creates humor by contrast with the rest of the sentence. The anticipation is built into the first part of the sentence, not the phrases in question. Rather than (A), these phrases are more understated than exaggerated.

9. **(B)** All of the phrases are indicative of the contrast between two

extremes. The first quotation in each pair contains wording indicating height of position or royalty, and the second quotation in each pair shows degradation or a "fallen" state. Although "duke" can be considered associated with a high position, "the head of the table" does not show any particular misfortune or change to a low position.

10. **(E)** The author ends his selection with the most exaggerated picture of all, the more humorous through the extreme exaggeration. The flies are not presented in a sympathetic light and have no inherent human qualities. There is no indication that any person in the stagecoach station wishes to die or will die due to unsanitary conditions.

11. **(A)** Throughout the poem, the narrator examines man's relationship with God and man's search for a close relationship with God. This search includes man's inadequate ability to communicate effectively with his "Deare Lord," choice (B), but the theme of the poem is not limited to the problem of communication because that would exclude the concept of the despair man feels when he no longer feels God's presence (stanzas 2 and 5). Although the poem certainly deals with (C), the main thrust is man's relationship with God. Choice (D) is a characteristic of God mentioned in many religious poems, and obliquely present in this poem, but (D) and (E) are not specifically mentioned by the narrator.

12. **(C)** The narrator knows "not what to say" (line 1) because his "Speech is too Course" (line 2) to express his love of God. The narrator feels nothing he can say will adequately describe his feelings. Although the narrator does say "Thy Love to mee's too great" (line 5), (B) includes the idea of that love's being too demanding, an idea not found in the poem. Partially implied is (E), but that idea is not developed as fully as the problem of communicating with God. God's distance from man (A) is not discussed in stanza 1. The "coarse web" in stanza 1 is not (D) but the crudeness of language to express sublime love.

13. **(D)** "Loath" means "dislike" or "hate." Although "web" is usually associated with snares or spiders, in this poem the speaker uses "web" to show that even the most gossamer filaments are too "Coarse" for the fine feelings he has. "To array" means "to clothe" and is used in the same context with "to make a mantle" (cloak) and "to shape/A Vesture" (covering or garment). The narrator holds his love for God in his heart, but he

cannot find words beautiful enough to express this love. God knows this love is there, but the narrator can only "clothe" his feelings in the coarse "garments" of the words in this poem as a means of communicating with God.

14. **(E)** In both stanzas 2 and 5, the trembling heart is associated with man's search for God. Stanza 2 uses the trembling heart running after God, and in stanza 5 the "trembling beating heart" shows man's despair at the absence of God's presence. The narrator describes in stanza 2 the heart running after God as a child runs after its nurse when the two have become separated. In stanza 5, the narrator expresses his fear that God will "hide thy shining face most fair/Away from me."

15. **(E)** A somewhat shocking metaphor is that of God as renting out his love to man and man as paying back interest but keeping the principal. Thus, God becomes a Usurer because man will never repay God his love. However, as the narrator points out, there is no "Extortion in such Usury" (line 16) and this "blessed Usury" (line 21) is profitable to both man and God because both exchange precious love; therefore, the loving relationship between man and Maker is extended indefinitely. In this loving harmony, man and God "shall not Jar" (line 20).

16. **(C)** Anson and Paula have known each other for three years, and it can be inferred that they have been dating for that time. That they know each other well can be seen by the close observation he makes of her face, the persistent looks, and the naturalness with which he goes outside with her. However, Anson's evaluation of Paula's face is not one of an infatuated man, for the details he notices are not those of beauty. To him, "her kind, serious face was wan and tired" — hardly those of (A). They have known each other for three years, so (D) is not accurate. Choice (B) is a logical answer, but not as significant a factor as (C). There is no indication in the passage of his feelings for Lowell Thayer.

17. **(C)** Paula probably dated casually for a year or two before she met Anson. It is logical to assume their relationship is serious and Paula has been expecting a proposal of marriage. However, Anson's observations are not those of a man madly in love and on the verge of a marriage proposal. Because "Thayer's glance fell between them," it is probable that Thayer is romantically interested in Paula, but she prefers Anson as shown

126

by the fact that the couple leaves with "scarcely a glance at Lowell Thayer." That the other person at the bridge table is described as "a casual fourth" and is not mentioned again underscores the importance of Thayer's role in the passage. There is no indication that (D) and (E) have occurred, and (A) and (B) are possible contributors to but probably not the overriding cause of Paula's strain.

18. **(E)** The fourth player is described as a "casual fourth" and is not mentioned again in the passage. This player is needed to make the game, forcing the players to sit at the same table and deal with all their emotional undercurrents. The cards are "hot." The glance Anson gives Paula "persistently" holds her eyes, even when "Thayer's glance fell between them." Paula's voice is "tense, low." The smoke in the room, although from cigarettes, is probably symbolic of smouldering emotions, as in the cliche "smoke gets in your eyes."

19. **(B)** Because Thayer's glances come between Paula and Anson, and because Thayer figures so prominently in this passage, it can be assumed that Thayer has secretly been courting Paula. Choices (C) and (D) are unlikely because Paula and Anson have probably been dating for three years. Because they are playing bridge, choice (E) might be possible but it is not probable. There is no evidence to give credence to (A).

20. **(E)** Paula seems to be "withering" due to lack of a marriage proposal. Lowell is "withering" due to lack of a commitment from Paula and through being an obvious second choice. There is no indication Anson is suffering, or that he is contemplating marriage.

21. **(E)** The cliche is, "you could cut the tension with a knife." In this selection, the smoke is so thick in the room that it "banked like fog" and swirls like ectoplasm when the opening of a door stirs the air currents. Therefore, both the tension created by strong emotions and the "blown swirls of ectoplasm" are probable antecedents of "it." The posturing of the Englishmen in the lobby might also be considered, but the other two answers are better, and there is no choice that lists all three considerations.

22. **(C)** Ectoplasm is the vaporous substance emanating from a spiritualist medium's body during a trance. "Blown swirls of ectoplasm" would provide cloudy vision, and there is a further unspoken suggestion that people deceive themselves, or allow themselves to be deceived, when they

attend a seance. The "Englishmen posing as Englishmen" are obviously exaggerating their habits in order to impress others, a deception on the part of the Englishmen and those who believe their posing. Therefore, what is portrayed in this portion of the passage is illusion and deception, or lack of clarity and honesty. Paula is not sure what to do about her problems in love. She is deceived in thinking Anson's jealousy of Lowell will spur Anson into a proposal. All three characters are involved in an elaborate but unspoken tension at the card table.

23. **(B)** By the end of the passage, Paula suddenly gets up and speaks to Anson; then, the two leave to walk hand in hand along the moonlit beach. Since Paula initiates the movement, it can be assumed she hopes Anson will now be "forced" by his jealousy into proposing marriage. There is no indication Lowell has proposed marriage (A), even though he seems interested in Paula. Anson is certainly aware (D) of the problem Lowell creates. The two men do not seem to be particular friends, nor is there apparent animosity emanating from Lowell, so choices (C) and (E) are incorrect.

24. **(A)** The fourth person at the table is a necessary factor in the author's presentation of a scene in which the lover's triangle creates an escalating tension, a tension which exists though it must be ignored for polite society's sake at the card table and which cannot be escaped for the duration of the rubber. The fourth person is a kind of convenient "prop" for the author. All other choices show Anson's attention to a person he obviously cares for, and has done so for some time as evidenced by the naturalness of their leaving and walking hand in hand on the beach.

25. **(A)** Because the author claims people gain "nobler resolutions" as the body ages, choice A does not contain opposites. The poet's thesis is that the body is mortal and subject to passions in its youth. The body is metaphorically portrayed as a dark cottage. The soul (portrayed as a female) becomes calmer with the addition of years, and as the body ages new light of resurrection shines throughout the chinks and cracks. Therefore, "soul," "her," "calm," and "new light" are contrasted with "body," "mortal parts," "passions," and "dark cottage."

26. **(D)** The interrupters in lines three and four make the passage a bit difficult to read. The sentence, with interrupters deleted, reads, "The soul

... does herself erect." Thus, lines five and six clearly mean the soul raises herself, without a body, to praise her Maker. "Her" refers to the immortal part of the human, not the aged body (A) or any of the other choices listed.

27. **(D)** A paradox is a statement that seems contradictory but is nevertheless true. At first glance, it would seem impossible for people to become stronger as they grow weaker, but there is no irony (A) in this passage. People get "stronger" spiritually as they become older (progress in physical "weakness").

28. **(C)** The author intimates that bodily age engenders wisdom. Old men are no longer swayed by the passions they once had in their youth, so their infirmities and their slower pace make them contemplative and wise. The more time people contemplate the transience of physical life, the more they are made aware of the soul and look forward to eternal life. Choice (D) is, therefore, only partially correct. Rather than age making a person appreciate his youth (E), the aging process makes him look forward to an eternal home. Although the paradox shows a weak and old man becoming wise, the poem does not deal with the converse (A). There is no evidence of (B) in the poem.

29. **(B)** The last sestet of the poem deals with the light emanating from the soul's new home. The tone is one of joyous anticipation. Although (C) is probably a logical effect of a body "battered and decayed," suffering is not the main emphasis. There is no indication of resentment of not being able to read and write (A) for age, nor is there (E) nostalgia for times past. The author displays no confusion about where he is going (D), as the soul at the end looks upon "both worlds" and stands "upon the threshold of the new."

30. **(C)** The word "indite" means "to compose or to write." This meaning can be gleaned from the context of the poem's first two lines. Line one can be paraphrased, "Even though we were so old that we could not read or write." Line two finishes that thought with the antithesis, "The subject enabled us to write." The title to this poem, "Of the Last Verses in the Book" illuminates the first two lines. The author, inspired by a growing appreciation of the soul's grandeur, is able to write down this poem of praise in the book of his life. Although he is old, and therefore is quite feeble, this advanced age has given the author a glorious insight; the

subject has provided the necessary insight for one more poem. The first sestet finishes this thought by stating that the soul does not need the body in order to raise herself to an erect position (A) so that she may praise her Maker (B). Choice (D) is too far away in the poem to be a plausible answer, and (E) is not found in the poem.

31. **(E)** Usually associated with youth, new beginning in this poem is a sign of extreme old age and imminent death. The last three lines describe men drawing near "to their eternal home," "leaving the old," and standing "upon the threshold of the new." Blowing winds (A) stir up the seas of youth (line 7). A close examination of lines ten through twelve refutes the remaining answers. When men are calm, they know how vain it is to boast of transient (B), "fleeting things." "Clouds" (D) conceal the "emptiness" (C) of youth.

32. **(B)** Clues in lines eleven and twelve point to the meaning "sees": when we are young, "clouds" hide or "conceal" something from our young "eyes." The logical conclusion is when we are old, we "see" that which was hidden from us in younger days. Although "sings about" (C) and "looks forward to" (E) seem good choices, they are not as good as (B) when the context of the two lines is considered. Choices (A) and (D) are illogical since the reward of old age is to be neither resented nor avoided.

33. **(A)** The last two lines picture humanity standing on a threshold from which "both worlds" can be seen. These two worlds are the earthly home with which we are familiar and the "eternal home" mentioned in line sixteen. Humanity is not blinded by this light (B), and we are not too weak to move forward (C) because the soul, as evidenced in the first sestet, can stand and move on its own volition.

34. **(C)** Evidence in the passage indicates the old clerk is still a good records keeper. Mr. Jonas observes that he "an't a bad clerk," to which Anthony adds, "A very good one." Mr. Jonas is obviously unconcerned about hurting the old clerk's feelings (B) as he says terribly rude things (E) in front of his father and the old clerk. Mr. Jonas says the clerk is "old" and he is not "pleased with him for that." Mr. Jonas' irritation with the old man shows through when he points out the clerk's inability (A) to hear no one but Mr. Jonas' father. Perhaps Mr. Jonas is trying to impress the young ladies (D) as he addresses them "apart."

35. **(A)**   Mr. Jonas' father is described in the passage as "honored parent." This wording might be taken ironically, and perhaps is humorous given the way he speaks in front of his parent, but Mr. Jonas goes on to say how the two old men are used to each other. As it would probably upset Mr. Jonas' father to do without his longtime companion, (A) is the logical conclusion. Choice (C) is a possible option, but "revere" is too strong a word given the tone Mr. Jonas uses. Choice (E) might be a possibility, but the highest praise the clerk receives is, "very good one." Mr. Jonas is more concerned with impressing than offending the young ladies (B), and there is no evidence to support (D).

36. **(E)**   Although "precious" can mean all of the definitions listed as possible answers, "very old" is the best meaning for "precious old" because the rest of the passage details the old clerk's eccentricities brought on by the passing of time. Choice (A) is directly refuted by "He an't a dear one." Choices (B) and (C) may apply to the way Mr. Jonas' father feels about the clerk, but they do not fit Mr. Jonas' feelings. Nowhere in the passage is (D) discussed.

37. **(C)**   When the old clerk took a fever "twenty years ago or so," he was delirious for three weeks. The entire time he had fever, he "never left off" running figures in his head, and the figures eventually became so high that his brain became addled. Choice (B) may have contributed to the clerk's problem, but it is not the immediate cause. Choice (A) is incorrect as the fever happened many years before he grew deaf. Choice (D) may have contributed, but there is no evidence in the passage to indicate it. Choice (E) is contradicted in the passage.

38. **(E)**   During the conversation between Mr. Jonas and Anthony about the clerk's worth as a worker, Mr. Jonas comments, "He an't a dear one" and then explains how he "earns his salt." The idiom "earns his salt" means he "earns his wages," so "dear" can be taken to mean "expensive" in this context: the old clerk does not have to be paid much but he earns his pay. Although (A) may be true, it is not the meaning in this context. There is no evidence to support (B), (C), or (D).

39. **(C)**   The clerk's being a good whist player seems to strike a bit of admiration in Mr. Jonas because the old man can play well even when he "had no more notion what sort of people he was playing against, than you

have." Even though he seems to be amazed at the old clerk's whist game, Mr. Jonas seems irritated the old man is unaware of anyone else but the "honored parent" (D). Mr. Jonas speaks disparagingly of the clerk's age (A), strangeness (B), and deafness (E).

40. **(B)** During his fever, the old clerk added numbers for three weeks. The numbers mounted steadily into "so many million at last." Choice (D) is a possibility, but evidence in the passage does not indicate this probability. The fever happened before (C) became a factor. Choice (E) is refuted by the passage, and choice (A) has no evidence to support it.

41. **(A)** The old clerk seems sharp enough dealing with accustomed things — clerking, whist, responding to Mr. Jonas' father — but he has difficulties with responding to new people and situations. There is no evidence (B) is correct, although he could hardly be blamed for getting a little of his own back. Keeping books and playing whist are not "the simplest of tasks" (C). What the old clerk "would like" (C) to do or is pleased (D) and (E) to do is not a consideration in this passage. It seems as if the old man's mind is permanently afflicted; Mr. Jonas says of him after the fever, "I don't believe he's ever been quite right since."

42. **(D)** The narrator and his companions return to the "nightmare ground" (line two) where they were almost killed. There does not seem to be any gloating (A) among the men, nor do they seem afraid of death (B). The picture of Steffi (C) could not have been sufficient reason to return, even if they had known the photo was there to begin with. Looking for salvageable spoils of war (E) is a common motive, but it is not borne out by these men because they do not carry off anything of value.

43. **(B)** The barrel of his gun is "frowning," an expression a person would have. As guns do not have a face to "frown," the literary device here is personification because the gun has been given human characteristics.

44. **(B)** Guns are an instrument of war and so carry the threat of destruction. The frowning barrel could express being upset over a defeat and death. Choice (B) carries both of these meanings. Since the German soldier is already dead, these two lines probably do not indicate a fear of dying.

45. **(A)**   There is no possibility a dead soldier could be "spoiling for a fight." The visitors to the scene do not appear particularly aggressive at this time; rather, the scene creates a feeling of melancholy at the terrible waste of life. All other meanings can apply. The man and his equipment have been rendered useless (B) and are now "waste" matter (D). The returning men have taken the territory (C) and can carry off any goods they find (E). Also, the soldier has been stripped of his life.

46. **(D)**   Both of the first two interpretations apply to line 14. The victors view the dead body "almost with content": they are content to have won, to have destroyed the enemy, and to be the ones alive. Taken in context, the "with content" can be paired with "abased" in line 14 and with "seeming to have paid" in line 14; in this case, the word "content" is intended to be ironic. The soldier is content because he is dead and therefore beyond the cares of this world. There is no indication the girlfriend will be content to have her boyfriend dead, although she may reach some degree of peace in having certain knowledge of how he died.

47. **(E)**   Two meanings apply here. The equipment which should have protected the soldier seems to mock him for two reasons. First, the equipment was the reason he was fired upon by enemy troops; thus, the protection is at the same time the cause of his destruction. Also, the gun is still "hard and good" (line 16) when the soldier is decaying. The man has paid with his life for having the military equipment. He has not had to pay for the equipment itself (II).

48. **(C)**   The tone of the poem conveys a pragmatism engendered by becoming accustomed to war and the destruction it causes. Perhaps the narrator and his companions are curious to see the aftermath of the "nightmare" battle, and there is a tinge of melancholy in the poem, a sadness for what cannot be made whole again. Mostly, the narrator observes the mortal wounds of the soldier and lover. The narrator is neither mocking nor sadistic. It is not beneficent to kill another, and it is impossible to be indifferent at the sight of torn flesh that could be one's own.

49. **(A)**   Although Kumalo does not know that particular hill, he knows (A) what a *kraal* is and can visualize a tall hill. These are things with which he is familiar. The other things are unfamiliar and therefore create fear because Kumalo is not accustomed to them or because he does not

know how they work. Kumalo gives up trying to understand the bottle and glass sign on the building (B). It is implied that the bustle of the crowd in the underground station (C) is overwhelming to him. The loud noise (D) of a rushing train "makes him jump in his seat," and Kumalo thinks the "noise is immense." The cars and buses (E) are "more than he has ever imagined."

50. **(C)** Kumalo is obviously not accustomed to the city. The two times the train stops at places with buildings and motorized vehicles, Kumalo thinks he might be at Johannesburg. It is possible that he might be (A) eagerly looking forward to his visit, but there is no evidence in the selection to support this. There is no evidence to support his being a visitor to the country; instead, a man traveling with Kumalo address him with a native title of respect, *umfundisi*. The men show signs of becoming tired at his questions (B), but they give no indication of wanting to sleep (D).

51. **(D)** Although Kumalo asks only two questions, there is an indication that there have been more. The men laugh and say the second stop is "nothing." It is at this point the men "are growing a little tired," the implication being that there have been earlier questions and explanations. There is no evidence of a long ride (B) or of any delays (E). It is likely some of the men are country people (C), but no one else is asking naive questions. All at least pretend to some knowledge and "Old hands some of them are." There is no evidence the men have been working (A) in the city.

52. **(E)** Kumalo thinks the number of railway-lines "is a wonder" and sees stations "more that he has ever imagined." His thinking the train has rushed past travelers, "leaving them disappointed," shows his ignorance of train schedules and timetables. Finally, his not knowing where to get off indicates that this is his first journey in a train because he is just now aware of the multiple stops a train makes and does not know how to look for the station signs.

53. **(C)** Although a bit tired of Kumalo's questions, none of the men display derisiveness (A) or irritation (B). They are certainly not indifferent (D) and even appear to enjoy showing off a bit, as the selection indicates their confidence and experience. There is no indication of obsequiousness (E) in any action or statement of the man.

54. **(D)** Kumalo is not illiterate because he can read the "black and white" on the sign's advertisement and wonder at the choice of colors in the neon bulbs. The selections shows Kumalo to be ignorant of the vast confusion and turmoil of the city, and frozen in fear at it all.

55. **(A)** Kumalo knows other people safely cross the street, and he gives no indication of fear for those individuals. However, something bad happened to Mpanza's son in crossing the street (B), so "he is afraid to follow" the stream of pedestrians. Even when the light is green, a bus cuts across so he thinks "there is some law of it that he does not understand" (C). His looking as if he is waiting there deliberately (D) is a defense mechanism to avoid ridicule. Calling upon *Tixo* to watch over him (E) is obviously an invocation to a higher force with protective powers.

56. **(B)** The husband enters in a bad mood reflected by his sour facial expression. He might be in a bad mood because he has heard idle gossip (C) or wishes to be left alone (D), but neither of these come out in the dialogue. Choice (A) is not a consideration here. Choice (E) is probably true of the husband but is not the immediate cause of his poor frame of mind.

57. **(B)** Mrs. Pinchwife, although longing to be more educated in the ways of the world, is probably a bit naive at this point. She confesses to her husband that Alithea has been scolding her for liking the actors, and she tells her husband she likes the players better than her husband because they are more refined. She may be a snob (A), but her naivete is the outstanding character trait. She knows little of society and so is probably not (E). Although there is no evidence in this scene of (C) or (D), she may yet attain those traits.

58. **(A)** Alithea denies she has kept company with women of scandalous reputation (B). However, when Pinchwife accuses Alithea of keeping the company of men of scandalous reputation, she replies, "Where? Would you not have me civil?" Thus, she admits to having entertained men of dubious reputation (A). Although (C) and (D) may be possible, or even probable given the circumstances, there is not enough evidence in this passage to prove either one. Choice (E) is a likely answer because Alithea is protective of her reputation and says quickly that her brother is her only censurer; however, the main drift of the argument leads to choice (A).

59. **(E)** Alithea has already taken Mrs. Pinchwife to the theater, at least, and perhaps to more places. Although Mr. Pinchwife would prefer to keep his wife ignorant of the town's pleasures, it is too late for that. In addition, Mr. Pinchwife leads his wife into more possibilities for misbehavior in his speech about the vices of the naughty town-women, "who only hate their husbands and love every man else, love plays, visits, fine coaches, fine clothes, fiddles, balls, treats, and so lead a wicked town-life." Mrs. Pinchwife, innocent as she is at this time, is only too eager to have fun in the city, for she states that these things her husband has listed make London "not so bad a place." The understatement of Mrs. Pinchwife and the exaggeration of the husband, combined with the cosmopolitan protestations of Alithea, create a humorous scene.

60. **(C)** Although Mr. Pinchwife is obviously familiar with the pleasures of town life, (E) is an answer that cannot be determined from this passage. Of the remaining possibilities, all are somewhat likely and can be supported. Fine clothes and coaches cost a great deal (D), and all that time spent in entertainment would keep Mrs. Pinchwife away from home (A) more than her husband would prefer. Once used to a faster-paced life, Mrs. Pinchwife might not be coaxed back to the much duller country life (B). However, most of Pinchwife's conversation with his wife concerns his wife's being attracted to the playermen (C); he does not want her to become one of the "notorious town-women" he accuses his sister of being.

Literature

TEST 3

Literature

TEST 3

1. (A) (B) (C) (D) (E)	21. (A) (B) (C) (D) (E)	41. (A) (B) (C) (D) (E)
2. (A) (B) (C) (D) (E)	22. (A) (B) (C) (D) (E)	42. (A) (B) (C) (D) (E)
3. (A) (B) (C) (D) (E)	23. (A) (B) (C) (D) (E)	43. (A) (B) (C) (D) (E)
4. (A) (B) (C) (D) (E)	24. (A) (B) (C) (D) (E)	44. (A) (B) (C) (D) (E)
5. (A) (B) (C) (D) (E)	25. (A) (B) (C) (D) (E)	45. (A) (B) (C) (D) (E)
6. (A) (B) (C) (D) (E)	26. (A) (B) (C) (D) (E)	46. (A) (B) (C) (D) (E)
7. (A) (B) (C) (D) (E)	27. (A) (B) (C) (D) (E)	47. (A) (B) (C) (D) (E)
8. (A) (B) (C) (D) (E)	28. (A) (B) (C) (D) (E)	48. (A) (B) (C) (D) (E)
9. (A) (B) (C) (D) (E)	29. (A) (B) (C) (D) (E)	49. (A) (B) (C) (D) (E)
10. (A) (B) (C) (D) (E)	30. (A) (B) (C) (D) (E)	50. (A) (B) (C) (D) (E)
11. (A) (B) (C) (D) (E)	31. (A) (B) (C) (D) (E)	51. (A) (B) (C) (D) (E)
12. (A) (B) (C) (D) (E)	32. (A) (B) (C) (D) (E)	52. (A) (B) (C) (D) (E)
13. (A) (B) (C) (D) (E)	33. (A) (B) (C) (D) (E)	53. (A) (B) (C) (D) (E)
14. (A) (B) (C) (D) (E)	34. (A) (B) (C) (D) (E)	54. (A) (B) (C) (D) (E)
15. (A) (B) (C) (D) (E)	35. (A) (B) (C) (D) (E)	55. (A) (B) (C) (D) (E)
16. (A) (B) (C) (D) (E)	36. (A) (B) (C) (D) (E)	56. (A) (B) (C) (D) (E)
17. (A) (B) (C) (D) (E)	37. (A) (B) (C) (D) (E)	57. (A) (B) (C) (D) (E)
18. (A) (B) (C) (D) (E)	38. (A) (B) (C) (D) (E)	58. (A) (B) (C) (D) (E)
19. (A) (B) (C) (D) (E)	39. (A) (B) (C) (D) (E)	59. (A) (B) (C) (D) (E)
20. (A) (B) (C) (D) (E)	40. (A) (B) (C) (D) (E)	60. (A) (B) (C) (D) (E)

LITERATURE

TEST 3

TIME: 60 Minutes
         60 Questions

DIRECTIONS: *This test consists of selections from literary works and questions on their content, form, and style. After reading each passage or poem, choose the best answer to each question and blacken the corresponding space on the answer sheet.*

NOTE: Pay particular attention to the requirement of questions that contain the words NOT, LEAST, or EXCEPT.

<u>QUESTION 1–7</u> are based on the following poem. Read the poem carefully before choosing your answers.

> After great pain a formal feeling comes
> The nerves sit ceremonious like tombs;
> The stiff Heart questions — was it He that bore?
> And yesterday — or centuries before?
>
> 5   The feet mechanical
> Go round a wooden way
> Of ground or air or Ought, regardless grown,
> A quartz contentment like a stone.
>
> This is the hour of lead
> 10 Remembered if outlived,

As freezing persons recollect the snow —
First chill, then stupor, then the letting go.

"After Great Pain," by Emily Dickinson

1. The "He" (line 3) is

    (A) the one who is instrumental in inflicting the pain

    (B) the pain itself which has been personified

    (C) the person who is inflicted with the pain

    (D) a disinterested observer trying to understand the cause of the pain

    (E) the poet himself

2. The word "stiff" in line three is best described by the phrase

    (A) protected by a shield

    (B) unwilling to bend

    (C) poorly prepared

    (D) insensitive and unfeeling

    (E) haughty and proud

3. Which other word is LEAST analogous to the word "ceremonious"?

    (A) stiff   (D) remembered

    (B) mechanical   (E) regardless

    (C) formal

4. Which of the following phrases is redundant and could be eliminated without altering the meaning of the poem?

    (A) if outlived   (D) a wooden way

    (B) like tombs   (E) like a stone

    (C) or centuries before

5. The phrase "recollect the snow" (line 11) means

   I.   Think of the formal whiteness of the snow

   II. Recall the quiet precision of the snowfall

   III. Remember the experience of freezing

   (A) I and III   (D) I only

   (B) II only   (E) III only

   (C) II and III

6. The word "regardless" (line 7) is best read as a synonym for

   (A) careless   (D) unwary

   (B) unmindful   (E) reckless

   (C) unthoughtful

7. "Ought" is an archaic word which the poet here uses to mean

   (A) nothing at all

   (B) everything which can be imagined

   (C) that which cannot be known

   (D) anything else

   (E) what may be misunderstood

QUESTIONS 8–15 are based on the following passage. Read the passage carefully before choosing your answers.

The widow was as complete a contrast to her third bridegroom, in everything but age, as can well be conceived. Compelled to relinquish her first engagement, she had been united to a man of twice her own years, to whom she had become an exemplary wife, and by whose death she was left in possession of a splendid fortune. A southern gentleman, considerably younger than herself, succeeded to her hand, and carried her to Charleston, where, after many uncomfortable years, she found herself again a widow. It would have been singular if any uncommon delicacy of feeling had survived through such a life as Mrs. Dabney's; it could not be crushed and killed by

her early disappointment, the cold duty of her first marriage, the dislocation of the heart's principles consequent on a second union, and the unkindness of her southern husband, which had inevitably driven her to connect the idea of his death with that of her comfort.
15 To be brief, she was the wisest, but unloveliest variety of women, a philosopher, bearing troubles of the heart with equanimity, dispensing with all that should have been her happiness, and making the best of what remained. Sage in most matters, the widow was perhaps the more amiable for the one frailty that made her ridicu-
20 lous. Being childless, she could not remain beautiful by proxy, in the person of a daughter; she therefore refused to grow old and ugly, on any consideration; she struggled with Time, and held fast her roses in spite of him, till the venerable thief appeared to have relinquished the spoil, as not worth the trouble of acquiring it.

by Nathaniel Hawthorne

8. From the first sentence we can assume that Mrs. Dabney is

   (A) much younger than her present groom

   (B) about the same age as her present groom

   (C) older than her present groom

   (D) much older than her present groom

   (E) impossible to tell for sure

9. Her first marriage can best be described as

   (A) an exercise in duty but without love

   (B) the one spot of romantic loveliness in an otherwise lackluster existence

   (C) an intellectually challenging relationship

   (D) an experience in poverty made bearable by mutual trust and understanding

   (E) a relationship marred by disloyalty and unchastity

10. Her second marriage to the southern gentleman was different from the first in that it was

    (A) based on mutual love and understanding

    (B) forced upon them by social pressures with which they could not cope

    (C) the result of her desire for status

    (D) founded upon greed and lack of tender feelings rather than upon love

    (E) an illegal arrangement unsanctioned by either civil or religious custom

11. The "early disappointment" mentioned in line 11 refers to

    (A) her first marriage

    (B) her second marriage

    (C) her contemplated third marriage

    (D) her first serious love

    (E) a combination of her romantic experiences up to this time

12. The last part of the paragraph involves the use of an interesting personification. Who is personified?

    (A) the bride   (D) beauty

    (B) her third husband   (E) time

    (C) marriage

13. How does a woman remain beautiful "by proxy" according to this author?

    (A) She has a beautiful daughter.

    (B) She refuses to grow old.

    (C) She gives way to a ridiculous fraility.

    (D) She avoids remaining single by marrying repeatedly.

    (E) She becomes a philosopher.

14. The passage is concerned primarily with the description of a woman who is

    (A) charming despite her age

    (B) without redeeming qualities

    (C) attempting to retain her youth

    (D) physically attractive to many men

    (E) incapable of sustained romantic love

15. In this context "roses" (line 22) represents

    (A) contentment in marriage

    (B) beauty of youth

    (C) hope for happiness

    (D) troubles of the heart

    (E) kindness of the married state

QUESTIONS 16–22 are based on the following passage. Read the passage carefully before choosing your answers.

> Strew on her roses, roses,
> And never a spray of yew!
> In quiet she reposes;
> Ah! would that I did too.
>
> 5   Her mirth the world required;
> She bathed it in smiles of glee.
> But her heart was tired, tired,
> And now they let her be.
>
> Her life was turning, turning,
> 10 In mazes of heat and sound.
> But for peace her soul was yearning,
> And now peace laps her round.
>
> Her cabin'd, ample spirit,
> It flutter'd and fail'd for breath.

15 To-night it doth inherit
   The vasty hall of Death.

"Requiescat," by Matthew Arnold

16. The poet looks upon the death of this person as

    (A) seasonable   (D) tragic

    (B) pathetic   (E) fortuitous

    (C) enigmatic

17. The tone or attitude assumed by the poet toward the subject of this poem is

    (A) playful and ironic

    (B) dispassionate and mocking

    (C) condescending and informal

    (D) formal and serious

    (E) sarcastic and poignant

18. How do we know that the poet refuses to think of her as dead?

    (A) He will not strew the yew.

    (B) He says she reposes.

    (C) He mentions her smiles of glee.

    (D) He says that her life was turning.

    (E) He tells us that her spirit was ample.

19. What is it that the poet contrasts with the vasty hall (line 16)?

    (A) peace that laps

    (B) roses

    (C) mazes of heat and sound

    (D) smiles of glee

    (E) a cabin'd spirit

20. Which of the following phrases describing her life can be considered as most ambiguous?

    (A) "She bathed it in smiles of glee"

    (B) "In quiet she reposes"

    (C) "Her life was turning"

    (D) "For peace her soul was yearning"

    (E) "Her mirth the world required"

21. Which of the following comes closest to the poet's conclusion in regard to the death of this person?

    (A) She will most certainly be missed.

    (B) She is surely more content now.

    (C) She was never fully appreciated.

    (D) History will deal harshly with her.

    (E) Her life could have been better spent.

22. The attitude of the poet toward the subject of the poem might best be described by which of the following?

    (A) He loved her to distraction.

    (B) He will greatly miss her.

    (C) His life has been little changed by her departure.

    (D) He felt toward her a hidden jealousy.

    (E) He envies her present condition.

QUESTIONS 23–28 are based on the following poem. Read the poem carefully before choosing your answers.

> Dark house, by which once more I stand
>   Here in the long unlovely street,
>   Doors where my heart was used to beat
> So quickly, waiting for a hand,

5   A hand that can be clasped no more —
        Behold me for I cannot sleep,
        And like a guilty thing I creep
     At earliest morning to the door.

        He is not here; but far away
10   The noise of life begins again,
        And ghastly thro, the drizzling rain
     On the bald street breaks the blank day.

"In Memoriam A.H.H.," by Alfred Lord Tennyson

23. The attitude of the speaker, the "I" of line 1, toward the "he" of the poem represented by the hand is one of

    (A) loathing based upon past misunderstanding of a bitter experience

    (B) terror as a result of "ghastly" experiences with which they have been associated

    (C) uncertainty, since he does not know how "he" will accept him when they eventually do meet

    (D) guilt since "I" has been at least to some extent responsible for the fact that "he" is dead

    (E) unqualified love, represented by his desire to clasp a hand that can no longer respond to him

24. The word "ghastly" in line 11 conveys which of the following ideas?

    I.   The empty (bald) street in the rain seems pale and ghostly.

    II. The individual who is dead haunts him in a spectral form.

    III. It seems to him horrible that the day should come to life again when the one he is writing of cannot do so.

    IV. The idea of a hand unconnected to a body causes terror.

    (A) I and IV   (D) I and III

    (B) III only   (E) I only

    (C) II and III

25. The general tone of the poem could best be described as

    (A) ironic   (D) condescending

    (B) gloomy   (E) satirical

    (C) playful

26. What image expressed at the beginning of the poem is repeated at the end but more specifically?

    (A) house and rain   (D) stand and breaks

    (B) unlovely and bald   (E) long and ghastly

    (C) dark and blank

27. The primary source of the irony in the poem is that

    (A) the hand once clasped can be clasped no more

    (B) life goes on despite the death of one's friend

    (C) the poet creeps like a guilty thing

    (D) the house on the unlovely street was dark

    (E) it begins to rain in the early morning

28. The lines of the poem are addressed to the

    (A) reader

    (B) drizzling rain

    (C) house

    (D) street on which the speaker stands

    (E) speaker's dead friend

QUESTIONS 29–31 are based on the following passage. Read the passage carefully before choosing your answers.

As no lady or gentleman, with any claims to polite breeding, can possibly sympathize with the Chuzzlewit family without being first assured of the extreme antiquity of the race, it is a great satisfaction to know that it undoubtedly descended in a direct line from Adam

5   and Eve; and was, in the very earliest times, closely connected with
    agricultural interest. If it should ever be urged by grudging and
    malicious persons, that a Chuzzlewit, in any period of the family
    history, displayed an overweening amount of family pride, surely
    the weakness will be considered not only pardonable but laudable,
10 when the immense superiority of the house to the rest of mankind, in
    respect of its ancient origins, is taken into account.

Martin Chuzzlewit, *by Charles Dickens*

29.   Which of the following is true of the meaning of this passage?

      (A)   The family is similar to every other family on earth.

      (B)   The family has genuine cause to be proud of its ancestry.

      (C)   The family earns its livelihood by tilling the soil.

      (D)   A great deal of research has been done on this family.

      (E)   The family is made up of polite, well-bred people.

30.   Which of the following terms could be said to apply to this passage?

      I.   Factual

      II.   Ironic

      III. Serious

      (A)   I and II   (D)   I, II, and III

      (B)   I and III   (E)   III only

      (C)   II only

31.   In reality the author is telling us in this passage that

      (A)   there is sufficient reason for one to admire this family

      (B)   all Englishmen are snobs

      (C)   this family really has little to commend it to our notice

      (D)   he wishes all families could be as well thought of as the Chuzzle-
            wits

      (E)   this family is characterized by an excessive amount of family
            pride

QUESTIONS 32–39 are based on the following poem. Read the poem carefully before choosing your answers.

Summer ends now; now barbarous in beauty, the stocks arise
    Around; up above, what wind-walks! what lovely behavior
    O silk-sack clouds! has wilder, wilful-wavier
Meal-drift moulded ever and melted across skies?

5 I walk, I lift up, I lift up heart, eyes,
    Down all that glory in the heavens to glean our Savior;
    And, eyes, heart, what looks, what lips yet gave you a
Rapturous love's greeting of realer, of rounder replies?

And the azurous hung hills are his world-wielding shoulder
10   Majestic-as a stallion stalwart, very-violet-sweet!
These things, these things were here and but the beholder
    Wanting; which two when they once meet,
The heart rears wings bold and bolder
    And hurls for him, O half hurls earth for him off under his feet.

"Hurrahing in Harvest," by Gerard Manley Hopkins

32. At what point does the poem cease to be merely a physical description of a landscape?

    (A) after the exclamation in line 2

    (B) at the beginning of line 5

    (C) after the third comma in line 7

    (D) at the beginning of the second stanza

    (E) after the semicolon in line 12

33. What part of speech is represented by "meal-drift" (line 4)?

    (A) It is a verb, representing a way of drifting.

    (B) It is an adjective describing a type of mold.

    (C) It is an adverb modifying "moulded."

    (D) it is a noun, the subject of "has ... moulded."

    (E) It is a noun joined to an adverb modifying "moulded."

34. The word "wanting" in line 12 seems to have no object. Which of the following best explains the function of the word?

(A) There was no one to behold these things.

(B) The beholder wants these things.

(C) These are the things the stallion wants.

(D) The heart wants wings.

(E) The person who describes these things wants them to be here.

35. Who is the "him" mentioned in line 14?

(A) the stallion   (D) the heart

(B) the poet   (E) the Savior

(C) the beholder

36. Which of the following defines "world-wielding shoulder" (line 9)?

I. A projection of the mountain

II. A round reply of rapturous love

III. The wings of the heart

IV. A part of the Savior's Body

(A) I only   (D) IV only

(B) II and IV   (E) II and III

(C) I and IV

37. The progress of the reader's perceptions as he reads the poem can best be described as

(A) from the particular to the general

(B) from truth to myth

(C) from beauty to ugliness

(D) from the distant to the immediate

(E) from obscurity to clarity

38. The word "barbarous" in line 1 can best be interpreted to mean

    (A) untamed and strong

    (B) violent and savage

    (C) wicked and devilish

    (D) misunderstood and hated

    (E) careless and foolish

39. By the word "moulded" in line 4 the poet implies that the

    (A) clouds appear moldy

    (B) sheaves of corn appear to be molded against the sky

    (C) Savior is he who has molded our lives

    (D) mealy whisps have formed into clouds

    (E) stocks appear to have molded to the landscape

QUESTIONS 40–45 are based on the following passage. Read the passage carefully before choosing your answers.

   While Caesar tarried where he was to fit out his ships, deputies came to him from a great part of the Morini to make excuse for their policy of the previous season, when in their barbarism and ignorance of our usage they had made war against Rome, and to promise that
5 they would carry out his commands. Caesar thought this overture exceedingly opportune. He did not wish to leave an enemy in his rear, nor had he a chance of carrying out a campaign because of the lateness of the season; nor did he think the settlement of such trivialities should take precedence of Britain. He therefore ordered
10 them to furnish a large number of hostages; and when they brought these he received them under his protection. When about eight transports — enough, in his opinion, to carry two legions across — had been collected and concentrated, he distributed all the ships of war he had over between his quartermaster-general, lieutenant-gen-
15 erals, and commandants. To the total stated eighteen transports should be added, which were detained eight miles off by the wind, and prevented from entering the port of concentration; these he allotted to the cavalry.

40. Which of the following best describes Caesar's attitude toward the deputies?

    (A) haughty disrespect   (D) angry hostility

    (B) cautious relief   (E) flippant disregard

    (C) unbounded optimism

41. What is meant by calling these men "deputies" in line 1?

    (A) They are law enforcement officers.

    (B) They represent only themselves.

    (C) They are a deputation from the Morini.

    (D) They are men of lesser importance.

    (E) They will be followed by another more important.

42. Caesar speaks of the barbarians' "ignorance of our usage." Of what could he be speaking?

    (A) bestiality   (D) concern

    (B) sympathy   (E) fairness

    (C) efficiency

43. When Caesar speaks of trivialities in line 9 he has reference to

    (A) the British

    (B) his policy toward the barbarians

    (C) his conflict with the barbarians

    (D) his campaign against the British

    (E) the hostages

44. When the fleet finally sails for Britain, how many ships will there be?

    (A) eight   (D) no way of knowing

    (B) eighteen   (E) depends on the wind

    (C) twenty-six

45. Why doesn't Caesar fight the Morini first before sending his troops against Britain?

(A) He has too few troops.

(B) The Morini are no threat.

(C) His generals are incompetent.

(D) The weather is unfavorable.

(E) The season is too far advanced.

QUESTIONS 46–52 are based on the following poem. Read the poem carefully before choosing your answers.

> I leant upon a coppice gate
>   When Frost was spectre-gray,
> And Winter's dregs made desolate
>   The weakening eye of day.
> 5 The tangled bine-stems scored the sky
>   Like strings of broken lyres,
> And all mankind that haunted nigh
>   Had sought their household fires.
>
> The land's sharp features seemed to be
> 10   The Century's corpse outleant,
> His crypt the cloudy canopy,
>   The wind his death-lament.
> The ancient pulse of germ and birth
>   Was shrunken hard and dry,
> 15 And every spirit upon earth
>   Seemed fervourless as I.
>
> At once a voice arose among
>   The bleak twigs overhead
> In a full-hearted evensong
> 20   Of joy illimited;
> An aged thrush, frail, gaunt, and small,
>   In blast beruffled plume,
> Had chosen thus to fling his soul
>   Upon the growing gloom.

25   So little cause for carolings
          Of such ecstatic sound
   Was written on terrestrial things
          Afar or nigh around,
   That I could think there trembled through
30   His happy good-night air
   Some blessed Hope, whereof he knew
          And I was unaware.

"The Darkling Thrush," by Thomas Hardy

46.   The attitude of the speaker toward the thrush could be described as

   (A)   puzzled admiration

   (B)   contemptuous indifference

   (C)   hostile repugnance

   (D)   fearful dismay

   (E)   unbounded love

47.   There is a marked change in the poet's mood during the course of the poem. Where does this change begin?

   (A)   line 29 with "I could think …"

   (B)   line 17 with "At once a voice arose …"

   (C)   line 9 with "The land's sharp features …"

   (D)   line 5 with "The tangled bine stems …"

   (E)   line 13 with "The ancient pulse …"

48.   Which of the following images is NOT used in describing the day?

   (A)   a tea cup   (D)   a grave

   (B)   a harp   (E)   the sun

   (C)   a fence

49.   The general mood of the speaker in the first 16 lines could be described as

   (A)   antagonistic and pugnacious

(B) lethargic and dull

(C) animated and agitated

(D) fearful and apprehensive

(E) puzzled and uncertain

50. Which of the following could be used to describe the thrush?

I.   Intimidating

II.   Courageous

III. Timorous

IV. Insightful

(A) I and III

(B) II only

(C) II and IV

(D) I only

(E) II and III

51. Using the evidence provided by the poem itself, what time of the year might the poem be describing?

(A) Christmas Day

(B) the winter solstice

(C) the autumnal equinox

(D) Thanksgiving

(E) New Year's Eve

52. The poem is full of good imagery. Which of the following is NOT included?

(A) the sun looking upon the earth

(B) the heavens as scratched

(C) the world with blood vessels

(D) roots clutching the soil

(E) the clouds covering a tomb

are based on the following passage. Read the passage carefully before choosing your answers.

Perchance he for whom this bell tolls may be so ill as that he knows not it tolls for him; and perchance I may think myself so much better than I am, as that they who are about me and see my state may have caused it to toll for me, and I know not that. The
5   church is catholic, universal, so are all her actions; all that she does belongs to all. When she baptizes a child, that action concerns me; for that child is thereby connected to that body which is my head too, and ingrafted into that body whereof I am a member. And when she buries a man, that action concerns me: all mankind is of one author
10 and is one volume; when one man dies, one chapter is not torn out of the book, but translated into a better language; and every chapter must be so translated.

From "For Whom the Bell Doth Toll," by John Donne

53. How is the writer most like the person for whom the bells tolls?

   (A) He does not realize that he has tolled the bell for others.

   (B) He thinks the bell tolls for himself.

   (C) He fears that the bell tolls for himself.

   (D) He does not realize that others may have caused the bells to toll for him.

   (E) They both know the bell tolls for them.

54. How is the poet related to the child who is baptized?

   (A) There is no relation except that they are both members of the church.

   (B) Their membership in the true church makes them brothers.

   (C) There is no relationship whatsoever.

   (D) The child is his brother regardless of what the church does to him.

   (E) After the child's baptism they are members of the same metaphorical body.

55. The final line of the passage indicates that

   (A) all will die and go to a better place

   (B) it is impossible to know what will happen to us at death

   (C) there is no better place than this

   (D) change is inevitable in the world

   (E) all men will die eventually

56. Which of the following describes the tone of this passage?

   I.   Playful

   II. Ironic

   III. Condescending

   IV. Serious

   (A) I and III   (D) none of these

   (B) IV only   (E) I and II

   (C) II only

QUESTIONS 57–60 are based on the following poem. Read the poem carefully before choosing your answers.

> My glass shall not persuade me I am old,
> So long as youth and thou are of one date;
> But when in thee time's furrows I behold,
> Then look I death my days should expiate.
> 5 For all that beauty that doth cover thee
> Is but the seemly raiment of my heart,
> Which in thy breast doth live, as thine in me.
> How can I then be elder than thou art?
> O therefore love, be of thyself so wary
> 10 As I not for myself, but for thee will,
> Bearing thy heart, which I will keep so chary
> As tender nurse her babe from faring ill.
> Presume not on thy heart when mine is slain;
> Thou gav'st me thine, not to give back again.

"Sonnet 22," by William Shakespeare

57. When does the poet believe he will grow old?

    (A) when he sees wrinkles in his face

    (B) when she holds up the glass for him to see his own face

    (C) when he sees wrinkles in her face

    (D) as long as he and she are both young

    (E) on the date she becomes as old as he is

58. If you were to search for it, where would you find her heart?

    (A) living in her own breast

    (B) in his breast

    (C) hidden by "seemly raiment"

    (D) covered by her beauty

    (E) it is impossible to find

59. Line 8 has reference to what other line(s) of the poem?

    (A) lines 5 and 11   (D) line 14

    (B) line 7   (E) lines 1 to 4

    (C) lines 3 and 6

60. What instructions does he give her in the poem?

    (A) she is never to die

    (B) she is not to try to repossess her heart

    (C) she is not to presume upon her beauty

    (D) she is to remain every young

    (E) she is to take back her heart after he is dead

TEST 3

ANSWER KEY

1. (C)	16. (A)	31. (C)	46. (A)
2. (A)	17. (D)	32. (B)	47. (B)
3. (D)	18. (A)	33. (D)	48. (C)
4. (E)	19. (E)	34. (A)	49. (B)
5. (E)	20. (C)	35. (E)	50. (C)
6. (B)	21. (B)	36. (C)	51. (E)
7. (D)	22. (E)	37. (A)	52. (D)
8. (B)	23. (E)	38. (A)	53. (D)
9. (A)	24. (D)	39. (D)	54. (E)
10. (D)	25. (B)	40. (B)	55. (A)
11. (D)	26. (B)	41. (C)	56. (B)
12. (E)	27. (B)	42. (E)	57. (C)
13. (A)	28. (C)	43. (C)	58. (B)
14. (C)	29. (A)	44. (D)	59. (E)
15. (B)	30. (C)	45. (E)	60. (B)

DETAILED EXPLANATIONS
OF ANSWERS
TEST 3

1.   **(C)**   One might say also that the heart itself is a bearer of the pain for it is the heart that questions the pain's reality. The reference of the poem is general and it describes a feeling experienced by anyone who goes through great pain.

2.   **(A)**   The point of the poem is that the formal feeling insulates or protects the emotions after pain much as we don a wetsuit when swimming in icy waters. Formal stiffness at such times is a defense against emotional disintegration.

3.   **(D)**   The words stiff, mechanical, formal and regardless all describe the character of the defenses raised by the heart to protect itself against the pain. The remembering of that feeling, if it comes at all, is done later and is not a defensive measure.

4.   **(E)**   The phrase "like a stone" repeats the meaning of the word "quartz" and therefore adds nothing to the poem's message. Because it is the essence of poetry to avoid unnecessary words, this phrase might be pointed out as a weakness. All of the other phrases are essential to what the poet is telling us.

5.   **(E)**   The word "snow" is here a poetic shorthand for the remembered experience. The meeting of the last stanza of the poem is that the formal feeling numbs or deadens one against the pain, just as a person who is freezing to death first becomes numb against the cold.

6.   **(B)**   The "stiff" heart and the "mechanical" feet of the one in great pain insulate themselves from that pain by becoming unmindful of it like the quartz is unmindful of blows which might be delivered to it.

7. **(D)** Line 7 is an inversion, a common practice of poets, with the phrases reversed. The poet's meaning is that the feet have grown regardless of ground or air or of anything else.

8. **(B)** Since we are told that she is a contrast to him in everything *but* age, we can assume that Mrs. Dabney and her third bridegroom are about the same age.

9. **(A)** Mrs. Dabney was during her first marriage an "exemplary" wife to a man twice as old as she was. The marriage was a "cold duty" (line 11) and therefore, it is presumed, was without love.

10. **(D)** We have to read between the lines for this one. We know he was an unkind husband (lines 7, 8 and 13) and that she had even considered suicide or at least wished for his death during this marriage (line 14). We also know that her first husband had left her well off financially (line 5). From these facts we must assume the nature of the relationship.

11. **(D)** Line 11 introduces a catalog of Mrs. Dabney's experiences, the first of which is the disappointment spoken of. It can only refer to the first engagement which she was compelled to relinquish (lines 2 and 3).

12. **(E)** Personification involves giving human qualities to a non-human or abstract object, so the first two answers could not be correct. Of the three abstractions which make up the last three answers, the last, time, is the one being personified. Time is the "venerable thief" (line 23) who at first tries to steal the "rose" of her beauty and finally gives up.

13. **(A)** Lines 20 and 21 clearly state that it is "in the person of a daughter" that a woman can maintain her beauty.

14. **(C)** Mrs. Dabney is pictured as slightly ridiculous as she approaches the altar for the third time in what must seem to the disinterested observer as a vain attempt to recapture the happiness which has eluded her twice already. The author feels that her attempting in this way to stay young makes her a sort of grimly comical figure.

15. **(B)** Mrs. Dabney is attempting to hold on to her youthful beauty

despite the attempts of time to remove it from her. The author here uses "roses" to describe the beauty of youth.

16. **(A)** The death of a friend is often looked upon as a tragedy or, if we see the victim as an innocent sacrifice, as pathetic, but the woman in this poem is neither a tragic nor a pathetic figure. If her death raised unanswerable questions, we might say it was enigmatic, but that is not the case here either. Fortuitous would indicate that it came by chance, as a random happening. But her death was not that; actually it came when it was welcome and looked for; it was seasonable, opportune and timely.

17. **(D)** Only (D) contains two elements that reflect the author's attitude or tone. Besides being formal and serious, the tone is also sombre, intimate, and certainly optimistic.

18. **(A)** The yew is the flower of death which he refuses to strew upon her remains, insisting rather on roses which are symbols of life and rebirth. To repose is a term often used for the dead and the other three descriptions are all of her before she died.

19. **(E)** The expansive halls of death are a great room, one in which her ample spirit can find the freedom of movement and the peace it wishes for on earth where she felt imprisoned. To "cabin" means to confine or to cramp. The poet hopes you will know that verb use of the word.

20. **(C)** All of these phrases are more or less metaphorical, but the one containing the least common metaphor and which is therefore most ambiguous and difficult to explain, is to say that life turns.

21. **(B)** The subject of the poem was much appreciated in this life and generally admired, but she was never content and always felt hedged in by her circumstances. Now that she is dead and in a place with infinite scope and possibilities, she must be much happier and less troubled.

22. **(E)** Only one line in the poem (line 4) gives us any direct evidence of his personal feelings. Every other passage in the poem limits itself to describing her life and death in dispassionate terms. From line 4 alone, therefore, we must draw our conclusions as to his personal feelings. In this line he tells us clearly that he wishes he could share her condition.

23. **(E)** Be careful not to read into the poem what is not there. Loathing, terror, uncertainty and guilt are not part of Tennyson's message.

24. **(D)** The word "ghashtly" may seem to you too strong for the feeling the poet is trying to achieve, but we can only deal with the poem in front of us, realizing that words take on new connotations as the years go by. There is nothing in the thought of his friend that causes terror. It is only in the real world and the contrast he feels between that world and the thought of his friend that he finds horror. He finds both the physical street itself and the incongruity between a living world and a friend who cannot live to be ghastly.

25. **(B)** The tone of the poem could be described as gloomy, though a number of other terms such as formal, sombre, and serious might also do. There is irony involved in the poet's description of his feelings, but irony is not the overall tone of the poem. Neither (C) nor (D) have anything to do with this poem.

26. **(B)** The street which the poet first sees as unlovely, he comes finally and more specifically to see as bald. The baldness represents the emptiness he feels at his friend's absence, and his examination of his feelings in the poem serve to clarify his first impression. Dark and blank at first may seem like unifying terms, but remember that it is morning by the end of the poem, so the blankness has nothing to do with the dark.

27. **(B)** The irony of life so often expressed by the grieving is that the world would dare to go on as if nothing had happened.

28. **(C)** This is called an apostrophe, a figure of speech by which some-one or something not present is addressed. In this case the first two words of the poem tell us who the speaker is addressing.

29. **(A)** Of course all families are descended in a direct line from Adam and Eve so there is no distinction to be derived from that fact and no need to do research to establish the fact. Likewise, all of the human race at first were farmers.

30. **(C)** Dickens is being his usual ironic self in this passage by saying

the opposite of what he means. He pretends to be serious and factual only to add to the humor of what he is saying.

31. **(C)**   Since there is apparently nothing but ancestry which the family has to commend it, and since tracing one's family back to Adam is manifestly a valueless exercise, it follows then that the Chuzzlewitts may be regarded lightly.

32. **(B)**   The poet has admired the fields and the clouds in the first four lines, but in line 5 he turns his thoughts to the identification of the Savior in nature.

33. **(D)**   Hopkins is asking a question (note the question mark at the end of line 4) beginning with the words in line 3 "has wilder, wilful-wavier ...." The "Meal-drift" is that which is moulded and melts across the skies.

34. **(A)**   The word "want" here means to lack. The poet's meaning is that all that was lacking was someone to recognize the things he is describing.

35. **(E)**   The message of the poem is that when the grandeur of the heavens and the presence of the Lord meet in the eyes of the beholder, his heart performs prodigious feats for the Savior.

36. **(C)**   The poet forces the reader to both understand and feel the strength and majesty of the Lord by comparing a mountain ridge to a part of his body.

37. **(A)**   As the poem begins, the reader is asked to visualize such specific objects as stocks and clouds, objects which are relatively close and tangible. By the end of the poem, however, the reader is nearly overwhelmed by the general and ponderous mass of the entire earth.

38. **(A)**   The reader, of course, does not know what the poet means by this adjective until he can conceive it in the context of the entire poem. The sky is seen as a fit environment for the Savior who is world-wielding, stalwart, and earth-hurling.

39. **(D)**   "Moulded" is the main verb in the sentence beginning in line 3 with the words "has wilder," the word "has" acting as a helping verb. The

subject of the sentence is "meal-drift" referring to the clouds which have moulded themselves into shapes from the meal drift.

40. **(B)** Caesar expresses the reassurance he feels in the knowledge that these people will not be threatening his rear while he is concentrating on an expedition across the North Sea to Britain.

41. **(C)** A deputation is a group of persons appointed to represent others. A deputy was originally a member of such a deputation.

42. **(E)** Though, in this case, we are forced to rely on context and our judgment, it seems unlikely that any of the answers from (A) to (D) would apply. From our general knowledge of the history of Rome we know that it was the purpose of the empire to subdue their enemies by the quickest and least difficult means possible. At least under Caesar the Roman armies had a reputation for being tough but fair.

43. **(C)** Caesar was obviously most concerned about the forthcoming expedition to Britain and did not want any lesser concern to trouble him. He seems to have felt that his troubles with the Morini, whatever they were, were of much less importance than was the British campaign.

44. **(D)** We have no way of knowing, because Caesar does not tell us how many ships of war will make the trip. We only know that eighteen transports will go.

45. **(E)** Caesar says (lines 7–8) that there is not time for both campaigns before winter sets in.

46. **(A)** The poet confesses that he does not understand why the bird is singing, since it seems to have so little to sing about, but he certainly feels a sense of respect toward the bird for doing it.

47. **(B)** As the poem begins, the poet experiences a lethargic stupor while viewing the dead winter world. It is not until line 17 that his spirits are revived by the singing of the old, dying thrush.

48. **(C)** The dregs in line 3 refer to the grounds in the bottom of the tea

cup, the broken lyre in line 6 is a harp, the crypt in line 11 is a grave, and the weakening eye of day (line 4) is the winter sun.

49. **(B)**   The weather, the time of day and the season all conspire to weigh down the poet's spirits. He describes himself as fervourless (line 16), a mood which seems to reflect his surroundings.

50. **(C)**   The poet first sees the bird as merely courageous as it braves the cold winter blast, but he then proceeds to question the bird's prophetic powers as it seemingly has so little to hope for and yet seems to see the world and its future prospects in such a hopeful light.

51. **(E)**   As a matter of fact the poem was written on December 31, 1900, the last day of the 19th century. The poet had every right to see in the day the corpse of a century.

52. **(D)**   This image has been used before, but not here. The others are all present in lines 4, 5, 13, and 11 respectively.

53. **(D)**   Lines 3 and 4 make it clear that his friends, seeing his advanced state of decline better than he can see it, may be tolling the bell for him without his knowing it.

54. **(E)**   The imagery in Line 4–8 is that of a body of which the church is the head and all baptized individuals are members of the body (arms and legs).

55. **(A)**   The imagery of lines 9–12 compare all men to a chapters in a book, each of which will be translated into a better language and find its place in a better book. Translating, then, is similar to going to one's reward, in a better life.

56. **(B)**   In defining man's relationship to his fellow men, the poet is serious and straightforward. He is, in effect, making a point which is so important that no writer's "trick" would be appropriate.

57. **(C)**   Line 3 makes it clear that he will admit he is old when he sees wrinkles (time's furrows) on her brow, and not before.

58. **(B)** Line 6 (last two words) and line 7 tell us that his heart lives in her breast, and the end of line 7 reverses the image, telling us that her heart is in his breast.

59. **(E)** As the poem began, the poet was explaining that he is eternally youthful because his beloved is young. In line 8, he concludes that he cannot be older than she is because of the exchange of hearts that has taken place. Lines 5-8, then, are the poet's explanation of the phenomena reported in lines 1-4.

60. **(B)** In Line 13 he orders her not to "presume" upon her heart after his death. From line 14 it is clear that he means by "presume" the act of taking back again, something she is not to do, for a heart once given (line 14) may not be recalled so easily.

Literature

TEST 4

Literature

TEST 4

1. Ⓐ Ⓑ Ⓒ Ⓓ Ⓔ
2. Ⓐ Ⓑ Ⓒ Ⓓ Ⓔ
3. Ⓐ Ⓑ Ⓒ Ⓓ Ⓔ
4. Ⓐ Ⓑ Ⓒ Ⓓ Ⓔ
5. Ⓐ Ⓑ Ⓒ Ⓓ Ⓔ
6. Ⓐ Ⓑ Ⓒ Ⓓ Ⓔ
7. Ⓐ Ⓑ Ⓒ Ⓓ Ⓔ
8. Ⓐ Ⓑ Ⓒ Ⓓ Ⓔ
9. Ⓐ Ⓑ Ⓒ Ⓓ Ⓔ
10. Ⓐ Ⓑ Ⓒ Ⓓ Ⓔ
11. Ⓐ Ⓑ Ⓒ Ⓓ Ⓔ
12. Ⓐ Ⓑ Ⓒ Ⓓ Ⓔ
13. Ⓐ Ⓑ Ⓒ Ⓓ Ⓔ
14. Ⓐ Ⓑ Ⓒ Ⓓ Ⓔ
15. Ⓐ Ⓑ Ⓒ Ⓓ Ⓔ
16. Ⓐ Ⓑ Ⓒ Ⓓ Ⓔ
17. Ⓐ Ⓑ Ⓒ Ⓓ Ⓔ
18. Ⓐ Ⓑ Ⓒ Ⓓ Ⓔ
19. Ⓐ Ⓑ Ⓒ Ⓓ Ⓔ
20. Ⓐ Ⓑ Ⓒ Ⓓ Ⓔ

21. Ⓐ Ⓑ Ⓒ Ⓓ Ⓔ
22. Ⓐ Ⓑ Ⓒ Ⓓ Ⓔ
23. Ⓐ Ⓑ Ⓒ Ⓓ Ⓔ
24. Ⓐ Ⓑ Ⓒ Ⓓ Ⓔ
25. Ⓐ Ⓑ Ⓒ Ⓓ Ⓔ
26. Ⓐ Ⓑ Ⓒ Ⓓ Ⓔ
27. Ⓐ Ⓑ Ⓒ Ⓓ Ⓔ
28. Ⓐ Ⓑ Ⓒ Ⓓ Ⓔ
29. Ⓐ Ⓑ Ⓒ Ⓓ Ⓔ
30. Ⓐ Ⓑ Ⓒ Ⓓ Ⓔ
31. Ⓐ Ⓑ Ⓒ Ⓓ Ⓔ
32. Ⓐ Ⓑ Ⓒ Ⓓ Ⓔ
33. Ⓐ Ⓑ Ⓒ Ⓓ Ⓔ
34. Ⓐ Ⓑ Ⓒ Ⓓ Ⓔ
35. Ⓐ Ⓑ Ⓒ Ⓓ Ⓔ
36. Ⓐ Ⓑ Ⓒ Ⓓ Ⓔ
37. Ⓐ Ⓑ Ⓒ Ⓓ Ⓔ
38. Ⓐ Ⓑ Ⓒ Ⓓ Ⓔ
39. Ⓐ Ⓑ Ⓒ Ⓓ Ⓔ
40. Ⓐ Ⓑ Ⓒ Ⓓ Ⓔ

41. Ⓐ Ⓑ Ⓒ Ⓓ Ⓔ
42. Ⓐ Ⓑ Ⓒ Ⓓ Ⓔ
43. Ⓐ Ⓑ Ⓒ Ⓓ Ⓔ
44. Ⓐ Ⓑ Ⓒ Ⓓ Ⓔ
45. Ⓐ Ⓑ Ⓒ Ⓓ Ⓔ
46. Ⓐ Ⓑ Ⓒ Ⓓ Ⓔ
47. Ⓐ Ⓑ Ⓒ Ⓓ Ⓔ
48. Ⓐ Ⓑ Ⓒ Ⓓ Ⓔ
49. Ⓐ Ⓑ Ⓒ Ⓓ Ⓔ
50. Ⓐ Ⓑ Ⓒ Ⓓ Ⓔ
51. Ⓐ Ⓑ Ⓒ Ⓓ Ⓔ
52. Ⓐ Ⓑ Ⓒ Ⓓ Ⓔ
53. Ⓐ Ⓑ Ⓒ Ⓓ Ⓔ
54. Ⓐ Ⓑ Ⓒ Ⓓ Ⓔ
55. Ⓐ Ⓑ Ⓒ Ⓓ Ⓔ
56. Ⓐ Ⓑ Ⓒ Ⓓ Ⓔ
57. Ⓐ Ⓑ Ⓒ Ⓓ Ⓔ
58. Ⓐ Ⓑ Ⓒ Ⓓ Ⓔ
59. Ⓐ Ⓑ Ⓒ Ⓓ Ⓔ
60. Ⓐ Ⓑ Ⓒ Ⓓ Ⓔ

LITERATURE

TEST 4

TIME: 60 Minutes
60 Questions

DIRECTIONS: *This test consists of selections from literary works and questions on their content, form, and style. After reading each passage or poem, choose the best answer to each question and blacken the corresponding space on the answer sheet.*

NOTE: Pay particular attention to the requirement of questions that contain the words NOT, LEAST, or EXCEPT.

QUESTIONS 1–5 are based on the following passage. Read the passage <u>carefully before ch</u>oosing your answers.

   Well, it was a curious country, and full of interest. And the
people! They were the quaintest and simplest and trustingest race;
why they were nothing but rabbits. It was pitiful for a person born in
a wholesome free atmosphere to listen to their humble and hearty
outpourings of loyalty toward their king and Church and nobility: as
5   if they had any more occasion to love and honor king and Church
and noble than a slave has to love and honor the lash, or a dog has to
love and honor the stranger that kicks him! Why, dear me, any kind
of royalty, howsoever modified, any kind of aristocracy, howsoever
pruned, is rightly an insult; but if you are born and brought up under
10   that sort of arrangement you probably never find it out for yourself,
and don't believe it when somebody else tells you. It is enough to

make a body ashamed of his race to think of the sort of froth that has always occupied its thrones without shadow of right or reason, and
15 the seventh-rate people that have always figured as its aristocracies — a company of monarchs and nobles who, as a rule, would have achieved only poverty and obscurity if left to their own exertions.

From A Connecticut Yankee in King Arthur's Court, *by Mark Twain.*

1. The speaker's tone in this passage can best be described as

    (A) wholeheartedly approving

    (B) wistfully sarcastic

    (C) mildly disappointed

    (D) reluctantly disapproving

    (E) shocked and indignant

2. As it is used in line 3, the word "rabbits" functions as a(n)

    (A) metaphor
    (D) literal descriptor

    (B) play on words
    (E) apostrophe

    (C) literary allusion

3. It can be inferred from this passage that the speaker believes

    (A) in a political system controlled by one person

    (B) that the aristocracy helps the people

    (C) in a society devoted to the pursuit of pleasure

    (D) in a free and democratic society

    (E) in the "divine right" of kings to rule

4. All of the following are true about lines 15–17 of the passage EXCEPT that they

    (A) suggest the uselessness of aristocracy

    (B) reinforce the earlier parts of the passage

    (C) change the meaning of the rest of the passage

(D)   contrast aristocrats and peasants

(E)   state that aristocrats would not do well if they had to earn their living

5.   In this passage, the animal imagery conveys which of the following ideas?

I.   The "people" are naive and obedient.

II.   The "king and Church and nobility" fear the "people."

III. The "people" fear the "king and Church and nobility."

(A) I only   (D) I and II only

(B) II only   (E) I and III only

(C) III only

QUESTIONS 6–11 are based on the following poem. Read the poem carefully before choosing your answers.

Shall I compare thee to a summer's day?
Thou art more lovely and more temperate:
Rough winds do shake the darling buds of May,
And summer's lease hath all too short a date:
5   Sometimes too hot the eye of heaven shines
And often is his gold complexion dimmed;
And every fair from fair sometimes declines,
By chance or nature's changing course untrimmed;
But thy eternal summer shall not fade,
10 Nor lose possession of that fair thou ow'st;
Nor shall death brag thou wander'st in his shade,
When in eternal lines to time thou grow'st:
So long as men can breathe, or eyes can see,
So long live this, and this gives life to thee.

"Sonnet 18," *by William Shakespeare*

6.   The poem is concerned primarily with the

     (A)   eternal nature of love

     (B)   idea that nature never changes

     (C)   transient nature of flowers

     (D)   idea that humanity creates eternal objects

     (E)   eternal nature of summer

7.   The metaphoric use of "a summer's day" (lines 1–2) suggests all of the following EXCEPT

     (A)   how much like a summer's day is the person addressed

     (B)   the shortness of life

     (C)   the contrast between the fleeting days of summer and the eternal quality of love

     (D)   the ugliness of life

     (E)   continuous, but ever-changing nature

8.   Lines 13 and 14 of the poem can best be described as

     (A)   blank verse   (D)   pastoral elegy

     (B)   rhymed triplet   (E)   rhymed couplet

     (C)   free verse

9.   Lines 5–6 employ the figure of speech called

     (A)   personification   (D)   apostrophe

     (B)   allusion   (E)   allegory

     (C)   alliteration

10. The speaker's attitude toward the person addressed can best be described as

     (A)   haltingly condescending

     (B)   admiringly romantic

     (C)   profusely deferential

(D) mildly derogatory

(E) thoroughly disgusted

11. The descriptive detail in lines 3–8 serves what specific purpose in the poem?

(A) personification of the speaker

(B) exemplification of the severity of nature

(C) allusion to classical sources

(D) imagery suggesting the joy of nature

(E) exemplification of unchanging nature

QUESTIONS 12–18 are based on the following poem. Read the poem carefully before choosing your answers.

> The world is too much with us; late and soon,
> Getting and spending, we lay waste our powers:
> Little we see in Nature that is ours;
> We have given our hearts away, a sordid boon!
> 5 This Sea that bares her bosom to the moon;
> The winds that will be howling at all hours,
> And are up-gathered now like sleeping flowers;
> For this, for every thing, we are out of tune;
> It moves us not. —— Great God! I'd rather be
> 10 A Pagan suckled in a creed outworn;
> So might I, standing on this pleasant lea,
> Have glimpses that would make me less forlorn;
> Have sight of Proteus rising from the sea;
> Or hear old Triton blow his wreathed horn.

"*The World is too Much With Us,*" *by William Wordsworth*

12. Which of the following ideas best describe the meaning(s) of this poem?

I. The purpose of life is to work hard in order to accumulate wealth.

175

II.   We have lost our ability to appreciate and be uplifted by nature.

III. The pursuit of materialism has weakened us.

(A) I only   (D) I and II only

(B) II only   (E) II and III only

(C) III only

13. What is the effect of the change from first person plural voice (lines 1–9) to first person singular voice (lines 9–14)?

(A) to suggest that we are all alike

(B) to emphasize the similarity between Pagans and Christians

(C) to contrast the speaker's appreciation of nature to the lack of appreciation of nature by most people

(D) to emphasize the difference between Pagans and Christians

(E) To suggest that each person is different from other people

14. From the context we can conclude that "Proteus" and "Triton" (lines 13–14) refer to

(A) flowers   (D) howling winds

(B) happy feelings   (E) ancient gods

(C) wasted powers

15. The speaker's tone in this poem can best be described as

(A) admonitory   (D) appreciative

(B) indifferent   (E) kind and gentle

(C) mocking

16. What is the effect of the personification of "This Sea" (line 5)?

(A) The human qualities of the "Pagans" (line 10) are underscored.

(B) The identity of "Proteus" (line 13) becomes clearer.

(C) An element of nature is portrayed as an object of romance to the speaker.

(D) The "Sea" is awake while the flowers sleep.

(E) The "Sea" is likened to God.

17. What is the function of the phrases "to the moon" (line 5) and "sleeping flowers" (line 7)?

(A) They suggest the nature of the "Sea" (line 5).

(B) They suggest that "Nature" (line 3) is asleep.

(C) They suggest that we are asleep.

(D) They suggest that the time setting of the poem is night.

(E) They suggest that the speaker mourns our wasted powers.

18. In its context, the phrase "I'd rather be/A Pagan suckled in a creed outworn" (lines 9–10) suggests which of the following beliefs of the speaker?

(A) A "Pagan" was closer emotionally to "Nature" (line 3) than the speaker's contemporaries.

(B) "Pagan" beliefs are no longer valid.

(C) A "Pagan" has no specific beliefs.

(D) The speaker wishes to fantasize about life.

(E) Contemporary religions bring people close to "Nature" (line 3).

QUESTIONS 19–25 are based on the following passage. Read the passage carefully before choosing your answers.

In short, I went on thus for a long time (I may say it without boasting), faithfully minding my business, till it became more and more evident that my townsmen would not after all admit me into the list of town officers, nor make my place a sinecure with a
5 moderate allowance. My accounts, which I can swear to have kept faithfully, I have, indeed, never got audited, still less accepted, still less paid and settled. However, I have not set my heart on that.

Not long since, a strolling Indian went to sell baskets at the house of a well-known lawyer in my neighborhood. "Do you wish to buy

10 any baskets?" he asked. "No, we do not want any," was the reply. "What!" exclaimed the Indian as he went out the gate, "do you mean to starve us?" Having seen his industrious white neighbors so well off, — that the lawyer had only to weave arguments, and, by some magic, wealth and standing followed, — he had said to himself: I
15 will go into business; I will weave baskets; it is a thing which I can do. Thinking that when he had made the baskets he would have done his part, and then it would be the white man's to buy them. He had not discovered that it was necessary for him to make it worth the other's while to buy them, or at least make him think that it was so,
20 or to make something else which it would be worth his while to buy. I too had woven a kind of basket of a delicate texture, but I had not made it worth anyone's while to buy them. Yet not the less, in my case, did I think it worth my while to weave them, and instead of studying how to make it worth men's while to buy my baskets, I
25 studied rather how to avoid the necessity of selling them. The life which men praise and regard as successful is but one kind. Why should we exaggerate any one kind at the expense of others?

From Walden, *by Henry David Thoreau*

19. As it is used in the passage, the word "sinecure" (line 4) means

    (A) job or position   (D) wealth

    (B) partial cure for illness   (E) insecurity

    (C) mathematical term

20. The narrator uses the story about the Indian (lines 8–20) trying to sell his baskets as

    (A) allusion   (D) paradox

    (B) metaphor   (E) simile

    (C) image

21. As used by the narrator, the effect of such phrases as "without boasting" (lines 1–2), "faithfully minding my business" (line 2), "accounts, which I can swear to have kept faithfully" (lines 5–6), and "never got audited" (line 6) is to

    (A) indicate the narrator's success in business

(B)   mock the ethics of his business partners

(C)   satirize the language of business

(D)   stress the narrator's ethical stance

(E)   reveal his townspeople's inattention to his abilities

22.   The narrator's attitude toward economic success as suggested by the phrase "wealth and standing" (line 14) and by lines 21–27, is best described as

(A)   ignorantly uncaring   (D)   heavily ironic

(B)   bitterly disapproving   (E)   shocked dismay

(C)   thoughtfully rejecting

23.   The idea in lines 25–27 is presented in which of the following ways?

(A)   as a categorical statement of truth

(B)   as a question to suggest the absolute truth about success

(C)   as a rhetorical question to prod the reader into thinking about different ways to be successful

(D)   as a rejection of anything but the conventional measure of success

(E)   as a comparison between the Indian and the lawyer

24.   As it is used in context, the phrase "Yet not the less, in my case, did I think it worth my while to weave them" (lines 22–23), suggests all of the following about the narrator's character EXCEPT his

(A)   idealistic philosophy

(B)   studied indifference about his image

(C)   relative indifference to wealth

(D)   whimsical behavior

(E)   relative indifference toward community status

25.   Weaving is used in the passage as which of the following?

I.   A metaphor for a life's work

II.   A symbol of economic success

III. A metaphor for the artist's work

(A) I only

(B) II only

(C) III only

(D) I and III only

(E) I, II, and III

QUESTIONS 26–30 are based on the following passage. Read the passage carefully before choosing your answers.

VLADIMIR:
Was I sleeping while the others suffered? Am I sleeping now? To-morrow, when I wake, or think I do, what shall I say of to-day? That with Estragon my friend, at this place, until the fall of night, I waited for Godot? That Pozzo passed, with his carrier, and that he spoke to
5 us? Probably. But in all that what truth will there be? (*Estragon, having struggled with his boots in vain, is dozing off again. Vladimir looks at him.*) He'll know nothing. He'll tell me about the blows he received and I'll give him a carrot. (*Pause.*) Astride of a grave and a difficult birth. Down in the hole, lingeringly, the grave-digger puts
10 on the forceps. We have time to grow old. The air is full of our cries. (*He listens.*) But habit is a great deadener. (*He looks again at Estragon.*) At me too someone is looking, of me too someone is saying, He is sleeping, he knows nothing, let him sleep on. (*Pause.*) I can't go on! (*Pause.*) What have I said?

From <u>Waiting for Godot</u>, *By Samuel Beckett. Reprinted with permission by Grove Press, Inc.*

26. The best paraphrase of "sleeping" (lines 1, 13) is

(A) deliberately ignoring reality

(B) peacefully slumbering

(C) dreaming

(D) closing one's eyes

(E) opening up a dream world

27. The tone of both the speaker and the passage is best described as

   (A) cheery   (D) sinister

   (B) bleak   (E) comic

   (C) sober

28. In this passage the metaphor in "Astride of a grave and a difficult birth." (lines 8–9) suggests which of the following?

   I.   Birth is the beginning of death.

   II. Birth is the beginning of life.

   III. Life is a struggle which ends in death.

   (A) I only   (D) I and II only

   (B) II only   (E) I and III only

   (C) III only

29. The speaker's attitude at the end of the speech can be described as all of the following EXCEPT

   (A) pessimistic   (D) desperate

   (B) optimistic   (E) ambivalent

   (C) confused

30. The meaning of the phrase "...habit is a great deadener" (line 11) is that habitual behavior

   (A) kills us   (D) keeps us going

   (B) sensitizes us   (E) slows us down

   (C) makes life fun

QUESTIONS 31–36 are based on the following poem. Read the poem carefully before choosing your answers.

'Twas mercy brought me from my *Pagan* land,
Taught my benighted soul to understand
That there's a God, that there's a *Saviour* too:

Once I redemption neither sought nor knew.
5   Some view our sable race with scornful eye,
    "Their colour is a diabolic dye."
    Remember, *Christians, Negroes*, black as *Cain*,
    May be refined, and join th' angelic train.

"On Being Brought from Africa to America," by Phillis Wheatley.

31. The best paraphrase of "angelic train" (line 8) is

    (A) celestial railroad

    (B) heaven's transportation

    (C) train car full of angels

    (D) saved souls bound for heaven

    (E) procession of Negroes

32. The phrase in line 5, "Some view our sable race with scornful eye"
    exemplifies which of the following?

    I.   Metaphor

    II. Allegory

    III. Alliteration

    (A) I only   (D) II and III only

    (B) II only   (E) I and III only

    (C) III only

33. As it is used in the poem, "diabolic" (line 6) can be understood in all of
    the following senses EXCEPT

    (A) Pagan   (D) satanic

    (B) devilish   (E) evil

    (C) fiendish

34. As it is used in line 2, the word "benighted" functions as a

    (A) literary allusion   (B) nonsense word

(C) play on words   (D) paradoxical term

(E) figure of speech

35. The speaker implies that some Christians are characterized by their

(A) belief in redemption

(B) belief that "Negroes" cannot be redeemed

(C) skepticism toward other Christians

(D) skepticism toward God

(E) belief in demons

36. According to the speaker, which of the following are NOT true about "Negroes"?

I.   They are compared to Cain.

II.   They are "diabolic."

III. They come from a Pagan land.

(A) I only   (D) I and II only

(B) II only   (E) I, II, and III

(C) III only

QUESTIONS 37–42 are based on the following passage. Read the passage carefully before choosing your answers.

The bell doth toll for him that thinks it doth; and though it intermit again, yet from that minute that that occasion wrought upon him, he is united to God. Who casts not up his eye to the sun when it rises? but who takes off his eye from a comet when that breaks out?
5   Who bends not his ear to any bell which upon occasion rings? but who can remove it from that bell which is passing a piece of himself out of this world? No man is an island, entire of itself; every man is a piece of the continent, a part of the main. If a clod be washed away by the sea, Europe is the less, as well as if a promontory were, as well
10 as if a manor of thy friend's or of thine own were. Any man's death

diminishes me, because I am involved in mankind; and therefore never send to know for whom the bell tolls; it tolls for thee.

"For Whom the Bell Doth Toll," by John Donne

37. As it is used in the passage, the word "intermit" (line 2) means

(A) start up   (D) interpose

(B) keep going   (E) interrupt

(C) continue

38. Given the context of the poem, the bell rings for which of the following reasons?

I. To note the time

II. To mark the change of watch at sea

III. To signify a person's death

(A) I only   (D) I and II only

(B) II only   (E) II and III only

(C) III only

39. The central idea of this passage can be suggested by all of the following EXCEPT

(A) "No man is an island, entire of itself"

(B) "If a clod be washed away by the sea, Europe is the less"

(C) "Any man's death diminishes me"

(D) "never send to know for whom the bell tolls"

(E) "every man is a piece of the continent"

40. The questions beginning in line 3 and continuing through line 7 function as

(A) plays on words   (D) alliteration

(B) figures of speech   (E) literary allusions

(C) analogies

41. "I" (line 11) can best be described as a(n)

   (A) social reformer   (D) alienated critic

   (B) philosophic observer (E) gentle fool

   (C) political activist

42. The person(s) addressed by the speaker can best be described as

   I.   Curious individualists

   II. Self-centered "islands"

   III. People frightened of death

   (A) I only   (D) II and III only

   (B) II only   (E) I, II, and III

   (C) III only

QUESTIONS 43–47 are based on the following poem. Read the poem carefully before choosing your answers.

> Hope is the thing with feathers
> That perches in the soul
> And sings the tune without the words
> And never stops at all.
>
> 5 And sweetest in the gale is heard;
> And sore must be the storm
> That could abash the little bird
> That kept so many warm.
>
> I've heard it in the chillest land
> 10 And on the strangest sea,
> Yet never in extremity
> It asked a crumb of me.

by Emily Dickinson

43. The metaphor of "Hope" (line 1) compared to a "bird" (line 7) is extended by all of the following EXCEPT

   (A) "never in extremity"

   (B) "thing with feathers"

   (C) "perches in the soul"

   (D) "sings the tune without the words"

   (E) "asked a crumb"

44. In the poem, the bird functions as which of the following?

   I.   A ubiquitous symbol of the persistence of life

   II. A symbol of freedom

   III. An undemanding, cheery companion

   (A) I only   (D) I and III only

   (B) II only   (E) I, II, and III

   (C) III only

45. As it is used in the poem, the word "sore" (line 6) means

   (A) severe   (D) ascending

   (B) painful   (E) afloat

   (C) aching

46. Which of the following does NOT suggest a meaning of the phrase "in extremity" (line 11)?

   (A) severe difficulty   (D) faraway lands

   (B) abundant times   (E) cold climates

   (C) stormy weather

47. The speaker can best be described as a(n)

   (A) pessimist   (D) clairvoyant

   (B) recluse   (E) explorer

   (C) optimist

QUESTIONS 48–53 are based on the following poem. Read the poem carefully before choosing your answers.

DREAM DEFERRED

What happens to a dream deferred?
Does it dry up
like a raisin in the sun?
Or fester like a sore —
5 And then run?
Does it stink like rotten meat?
Or crust and sugar over —
like a syrupy sweet?

Maybe it just sags
10 like a heavy load.

Or does it explode?

48. The poem is concerned primarily with the

    (A) inevitability of dreams

    (B) gradual change from dream to reality

    (C) necessity of living in the real world

    (D) nature of unfulfilled dreams

    (E) consequences of dreams and reality

49. The effect of such phrases as "dry up" (line 2), "fester like a sore" (line 4), "stink like rotten meat" (line 6), "crust and sugar over" (line 7), "sags like a heavy load" (lines 9–10), and "explode" (line 11) is to

    (A) catalog the many negative possibilities of deferred dreams

    (B) stress the speaker's dissatisfaction with reality

    (C) satirize those who defer dreams

    (D) underscore the necessity to dream

    (E) suggest the fruits of dreaming

50. As it is used in the poem, "explode" (line 11) can be understood in all of the following senses EXCEPT

   (A) blow up   (D) erupt

   (B) expand   (E) madden

   (C) destroy

51. The effective meaning of the simile in lines 7–8 is to

   (A) parody children's visions at Christmas

   (B) suggest sweetness allays the burden of dreams

   (C) suggest the speaker's craving for sweets

   (D) satirize those who refuse to dream

   (E) suggest that sweet on the outside might mean sour on the inside

52. In the context of the poem as a whole, the speaker's attitude toward "a dream deferred" (line 1) can best be described as

   (A) mocking   (D) dispassionate

   (B) disappointed   (E) sympathetic

   (C) deferential

53. Which of the following changes is introduced in line 11?

   (A) The deferred dream could lead to violence.

   (B) The deferral of dreams is accepted.

   (C) The deferral of dreams is rejected.

   (D) The question in line 1 is answered.

   (E) The deferred dream is defined.

QUESTIONS 54–60 are based on the following passage. Read the passage carefully before choosing your answers.

   Kilgore Trout became Billy's favorite living author, and science fiction became the only sort of tales he could read.
   Rosewater was twice as smart as Billy, but he and Billy were

dealing with similar crises in similar ways. They both had found life
5   meaningless, partly because of what they had seen in war. Rosewater, for instance, had shot a fourteen-year-old fireman, mistaking
him for a German soldier. So it goes. And Billy had seen the greatest
massacre in European history, which was the fire-bombing of Dres-
den. So it goes.
10   So they were trying to re-invent themselves and their universe.
Science fiction was a big help.
      Rosewater said an interesting thing to Billy one time about a
book that wasn't science fiction. He said that everything there was to
know about life was in *The Brothers Karamazov*, by Feodor Dos-
15 toevsky. "But that isn't *enough* any more," said Rosewater.
      Another time Billy heard Rosewater say to a psychiatrist, "I
think you guys are going to have to come up with a lot of wonderful
new lies, or people just aren't going to want to go on living."

Excerpt from Slaughterhouse-Five *by Kurt Vonnegut, Jr., copyright 1968, 1969 by
Kurt Vonnegut, Jr. Reprinted by permission of Delacorte Press/Seymour Lawrence, a division of Bantam, Doubleday, Dell Publishing Group, Inc.*

54. As it is used in the context of this passage, "science fiction" (lines 2,
11) suggests which of the following?

    I.   A metaphoric contrast between real and fantasy lives

    II.   A metaphor for a secure and stable life

    III. A metaphor suggesting we need lies to survive life

    (A) I only   (D) I and III only

    (B) II only   (E) I, II, and III

    (C) III only

55. The speaker's tone in the whole passage is best described as

    (A) mildly disappointed

    (B) mildly skeptical

    (C) interested and sympathetic

    (D) totally indifferent

    (E) mostly ironic

56. As it is used in lines 7 and 9, the sentence "So it goes" suggests

   (A) verbal irony

   (B) apparent empathy toward tragedy

   (C) sensitivity toward tragedy

   (D) excuses for accidents

   (E) a verbal "shrug of the shoulders"

57. It can be inferred from the context that the book *The Brothers Karamazov* (line 14)

   (A) is a science fiction book

   (B) is about people "trying to re-invent themselves and their universe" (line 10)

   (C) is not a science fiction book

   (D) represents a type of fiction that answers life's questions

   (E) represents fantasy or escape fiction

58. It can be inferred from the context of this passage that "Billy" (line 1) and "Rosewater" (line 3) are

   (A) in prison

   (B) old friends

   (C) undergoing treatment for mental problems

   (D) in business together

   (E) related to each other

59. All of the following are suggested by Rosewater's comments in lines 13–18 EXCEPT

   (A) survival requires beliefs which mask reality

   (B) life is meaningful only if confronted directly

   (C) life is meaningless without fantasies

   (D) psychiatrists and novelists provide useful lies to help us survive

   (E) old solutions do not solve new problems

60. The phrase "twice as smart as Billy" (line 3), as well as other clues in the context, suggest that the relationship between "Rosewater" and "Billy" can best be described as

   (A) father and son

   (B) childhood friends

   (C) college students

   (D) neighbors

   (E) mentor and follower

TEST 4

ANSWER KEY

1.	(B)	16.	(C)	31.	(D)	46.	(B)
2.	(A)	17.	(D)	32.	(E)	47.	(C)
3.	(D)	18.	(A)	33.	(A)	48.	(D)
4.	(C)	19.	(A)	34.	(C)	49.	(A)
5.	(E)	20.	(B)	35.	(B)	50.	(B)
6.	(A)	21.	(D)	36.	(B)	51.	(E)
7.	(D)	22.	(C)	37.	(E)	52.	(B)
8.	(E)	23.	(C)	38.	(C)	53.	(A)
9.	(A)	24.	(D)	39.	(D)	54.	(E)
10.	(B)	25.	(A)	40.	(C)	55.	(C)
11.	(B)	26.	(A)	41.	(B)	56.	(E)
12.	(E)	27.	(B)	42.	(E)	57.	(D)
13.	(C)	28.	(E)	43.	(A)	58.	(C)
14.	(E)	29.	(B)	44.	(D)	59.	(B)
15.	(A)	30.	(D)	45.	(A)	60.	(E)

DETAILED EXPLANATIONS
OF ANSWERS

TEST 4

1.   **(B)**   Choice (B) edges out the two next best choices, (E) and (D). "Wistfully" means "with pensive or thoughtful yearning"; "sarcastic" means "bitter, cutting, or contemptuously derisive." Those phrases characterize the speaker's tone: he does think and yearn for change in the status quo; he also shows contempt for both the nobility and the peasants who cower before them like rabbits or dogs kicked by strangers. Choice (E) contends for the correct answer because the speaker does show indignation, but he is not really "shocked" (surprised and curious, yes, but not shocked), and his indignation pours out through the sarcasm. The speaker certainly disapproves of all he observes, but he shows no reluctance to condemn, thus leaving choice (D) a distant third. From the explanation so far, choice (A) does not even compete, and (C) is too tame to describe the speaker's attitude toward his description (tone).

2.   **(A)**   A pun is a play on words, an allusion a reference to another literary or historical work, an apostrophe a direct address to (usually) an inanimate object or concept, and a literal descriptor an actual description of a sight, sound, etc. Last, but most important, a metaphor makes an implied analogy (comparison between familiar and unfamiliar). Here, the speaker calls the people rabbits to show an analogy between their behavior in the face of the ruling class and the behavior of rabbits in the face of predators. Hence, (A) becomes the only logical choice.

3.   **(D)**   None of the choices except (D) could be forced to describe the probable beliefs of the speaker. He clearly stands against the aristocrats and the monarchy, who, he states are "rightly an insult." This obviously rules out choices (B) and (E). His disdain for the monarchy (defined as rule by a monarch or single person) also stands out clearly and, therefore, rules out choice (A). The search for personal pleasure, choice (C), hardly applies to the speaker in this passage, since no specific statements indicate that he

believes in hedonism. To the contrary, he suggests that the aristocracy does, in fact, seek pleasure instead of useful occupation and are, as a result, morally bankrupt. Rather, the speaker seems to want a freely competitive economy, within a classless or egalitarian society. One's own exertions, then, would stand as the arbiter of one's fortune.

4. **(C)** Choice (C) stands out clearly as the answer because it incorrectly states that the lines differ from the rest of the passage. Quite obviously, they build on or reinforce it. In that reinforcement, the lines contrast the uselessness of the aristocracy (which whips and kicks the peasants and is "an insult") with the peasants who, at least, work for their king or lord. Also very clearly, the "aristocracies" would not rise above "poverty and obscurity," these lines state, "if left to their own exertions." Thus, all the choices with the exception of (C) correctly characterize the lines in question.

5. **(E)** All three statements could be true of the whole passage (although no direct statement of fear of the "people" by the nobility is made or implied in the passage). Indeed, history shows that nobility should fear an uprising of the people they treat like rabbits or dogs. However, the passage shows no such fear on the part of the aristocracy. So, it is through the meek animals associated with the "people" that both I and III — choice (E) are accurate descriptions of the effect of the imagery. Surely, dogs can bite "the hands that feed them," but these dogs are the ones even strangers can abuse with impunity. Dogs, after all, are supposed to be their master's best friend, slavishly obedient, even against their own best interests. Rabbits, besides being associated with multiplication, are notoriously timid, frightened. Choices (A) and (C), then, are only partly correct; (B) has no logical inferential base, thus negating (D).

6. **(A)** The poem leaves us with no basis for choosing (D) since it neither alludes to nor mentions human artifacts at all. Choices (B) and (E) echo each other and contradict what the poem tells us. In the poem "summer's lease hath all too short a date" (line 4); the only "eternal summer" (line 9) belongs to the female love addressed by the speaker. The idea that nature indeed changes rather quickly pops up often in the poem (e.g., lines 5–8). Choice (C) could serve as a subject for a poem, but this one uses the "transient nature of flowers" — "Rough winds do shake the darling buds of May" (line 3) — as a contrast to the "eternal nature of love" embodied in the lover's description of his object of desire in line 9 (and lines 10-14). Thus

choice (A) correctly identifies the main idea of the poem.

7.   **(D)**   Nothing about summer mentioned in the poem suggests "ugliness of life," nor can we infer such a concept from it; thus choice (D) is the correct answer. Choice (A) comes close because the poem shows how different "thee" is from a summer's day. However, an initial possibility exists, or the comparison would appear ludicrous. "Thee" addressed obviously has some of the loveliness of a summer's day, but far exceeds it, according to the speaker. Summer's connotation, in fact, brims over with the idea of the transient; the fleeting days of summer quickly fade. Choices (B) and (C) echo that connotation. And since summer, all too quickly departing, stands as part of the continuity of nature, choice (E) likewise reinforces the metaphor.

8.   **(E)**   If one has even a nodding acquaintance with the terms used as choices, (E) stands out as the obvious correct one. This particular sonnet form conventionally ends with a rhymed couplet. Neither (A) nor (C) applies as neither blank nor free verse rhymes. A triplet by definition is three lines, so choice (B) is incorrect. And even though the poem praises nature, perhaps engendering a pastoral atmosphere, it does not meet the definition of an elegy; nor does it fulfill its particular requirements, including the most common one: the death of an admired person.

9.   **(A)**   An allegory uses abstract ideas in the form of characters, so it would not apply and would negate choice (E). Similarly, apostrophe, a speaker's address to an inanimate object or concept (usually) does not appear in lines 5-6. Choice (D) fails the test. An allusion refers to another literary or historical work; and these lines, although they may vaguely suggest Biblical definitions, hardly allude to any single identifiable passage. Choice (B) falls out. Alliteration, the repetition of similar sounds, admittedly appears in line 6 ("is his"), but not in line 5; so choice (C) must yield to choice (A) as the correct one. Both the "eye of heaven" and "his gold complexion" ascribe human characteristics to a concept or place, which defines personification.

10. **(B)**   Both choices (D) and (E) make no sense; the speaker shows neither disgust nor dislike for "thee" addressed in the poem. Nor does the speaker condescend to his love — choice (A). If anything, he seems to treat her as an equal in wit if not as an equal in gender. He does, after all, put her

on a pedestal. The latter act suggests choice (B) as the correct one. The speaker certainly uses romantic speech to profess admiration, eternally. "Deferential" describes one who yields personal judgment to another. However, the speaker does not defer judgment; he boldly proclaims it, so choice (C) does not stand.

11. **(B)**   Choice (B) stands out as the best one here. The first line poses the question of comparing "thee" to a summer's day; the second states that a summer's day is neither as lovely nor as even-tempered as "thee." Lines 3–8, then, illustrate the ways in which a summer's day can be less lovely and less temperate. Choice (A) has no logical base, since the speaker is already a human being and does not need personification. Likewise, choice (E) fails the test because the lines in question show just the opposite. No obvious classical allusions appear in these lines, so choice (C) also fails to qualify. Rather than "the joy of nature," these images suggest its extremes, thus eliminating choice (D) .

12. **(E)**   The first two lines of the poem eliminate the possibility that the purpose of life is to work to accumulate wealth. They state the exact opposite view. Having said that, we can throw out choices (A) and (D). Choices (B) and (C) characterize two complementary ideas: distance from nature and spirits weakened by materialism. The latter may be said to have caused the former as the poem suggests. So neither stands by itself as correct. Choice (E) includes both and identifies the major themes of the poem.

13. **(C)**   The speaker indicts all of humanity as he knew it when he wrote the poem, thus the use of first person plural in the first nine lines to characterize the dismal spiritual state of humanity. The very act of recognition sets the speaker apart from the rest, and he shows it beginning in line 9 by using first person singular in the rest of the poem. Choice (C) then is the best answer. The foregoing eliminates (A) as a choice; it also weakens (E) as a possibility. Only those who respond to nature and reject the cult of materialism stand out here. The last six lines of the poem suggest a strong difference between the ancients (Greeks and Romans, i.e., Pagans) and the contemporaries of the speaker, presumed to be Christians, eliminating choice (B). The change to "I" does suggest that difference, but choice (D) pales in comparison to (C) as the best one.

14. **(E)** The acts of "rising from the sea" and blowing a horn suggest that choices (A), (B), and (C) will not do, not even remotely as symbols. That leaves (D) and (E). Since the speaker has identified his preference to be a "Pagan" (one who believes in multiple gods), one could infer that pagans would, in fact, see their gods in nature. The two mentioned are, in fact, sea gods from ancient Greece. Choice (D) has less realistic contextual meaning, even though winds can rise from the sea and figuratively, at least, blow a horn.

15. **(A)** The exclamations in lines 4 and 9 suggest that the speaker is anything but gentle, so choice (E) stands far afield, as does choice (B). The speaker may be accused of many things, but not indifference. He also does not appreciate what he sees, as evidenced by his preference for paganism so as to be closer to nature than we readers. At the same time, he does not really mock us readers, but rather he admonishes (reproves or warns) us to veer off our foolish path of materialism. The current cliché is "stop to smell the roses." Thus choices (C) and (D) do not pass muster; (A) correctly identifies the speaker's tone.

16. **(C)** Choice (C) stands out as best here because the image of baring "her bosom" is an overtly sexual one. It also suggests a kinship among souls characterized by keeping no secrets, not even a covered (secret) bosom. So it announces a kind of intimacy associated with romantic relationships. The personification by itself does not support choice (D); and the type personification, as noted, likens the sea more to an amorous woman than to God, eliminating choice (E). Neither (A) nor (B) is supported by personification. Proteus was a male god, so personifying the sea as female contradicts choice (B). The human qualities of "Pagans" are not at issue because the speaker sides with them, so choice (A) is out.

17. **(D)** How does a poet suggest the setting of a poem? This question is addressed by test question 17. We can picture the poet standing by the sea one evening and reflecting on his culture's materialistic bent, to the exclusion of the appreciation of nature's splendor. He then transforms that time into poetic language of the sea baring her bosom to the moon (not the sun) and of the flowers sleeping (not awake and "catching some rays"). Choice (D), then, is correct. None of the other choices makes sense except (C), possibly. But we are told that we are busy, active, not sleeping. Our intense pursuit of the materialistic blinds us to nature, not our eyes closed in sleep.

18. **(A)**   For most of the poet's audience, "Pagan" beliefs were not only invalid but also sinful. However, the poet/speaker chooses them. So choice (B) does not really work. Choice (C) also proves false by the language of the poem: a creed is a set of specific beliefs (even if "outworn"). Choice (E) is negated by the first four lines and lines 8–9; the speaker's preference for a "Pagan" creed also suggests the inadequacy of contemporary religions to bring people close to "Nature." Even though the speaker has a rich imagination, he recognizes and wishes to live in reality. Indeed, he wishes for us to re-think our reality, so choice (D) misses the mark. Choice (A) correctly defines both "Pagan" and the speaker's beliefs.

19. **(A)**   We can relatively quickly eliminate choices (B) and (C) as either inappropriate or as misleading. The context suggests nothing about illness, and the notion of "accounts" should not mislead us into thinking the term has much to do with mathematics. Likewise, choice (E) fails the test of logic when substituted for "sinecure" in the passage. The phrase following "sinecure," i.e., "with a moderate allowance," negates the idea of choice (D). That leaves choice (A) as the correct answer, both in the context and from the definition of "sinecure" as an "office or position that requires little or no work."

20. **(B)**   Refer to the explanations for questions 2 and 9 preceding this one and to the explanations for questions 32, 34, and 40 following this one for definitions of "allusion," "paradox," and "metaphor." A "simile" is essentially the same as a metaphor except that it usually requires a comparative word such as "like" or "as" to make the comparison. An "image" is a broad term referring to anything that can be perceived through the senses (sight, sound, smell, taste, and touch). Clearly, the story serves as an example or an implied comparison between the Indian and the narrator; hence it is a "metaphor," and choice (B) correctly identifies the function. The story is not a "simile" because the narrator does not use "like" or "as" to make the comparison; instead he simply says "I too" did what the Indian did, thereby equating the two.

21. **(D)**   A couple of choices compete here. However, we can dismiss (B) because the narrator never mentions any "business partners," nor do the phrases imply such a possibility. Likewise, choice (E) does not directly relate to the use of the phrases. Choice (A) fails because the phrases have little to do with business success, except in the sense of keeping accounts,

and because choices (C) and (D) could serve as better answers than (A). Choice (C) yields to (D) — the correct answer — because there is no "satire" present in the passage. The term means, in essence, the use of ridicule to try to change a situation. We could argue that ridicule can be found in the passage and maybe even in the specific phrases, but they seem to exude, if anything along that line, mild parody or gentle humor applying business language to life. Nonetheless, choice (D) accurately describes the author's sense of ethics (upright behavior) and, to a lesser extent, humility ("without boasting"), which would be considered an appropriate stance to take.

22. **(C)** The narrator fairly clearly rejects after much thoughtful and deliberate consideration the idea of economic success admired by his "townsmen" and by both the "lawyer" and the "Indian." If we recognize this passage as part of Henry David Thoreau's *Walden*, we know that the work itself argues against pursuing conventional American economic success as epitomized by materialism. But even without that recognition, we should see that the narrator is not ignorant (unknowing); nor is he "shocked" or dismayed. Likewise, he does not sound bitter, although we could say he is "disapproving." That eliminates choices (A), (E), and (B), respectively. We can probably reject choice (D) in favor of the correct choice (C) because the narrator does show a thoughtful rejection of "economic success," without really heavy irony. The ending of the passage simply suggests that many different "successful" lives exist outside of the economic realm. His use of business language in the passage is somewhat ironic, but that is not the question here.

23. **(C)** This question gives us a relative break because the choices differ so greatly. Choices (D) and (E) clearly miss the target. Likewise, choice (A) fails out of hand because the lines in question do not make a categorical statement about truth but, instead, question the idea that only one type of successful life exists. Thus, we can eliminate choice (B) and settle on choice (C) as the correct one. Arguably, a "truth" is stated about success, but not an absolute one upon which all readers would agree.

24. **(D)** We know the narrator rejects conventional definitions of success at the end of the passage, so we can eliminate choices (B), (C), and (E). They characterize him appropriately, and we are looking for exceptions. The phrase says, in effect, "I know they [his "baskets"] won't sell, but I'll make

them anyway." That means his behavior is a thoughtful or philosophical choice (rather than whim) which reflects ideals (idealism) because it is done without thought of immediate economic reward. Choice (D) wins because it incorrectly characterizes the narrator's attitude shown in the phrase in question.

25. **(A)** First, weaving cannot stand as symbolic of economic success because both the Indian and the narrator fail economically when they "weave" their "baskets." Therefore, choices (B) and (E) fall out of the running. Likewise, weaving is used to describe the lawyer's "arguments," which even though we might admit there is an "art" to winning legal arguments, it is not art in the sense used in the passage. That eliminates choices (C) and (D). Choice (A) correctly identifies the use of weaving as metaphorically describing life's work, whether success or failure, in the conventional sense.

26. **(A)** Line 1 suggests that sleeping does not mean "peacefully slumbering," "opening up a dream world," or simply "closing one's eyes" — choices (B), (E), and (D), respectively. Line 13 reinforces that statement and suggests ignorance ("knows nothing"). "Dreaming" — choice (C) — almost makes it because we do daydream as escape from reality; but (A) better describes the paraphrase of "sleeping" in this passage, and "dreaming" does not differentiate day- and night dreams. "Deliberately ignoring reality" — choice (A) has support in "while the others suffered" and in "he knows nothing, let him sleep on."

27. **(B)** Unless we stretch quite a bit to irony, choices (E) and (A) immediately drop out of the realm of possibility. Nothing is comic here, and the same can be said for cheer. Sinister — choice (D) — means evil, bad, or corruptive; it too does not apply exactly. Choice (C), sober, comes close to the mood of the piece; but bleak — choice (B) — describes the passage almost completely. Sober means realistic, upright, not drunk, and perhaps a bit on the melancholic side; bleak, however, means relatively hopeless, desperate, depressing, etc. Taken as a whole, even with the mention of "Tomorrow" (lines 1–2), little hope shows up in this passage.

28. **(E)** Normally, we would think birth is the beginning of life (II). But then if we look at a glass with water at the halfway point, do we see it as half-full or half-empty? If you will allow a mixed metaphor, the image of the

grave-digger as obstetrician or midwife, certainly suggests the glass is half empty. Furthermore, life, as defined by the distance between the mother astride of a grave and the grave itself, allows for little time or comfort. Therefore, life, as embodied in the metaphor is also a struggle. So, the best answer is (E), which comprises both I and III.

29. **(B)** This one should be fairly obvious, the correct exception being choice (B). Certainly at the end no hope appears. "I can't go on!" emphasizes the apparent pessimism and despair — choices (A) and (D). Likewise, the speaker appears both confused and ambivalent, as noted in the pauses and the references to sleeping, as well as the final "What have I said?"

30. **(D)** In the immediate context of the phrase, choice (D) makes the most sense. We do not think when we act out of habit; so if life is miserable, we simply dull ourselves to it and go on living — or at least that seems to be the speaker's suggestion. As used here, "deadener" kills only our spirit or our thought, not our physical presence, so (A) is not correct. Likewise, (B) means the exact opposite. Choice (C), fun, in this context seems out of place and, therefore, incorrect. Finally, if habitual behavior allows us to plod through life, it does not slow us down any further than we already are, so (E) does not quite work.

31. **(D)** Choices (A), (B) and (C) divert us frivolously from meaning here for what should be obvious reasons (angels have wings, right?). In the context, the "angelic train" already exists with white angels, and "Negroes.../May be refined" enough to join the train, so (E) quite obviously fails. Consequently, the best paraphrase is choice (D), suggesting that the "angelic train" serves as mass transportation between life on earth and life in heaven (for saved souls only — white, black, red, yellow).

32. **(E)** A difficult item this one; you must know the terms and decide if they apply. A metaphor can be an implied comparison as in "sable race," which suggests not only color (black), but sadness, gloom, evil, mystery, or threat. An allegory, already defined in another explanation, is a story told using people as abstractions (ideas, concepts) rather than as individuals. Finally, alliteration is the repetition of similar sounds. No real allegory can be detected in this line, nor in the poem as a whole. But notice the repetition of the hard or hissing "s" sound in four of the eight words of line 5: "Some...sable race...scornful...." Actually, this is a special kind of allitera-

tion called consonance, the repetition of consonant sounds. Given the explanation, choice (E) stands as the best answer.

33. **(A)** "[D]iabolic" derives from the word meaning "devil," so choices (B), (C), (D), and (E) all serve as fairly obvious meanings. "Pagan," on the other hand, means, in essence, a believer in multiple gods, not necessarily an evil person, unless you define anyone who doesn't believe in monotheism (single god) as evil. So (A) is the correct choice here.

34. **(C)** "[B]enighted" serves as a pun or play on words because it means "overtaken by darkness" or "in a state of intellectual, moral, or social darkness." Its literal meaning, then, denotes the race of the speaker and her soul; and it figuratively suggests her state of moral darkness (not yet redeemed). But beyond that, it sounds like "beknighted," which suggests, playfully, an elevation in class rank (as in given the title of "Knight of the Realm"). So, choice (C) outdistances the others. A paradox is a word or phrase comprising an inherent contrast, which does not apply here. A pun is a figure of speech, but when faced with a choice of either the general or the specific term, choose the specific one. Choices (A) and (B) do not really compete here.

35. **(B)** The last two lines of the poem are the key to this question. In those lines, the speaker reminds "Christians" that "Negroes.../May be refined," implying that some (all?) "Christians" believe that "Negroes" are a "diabolic" race. Choice (B) clearly fits as the best answer. The others may be true, but are not implied by the speaker in the poem.

36. **(B)** Put each statement to the test of NOT true according to the speaker. Statement I is true (line 7), and so is statement III (line 1). Both are in the speaker's voice. Statement II comes from line 6, which is a quote by "Some" others, presumably white Christians. It thus fails the test, i.e., it is not true according to the speaker; so choice (B) is the correct one.

37. **(E)** If you do not know the word "intermit," this one becomes more difficult. "Intermittent," an adjective more likely known (meaning occurring or coming and going in intervals), derives from "intermit," a verb meaning to occur at intervals. Therefore, "start up" (A), "keep going" (B), "continue" (C), and "interpose" — to put between — (D) do not work as

well as "interrupt" (E). In context, the bell is ringing, but it intermits (interrupts ringing, then recurs).

38. **(C)**   Bells ring for many reasons, any of which is generally possible from the three choices. However, the only mention of sea in the passage does not imply bells signifying a change of watch. Likewise, no evidence supports the idea that bells ring in the passage to note the time of day (like Big Ben, Westminster chimes). Indeed, the passage speaks of death and refers to the death knell when the funeral bier and procession pass by, an uncommon practice in the United States. Only choice (C) gives the correct reason.

39. **(D)**   Choices (A), (C), and (E) all suggest the speaker's apparent theme that all humanity is one. Choice (B) might trip us just a bit, but it also announces, figuratively, the theme of human kinship (clod [of dirt] = a man; Europe = humanity). Choice (D), the correct one, could spark an argument, but it stands clearly a step or two farther away from the central idea than (B). It requires the next statement, "it tolls for thee," to qualify as theme statement.

40. **(C)**   Previous explanations have defined plays on words (A), alliteration (D), and literary allusions (E), none of which serves as a function of the questions noted. Figures of speech (B) covers a broad category of specific terms; and it, too, at least in comparison to (C), fails to convey specific function. Analogies are comparisons of the unfamiliar to the familiar so as to define the unfamiliar or abstract. These questions serve as analogies to define the idea that the "bell doth toll for him that thinks it doth." Thus, choice (C) defines the function best.

41. **(B)**   The speaker sounds more like a philosophic observer (B) than any of the other choices. He is pondering the meaning of humanity and the relationships between God and humanity and within humanity itself. Thus, while he may be gentle, we could hardly call him a fool (E). Far from being alienated, he is "involved in mankind" (D). His text does not cover politics, however, so choice (C) seems inappropriate. Nor does he propose to reform society, although that choice (A) almost hits the stake. Neither is it a "leaner."

42. **(E)** The people addressed by the speaker probably fear death, because the speaker says that upon hearing the death knell one "is united to God," a hopeful act of redemption. He also suggests that they might not think of themselves as enmeshed with the rest of humanity, that is, they might consider themselves separate islands and individualists curious to find out who has died. His statements incorporating all mankind into himself suggest that his audience does not yet think that way. The best description of the audience, then, comprises all three statements (I, II, and III), choice (E).

43. **(A)** Choices (B) through (E) all underscore the bird imagery by repeating characteristics of birds. Choice (A), the correct answer, however, does not necessarily apply solely to birds.

44. **(D)** That the bird symbolizes persistence of life (hope) should not surprise you (statement I). That it serves also as an undemanding, cheery companion (statement III) may take a bit of convincing. Note "sweetest in the gale," along with other clear statements that the bird (hope) accompanies the speaker, demands nothing, and sings uninterrupted. Often, birds function as symbols of freedom (statement II) because of their ability to fly; but in this poem, no apparent freedom is implied in the metaphor of hope = bird. Thus, choice (D), incorporating statements I and III, states the functions most accurately.

45. **(A)** Usually, sore does mean painful (B) or aching (C), but in this case, it means severe (A), the correct choice. The storm has to reach a high level of intensity to "abash" or slow down the bird's persistently cheerful, sweet song. Choices (D) and (E) both represent "trick" meanings of the homonym "soar," which, as a verb, means to scale heights, fly upwards, float in the air.

46. **(B)** All but (B) "abundant times" suggest meanings of "in extremity." Certainly (A) carries that meaning. Choices (C), (D), and (E) stem from specific references within the poem, all of which exemplify extremity. Extremes include polar opposites, which could include (B), but it should be clear from the context that "extremity" is limited to the one negative pole.

47. **(C)** The two most inviting choices here include (E) and (C). We can dismiss out of hand, given the context, choices (A), (B), and (D) . How

could a pessimist speak so lovingly of hope? The speaker claims to have travelled to the "chillest land" and to the "strangest sea." No evidence or inference suggests the ability to foretell the future, as would a clairvoyant be able to do. Is the speaker an explorer, or merely a world traveller? We can not choose conclusively, but we can conclude that the poem exudes optimism from the speaker, thus choice (C) is correct.

48. **(D)**   Again, you should be able to narrow down the choices fairly quickly to either (D) or (E). Nothing in the poem can support the notion that its main concern is either the inevitability of dreams (A), the gradual change from dream to reality (B), or the necessity of living in the real world, the last of which is a given (C). No, we have to focus on the correct choice, (D), which clearly states the main concern of the poem as it questions the fate of unfulfilled (deferred) dreams. We can eliminate (E) on the grounds of fuzziness or vagueness. Had the language of that choice been more precise than it is, it could have been a contender.

49. **(A)**   Perhaps this question could challenge you a bit more than it does. Looking at the cumulative effect leaves us with several tantalizing possibilities which do not hold up to scrutiny. For example, (E) looms large as a choice, but the speaker does not imply that dreams should cease because the fruits of dreams are rotten otherwise forbidden. Neither does (D) hold up well. If anything, the results of dreams deferred might lead one to quit dreaming instead of reinforcing the necessity of dreaming. Choice (C) also falls out of contention because, rather than satirize, the speaker seems to empathize with those whose dreams are deferred. Choice (B) comes closer to a possibility of truth about the poem. Yes, the speaker does seem dissatisfied with a reality that forces people to defer their dreams, but is that the effect of the phrases? No. In fact, the phrases suggest what the best choice, (A), states: deferred dreams lead to negative consequences of different sorts (possibilities).

50. **(B)**   These choices should settle out relatively easily. The word "expand" suggests a positive power in one meaning (i.e., mind expansion), but here, "explode" does not have that connotation. Instead, "explode" suggests an eruption of violence that blows up madly from frustration and ends with destruction, choices (D), (A), (E), (C). So, the correct choice, (B), is the exception.

51. **(E)** Choice (A) can be easily dismissed. Likewise, choices (C) and (D) seem not germane to the meaning of the similie. Sweetness does not allay the burden of dreams (B); it further defers them. The best choice, (E), specifies the exact meaning of sugar-coating a problem.

52. **(B)** We can dismiss rather quickly choices (D) and (A) because the speaker feels passionate about the subject (evidenced especially in lines 9-11) and does not mock the dreamers. Neither does he defer his own sympathies, choice (C), although one could argue that the lack of a conclusive answer suggests not a dream deferred but a solution deferred. The speaker does show sympathy with the dreamers, choice (E), but he shows more disappointment about the deferred dreams than he shows sympathy for them (for the dreams, not for the disappointed dreamers). Thus, choice (B) edges out (E) because of the specific attitude which is the subject of the question.

53. **(A)** The meaning of the question in line 11 most certainly negates choices (B) and (E). That it remains a question negates to a certain extent choice (D). Between choices (C) and (A), we must discriminate carefully. The question does, in fact, reject the deferral of dreams by exploding the pent up frustration into violence. That is exactly and specifically what the best choice, (A), tells us, albeit with ambivalence: it could explode, but the phrasing in question form leaves other possibilities as well.

54. **(E)** Science fiction, also known as fantasy or escape fiction, does in fact lead us to a contrast between real and fantasy lives (statement I). In this passage, science fiction also connotes security and stability in lines 10–11 (statement II). Finally, since it can be fantasy and it is fiction that may help the characters deal with crises in their lives, it could also serve as a metaphor suggesting the need for lies to escape ugly moments in life (statement III). Having read the foregoing, it should become obvious that choice (E), inclusive of statements I, II, and III, is the correct one.

55. **(C)** We would be hard pressed to detect disappointment, choice (A), in the speaker's tone. Nor can we find total indifference; at least it makes a good story, so we can eliminate choice (D). While Rosewater exhibits skepticism, the speaker seems to accept everything stated as if it were true, so choice (B) falls out. One could argue about irony, choice (E), in this passage, largely embodied in the repetition of "So it goes." However, it just does not quite arrive at irony, again because the speaker seems not to dispute

or lampoon the possibly unorthodox ideas espoused by Rosewater and Billy. Therefore, choice (C) appears to describe accurately the speaker's tone.

56. **(E)** Taking just this passage into consideration, we would be hard pressed once again to find irony, choice (A), in the use of the phrase. (See explanation 55.) In the whole novel, the author uses the phrase more than a hundred times, about once every two pages; and it does accumulate to verbal irony, but not in this passage, which is all you have to use as a text. Both choices (B) and (C), however, miss the target as well. The phrases have the feel of insensitivity and lack of empathy rather than the opposite, as the choices state. Nor does the phrase strike us as excuses, so choice (D) is not the best one. We are left with the correct choice (E). "So it goes" does seem to describe a shrug of the shoulders, a sense that something may be unpleasant but unavoidable. least, the speaker using the phrase seems to be saying he is not responsible for unfortunate accidents or tragedies.

57. **(D)** Choice (A) is not correct because the text states directly the book is not science fiction. Inferences must be deduced from what is said and what is suggested, not what is stated without interpretation. For the same reason, we can eliminate choices (C) and (E), although the latter stands closer to the set of correct answers than does (C). Choice (B) sounds like a reasonable answer that contends with the correct or best choice (D). The reason (B) loses stems from the context: re-invention of self goes with science fiction; the book is not science fiction. Therefore, it is not necessarily about re-invention of self. The context of lines 16-20, does, however, support choice (D).

58. **(C)** No evidence, either direct or inferential, supports choices (A), (B), (D), or (E). Likewise, no evidence in this passage, absolutely refutes any of those choices. However, we do have inferential evidence that the pair are undergoing treatment for mental problems, the correct choice (C). We find it in lines 3–5 and 16 (psychiatrist), particularly. But those lines are supported by more general inferential evidence in lines 1–2 and 10–18, virtually the rest of the passage.

59. **(B)** The correct choice, (B), stands out here and even calls attention to itself by its clear difference from the other choices. The whole passage seems to argue against (B), but particularly the last six lines. Choice (A) is

supported particularly by lines 17–18, as are choices (C), (D), and (E), the latter also being reinforced by lines 12–15.

60. **(E)** Neither childhood friends nor college students, neighbors, nor fathers and sons absolutely define their relationships either in part or in the whole by relative intelligence. Mentors, however, usually teach their followers, pupils, or protégés, thus requiring some measure of knowledge or skill or art superior to the follower. Thus, choice (E) seems correct as judged by the phrase in question.

Literature

TEST 5

Literature

TEST 5

1. (A) (B) (C) (D) (E)	21. (A) (B) (C) (D) (E)	41. (A) (B) (C) (D) (E)
2. (A) (B) (C) (D) (E)	22. (A) (B) (C) (D) (E)	42. (A) (B) (C) (D) (E)
3. (A) (B) (C) (D) (E)	23. (A) (B) (C) (D) (E)	43. (A) (B) (C) (D) (E)
4. (A) (B) (C) (D) (E)	24. (A) (B) (C) (D) (E)	44. (A) (B) (C) (D) (E)
5. (A) (B) (C) (D) (E)	25. (A) (B) (C) (D) (E)	45. (A) (B) (C) (D) (E)
6. (A) (B) (C) (D) (E)	26. (A) (B) (C) (D) (E)	46. (A) (B) (C) (D) (E)
7. (A) (B) (C) (D) (E)	27. (A) (B) (C) (D) (E)	47. (A) (B) (C) (D) (E)
8. (A) (B) (C) (D) (E)	28. (A) (B) (C) (D) (E)	48. (A) (B) (C) (D) (E)
9. (A) (B) (C) (D) (E)	29. (A) (B) (C) (D) (E)	49. (A) (B) (C) (D) (E)
10. (A) (B) (C) (D) (E)	30. (A) (B) (C) (D) (E)	50. (A) (B) (C) (D) (E)
11. (A) (B) (C) (D) (E)	31. (A) (B) (C) (D) (E)	51. (A) (B) (C) (D) (E)
12. (A) (B) (C) (D) (E)	32. (A) (B) (C) (D) (E)	52. (A) (B) (C) (D) (E)
13. (A) (B) (C) (D) (E)	33. (A) (B) (C) (D) (E)	53. (A) (B) (C) (D) (E)
14. (A) (B) (C) (D) (E)	34. (A) (B) (C) (D) (E)	54. (A) (B) (C) (D) (E)
15. (A) (B) (C) (D) (E)	35. (A) (B) (C) (D) (E)	55. (A) (B) (C) (D) (E)
16. (A) (B) (C) (D) (E)	36. (A) (B) (C) (D) (E)	56. (A) (B) (C) (D) (E)
17. (A) (B) (C) (D) (E)	37. (A) (B) (C) (D) (E)	57. (A) (B) (C) (D) (E)
18. (A) (B) (C) (D) (E)	38. (A) (B) (C) (D) (E)	58. (A) (B) (C) (D) (E)
19. (A) (B) (C) (D) (E)	39. (A) (B) (C) (D) (E)	59. (A) (B) (C) (D) (E)
20. (A) (B) (C) (D) (E)	40. (A) (B) (C) (D) (E)	60. (A) (B) (C) (D) (E)

LITERATURE

TEST 5

TIME: 60 Minutes
60 Questions

DIRECTIONS: *This test consists of selections from literary works and questions on their content, form, and style. After reading each passage or poem, choose the best answer to each question and blacken the corresponding space on the answer sheet.*

NOTE: Pay particular attention to the requirement of questions that contain the words NOT, LEAST, or EXCEPT.

QUESTIONS 1–9 are based on the following poem. Read the poem carefully before choosing your answers.

> I went to the Garden of Love,
> And saw what I never had seen:
> A Chapel was built in the midst,
> Where I used to play on the green
>
> And the gates of this Chapel were shut,
> 5 And "Thou shalt not" writ over the door;
> So I turned to the Garden of Love
> That so many sweet flowers bore;
>
> And I saw it was filled with graves,
> And tomb-stones where flowers should be;
> 10

And Priests in black gowns were walking their rounds,
And binding with briars my joys and desires.

"The Garden of Love," by William Blake

1. What best explains the Chapel?

    (A) The Chapel symbolizes pure love.

    (B) The Chapel represents rules that religion enforces over free love.

    (C) The Chapel symbolizes the power the Church holds over secular love.

    (D) The Chapel is an image of the strict love of God rather than of religious fervor.

    (E) The Chapel represents the strict rules of commitment in marriage.

2. The words "Thou shalt not" on the closed gates suggests

    (A) religion sets up a barrier to the human experience of love

    (B) the poet rebels against the Ten Commandments

    (C) religion has closed the gate on human happiness

    (D) the poet has rejected religion

    (E) the poet feels shut out by the Church

3. What best explains the verbs "play" (line 4) and "bore" (line 8)?

    (A) As a child the poet felt free in this garden with so many beautiful flowers that now simply bore him.

    (B) In his youth the poet felt no limits to the way he loved, now he feels hemmed in by the garden.

    (C) In his youth the poet revelled in free, untrammeled love which seemed to surround him like flowers.

    (D) As a child the poet was surrounded by people who loved him as if by flowers in the garden.

    (E) In the past the poet was able to give love freely which he did as if giving away flowers.

4. The Garden is now filled with graves and tombstones because

    (A) the Industrial Revolution has blighted the "garden," turning countryside into wasteland

    (B) industry has turned gardens into factory sites — graveyards for the workers

    (C) strict rules of society have turned free expression of poets and writers into dead things.

    (D) religious rules have turned the beautiful free expression of human love into something dead and ugly

    (E) religion has taken away individuality and turned people into automatons, dead inside, incapable of loving

5. What figure of speech is "binding with briars"?

    (A) Onomatopoeia   (D) Feminine rhyme

    (B) Alliteration   (E) Assonance

    (C) Internal rhyme

6. The poet's tone in the last line is

    (A) wistful   (D) angry

    (B) sad   (E) anxious

    (C) lonely

7. The change of rhyme scheme in the last stanza gives the effect of

    (A) breaking the mood of pensiveness and simplicity.

    (B) rounding off the poem with a satisfying conclusion.

    (C) emphasizing the poet's swing from love to hate.

    (D) completing the circle suggested by binding and "rounds."

    (E) emphasizing the very last word — "desires" — as the focus of the poem.

8. The repetition of the conjunction in the last stanza suggests

    I.   The poet is building to a climax.

    II. The poet is growing more and more frustrated.

    III. The poet's hatred of the priests is about to erupt.

    (A) I and III   (D) I, II and III

    (B) I only   (E) I and II

    (C) III only

9. The poem is a(n)

    (A) fable   (D) fabliau

    (B) parable   (E) allegory

    (C) dramatic monologue

QUESTIONS 10–18 are based on the following passage. Read the passage carefully before choosing your answers.

    The high-tech world of clocks and schedules, computers and programs was supposed to free us from a life of toil and deprivation, yet with each passing day the human race becomes more enslaved, exploited and victimized. Millions starve while a few live in splendor. The human race remains divided from itself and severed from the natural world that is its primordial community.

    We now orchestrate an artificial time world, zipping along the electronic circuits of silicon chips, a time world utterly alien from the time a fruit takes to ripen, or a tide takes to recede. We have sped ourselves out of the time world of nature and into a fabricated time world where experience can only be simulated but no longer savored. Our weekly routines and work lives are punctuated with artificial rhythms, the unholy union of perspective and power. And with each new electric dawn and dusk, we grow further apart from each other, more isolated and alone, more in control and less self-assured.

From Time Wars *by Jeremy Rifkin. Copyright © 1987 by Jeremy Rifkin. Reprinted by permission of Henry Holt and Company, Inc.*

10. All of the following pairs belong in the high-tech world EXCEPT

   (A) enslavement and exploitation

   (B) perspective and power

   (C) toil and deprivation

   (D) isolation and aloneness

   (E) in control and less self-assured

11. Which of the following most closely explains the use of "fruit" and "tide"?

   (A) to compare natural processes in the world of time

   (B) to emphasize the uncontrollable natural processes in the world of time

   (C) to contrast well-known natural processes with the modern world

   (D) to contrast the fast high-tech world with the slow world of nature

   (E) to contrast the time processes of the natural world with the time of the modern world

12. The expression "electric dawn and dusk" functions as a(n)

   (A) symbol of humanity's tampering with nature

   (B) image of humanity's power over nature

   (C) symbol of the computerized world of time

   (D) personification of light

   (E) symbol of the elongated day in the modern world

13. What differentiates the two worlds of time?

   (A) People are deprived in one, fulfilled in the other.

   (B) People enjoy life in one but play at life in the other.

   (C) People experience power in one but fantasize over power in the other.

   (D) People move speedily in one and at leisure in the other.

   (E) People experience full life in one but copy life in the other.

14. The author uses the adjectives in the comparative in the last sentence in order to

    (A) show the balance and rhythm in the computerized world

    (B) emphasize the regret he feels at the loss of rhythm and balance

    (C) highlight the orchestration of the new world of time

    (D) draw attention to the "artificial rhythms" of our lives

    (E) build to a satisfying climax expressing the loss in our lives

15. Why does the author change from "human race" to "we" in the second paragraph?

    (A) to make us feel guilty at orchestrating a new time world

    (B) to make us feel proud that we are involved in the high-tech world

    (C) to emphasize everyone's involvement in the changing of the two worlds

    (D) to emphasize his distance from the high-tech world

    (E) to emphasize it is not our fault that the time worlds have changed

16. Which expression best describes the notion that we have become automatons in the new time world?

    (A) "severed from the natural world that is its primordial community"

    (B) "zipping along the electronic circuits of silicon chips"

    (C) "sped ourselves out of the time world of nature"

    (D) "unholy union of perspective and power"

    (E) "more in control and less self-assured"

17. Which pairing best captures the author's tone?

    (A) lecturing and misanthropic

    (B) pedantic yet sensitive

    (C) sensitive and nostalgic

(D) sentimental and sad

(E) understanding yet stern

18. What is the role of the author here?

    (A) prophet of doom   (D) humanist

    (B) philanthropist   (E) scientist

    (C) misogynist

QUESTIONS 19–27 are based on the following passage. Read the passage carefully before choosing your answers.

A perfectly healthy sentence, it is true, is extremely rare. For the most part we miss the hue and fragrance of the thought; as if we could be satisfied with the dews of the morning or evening without their colors, or the heavens without their azure. The most attractive sentences are, perhaps, not the wisest, but the surest and roundest. They are spoken firmly and conclusively, as if the speaker had a right to know what he says, and if not wise, they have at least been well learned. Sir Walter Raleigh might well be studied if only for the excellence of his style, for he is remarkable in the midst of so many masters. There is a natural emphasis in his style, like a man's tread, and a breathing space between the sentences, which the best of modern writing does not furnish. His chapters are like English parks, or say, rather like a western forest, where the larger growth keeps down the underwood, and one may ride on horse-back through the openings. All the distinguished writers of that period possess a greater vigor and naturalness than the modern, — for it is allowed to slander our own time, — and when we read a quotation from one of them in the midst of a modern author, we seem to have come suddenly upon a greener ground, a greater depth and strength of soil....The little that is said is eked out by the implication of the much that was done. The sentences are verduous and blooming as evergreen and flowers, because they are rooted in fact and experience, but our false and florid sentences have only the tints of flowers without their sap or roots.

From "A Week on the Concord and Merrimack Rivers." by Henry David Thoreau.

19. The passage centers around

    (A) the metaphor of the garden

    (B) a simile of nature

    (C) an analogy of horseback riding

    (D) an analogy of vigorous verdant life

    (E) the personification of Nature

20. Which of the following best describes the "healthy sentence"?

    (A) one full of wisdom and truth

    (B) one firmly delivered and open to interpretation

    (C) one spoken loudly and full of erudition

    (D) one which says a great deal in a short space

    (E) one which is full and leaves no unanswered questions

21. The author prefers the comparison of "Western forests" over "English parks" because

    (A) Raleigh was English but knew America well

    (B) English parks are too cluttered

    (C) English parks are too ornamental

    (D) Western forests are more accessible

    (E) Western forests are deeper and lush

22. The author admires Raleigh because

    I.   Raleigh was much revered by other great writers

    II.   There is an openness and space in Raleigh's style

    III. Raleigh expresses facts in a unique style

    (A) I only   (D) I and II

    (B) I and III   (E) I, II and III

    (C) II only

23. What does the author criticize in modern writers?

    (A) They are loud and do not say enough about life's experiences.

    (B) They are verbose and exaggerate trivial matters.

    (C) They are verbose yet say little that is substantial.

    (D) They are wordy and deal with too many facts.

    (E) They are overly colored and hold little of importance.

24. All of the following describe the sentences of Raleigh's contemporaries EXCEPT

    (A) there is profound substance to them

    (B) they hold a certain life and force

    (C) there is a natural strength in them

    (D) they exercise brevity but describe action forcefully

    (E) they say very little but say it beautifully

25. In its context "verduous" means

    (A) robust   (D) venal

    (B) virtuous   (E) everlasting

    (C) healthy

26. Which best describes the notion of "riding horse-back through the openings" when applied to a writing style?

    (A) One can read between the lines.

    (B) One has to work at the meaning.

    (C) One can read fast, at a gallop.

    (D) One can read steadily and smoothly.

    (E) One has to rein in the imagination.

27. Which best describes the word choice of "hue" and "fragrance"?

    (A) The words fit the theme of flowering and growth.

(B)   The words describe the verbosity of the modern sentence.

(C)   The words fit the floweriness of Raleigh's contemporaries.

(D)   The words describe the state of the healthy sentence.

(E)   The words fit the idea of the English parks.

QUESTIONS 28–35 are based on the following passage. Read the passage carefully before choosing your answers.

He lived in a large new house of red brick standing outside a mass of homogeneous red-brick dwellings, called Wiggiston. Wiggiston was only seven years old. It had been a hamlet of eleven houses on the edge of heathy, half-agricultural country. Then the great seam of coal had been opened. In a year Wiggiston appeared, a great mass of pinkish rows of thin, unreal dwellings of five rooms each. The streets were like visions of pure ugliness; a grey-black macademized road, asphalt causeways, held in between a flat succession of wall, window, and door, a new brick channel that began nowhere, and ended nowhere. Everything was amorphous, yet everything repeated itself endlessly. Only now and then, in one of the house windows, vegetables or small groceries were displayed for sale.

In the middle of the town was a large, open, shapeless space, or market place, of black trodden earth, surrounded by the same flat material of dwellings, new red-brick becoming grimy, small oblong windows, and oblong doors, repeated endlessly, with just, at one corner, a great and gaudy public house, and somewhere lost on one of the sides of the square, a large window opaque and darkish green, which was the post office.

The place had the strange desolation of a ruin. Colliers hanging about in gangs and groups, or passing along the asphalt pavements heavily to work, seemed not like living people but like spectres. The rigidity of the blank streets, the homogeneous amorphous sterility of the whole suggested death rather than life. There was no meeting place, no centre, no artery, no organic formation. There it lay, like the new foundations of a red-brick confusion rapidly spreading, like a skin disease.

From "The Rainbow," by D.H. Lawrence. Copyright 1964 by D.H. Lawrence. Reprinted with permission of Viking-Penguin, Inc.

28. The passage represents all of the following EXCEPT the

    (A) Industrial Revolution

    (B) ugliness of modern industry

    (C) sterility of 20th century life

    (D) regret for the agrarian days

    (E) emptiness in the colliers' lives

29. The word "hamlet" functions to

    (A) emphasize the place's original smallness

    (B) promote the "bad" old days and the good new ones

    (C) suggest the largeness of Wiggiston

    (D) suggest the change from rural to industrial

    (E) show the author's wistfulness for the past

30. The "He" of the first line is never mentioned again here because he

    (A) is giving a purely objective view

    (B) wants to meld into the whole description

    (C) is not important in the description of place

    (D) symbolizes the non-importance of humans in this place

    (E) is one of the spectres

31. Which is the closest explanation for the expression "homogeneous amorphous sterility" of the place?

    (A) The houses are all alike yet distinct in their emptiness.

    (B) The houses are all alike but without form in their death-like appearance.

    (C) Everything was essentially alike yet shapeless in a sterile death-like way.

    (D) The post office and the market place were devoid of life.

    (E) The market place and the earth blended into each other in a sterile whole that resembled death.

32. The author uses the words "repeated" and "endlessly" in order to stress the

    (A) repetition in the colliers' lives

    (B) repetition in the world of technology

    (C) repetition of the place's ugliness

    (D) repeated quality of death

    (E) spreading quality of the disease of modernism

33. Which pair best describes the word choice for the public house description?

    (A) alliteration — to draw attention to the crassness of the building

    (B) simile — to show sensitivity for the people who have nothing but this building to enjoy

    (C) alliteration — to show scorn for the people who have nothing but this building to enjoy

    (D) assonance — to show how ugly the building is because of the sound of the words

    (E) analogy — to show how the people waste their time

34. Which pair best describes the narrator's tone?

    (A) nostalgic and depressed

    (B) reminiscent and cold

    (C) reminiscent and sad

    (D) sad and depressing

    (E) cold and distant

35. The gradual buildup of "meeting place" "centre" "artery" "organic formation" suggests that the

    (A) author envisions the place as a human being

    (B) place becomes more and more inhuman

    (C) author does not see the place in human terms

(D)   place becomes more and more death-like

(E)   place becomes an organ open to disease

QUESTIONS 36–44 are based on the following dramatic excerpt. Read the excerpt carefully before choosing your answers.

> [Volpone in a large bed. Enter Mosca. Volpone awakes]
> Volpone: Good morning to the day; and next, my gold!
> Open the shrine, that I may see my saint.
> [Mosca draws a curtain, revealing piles of gold]
> Hail the world's soul, and mine! More glad than is
> The teeming earth to see the longed-for sun
> 5   Peep through the horns of the celestial Ram,
> Am I, to view thy splendour darkening his;
> That lying here, amongst my other hoards,
> Show'st like a flame by night, or like the day
> Struck out of chaos, when all darkness fled
> 10   Unto the centre. O, thou son of Sol
> (But brighter than thy father) let me kiss,
> With adoration, thee, and every relic
> Of sacred treasure in this blessed room.
> Well did wise wise poets by thy glorious name
> 15   Title that age which they would have the best,
> Thou being the best of things, and far transcending
> All style of joy in children, parents, friends,
> Or any other waking dream on earth.

From "Volpone, or the Fox," *by Ben Jonson.*

36.   Volpone's greeting of the day and then his gold is a(n)

(A)   satire

(B)   ode

(C)   parody of an ode

(D)   aubade

(E)   parody of an aubade

37.   Which best explains the greeting "Hail the world's gold and mine!"?

(A)   Money has become the centre of both the world and Volpone.

(B)   Like everyone else, Volpone loves money more than his soul.

(C) Volpone has replaced the goodness of his soul with worldly commodities like gold.

(D) Volpone worships worldly goods like gold.

(E) Volpone has sold his soul for the world's acclaim for his gold.

38. The term "celestial Ram" suggests that the time of year is

(A) Christmas
(D) winter
(B) Easter
(E) summer
(C) spring

39. Which best explains the use of the word "relic"?

(A) The playwright puns on the idea of religious antiques.

(B) The playwright pokes fun at Volpone kissing the gold.

(C) The playwright puns on the idea of people kissing religious relics.

(D) The playwright satirizes people who kissed old bones thinking they were religious relics.

(E) The playwright stresses the fact Volpone worships his treasures as if they were religious relics.

40. Volpone is all of the following EXCEPT

(A) a mendicant
(D) irreligious
(B) an idolatrist
(E) a miser
(C) venal

41. The age referred to in lines 14–15 is the

(A) Age of Affluence
(D) Age of the Poets
(B) Renaissance
(E) Age of the Alchemists
(C) Golden Age

42. The father in line 11 refers to

    (A) God the Father   (D) the Earth

    (B) Volpone's father   (E) Volpone's soul

    (C) the Sun

43. Thou in line 16 refers to

    (A) Volpone's soul   (D) the saint in the shrine

    (B) Mosca   (E) the Sun

    (C) the shrine

44. The last three lines suggest Volpone

    (A) is transcended by the love of his gold

    (B) has become a transcendentalist preferring fantasy to reality

    (C) assumes that everyone loves gold to the same extent he does

    (D) has sacrificed human attributes for the love of his gold

    (E) finds joy in the simple attributes that money cannot buy

QUESTIONS 45–53 are based on the following passage. Read the passage carefully before choosing your answers.

But his Honour, out of Curiosity, and perhaps (if I may speak it without Vanity) partly out of Kindness, was determined to see me in my Canoo; and got several of his neighboring Friends to accompany him. I was forced to wait above an Hour for the Tide, and then observing the Wind very fortunately bearing towards the Island, to which I intended to steer my Course, I took a second Leave of my Master: But as I was going to prostrate myself to kiss his Hoof, he did me the Honour to raise it gently to my mouth. I am not ignorant how much I have been censured for mentioning this last Particular. Detractors are pleased to think it improbable, that so illustrious a Person should descend to give so great a Mark of Distinction to a Creature so inferior as I. Neither have I forgot, how apt some travellers are to boast of extraordinary Favours they have received. But, if these Censurers were better acquainted with the noble and courteous Disposition of the Houyhnhnms, they would soon change their Opinion.

From "Voyage to the Houyhnhnms" in Gulliver's Travels, *by Jonathan Swift.*

45. His Honor is

    (A) mayor   (D) chief

    (B) mare   (E) captain

    (C) horse

46. The narrator is a

    (A) native of the island   (D) horse

    (B) journalist   (E) canoeist

    (C) travel writer

47. Which best describes why the *narrator* thinks he has been censured for "this last particular"?

    I.   He is lying about the favour bestowed upon him.

    II. Travellers very often lie about the way they treat inferiors.

    III. He is making up the entire story.

    (A) I and III   (D) III only

    (B) I only   (E) II and III

    (C) II only

48. Which best describes why *readers* censure the narrator?

    I.   He should not be so sycophantic to an animal.

    II. He is not a reliable narrator.

    III. Such a narrator always has tall tales to tell.

    (A) I only   (D) II and III

    (B) I and II   (E) I and III

    (C) II only

49. Which pair best describes the narrator's attitude to the Houyhnhnms?

    (A) supercilious and arrogant

    (B) humble and demeaning

    (C) humble and demanding

    (D) vain yet kind

    (E) respectful yet equal

50. Which best explains the narrator's tone?

    (A) frustrated at the wait for the tide

    (B) sad at having to leave his Honour

    (C) eager to set sail and leave such a place

    (D) prostrate at having to leave the Islands

    (E) regretful at having to leave such a beautiful place

51. "so illustrious a Person" refers to

    (A) a Houyhnhnm

    (B) a fellow traveller

    (C) chief of the Islands

    (D) the owner of the canoo

    (E) a detractor

52. The use of the word Master suggests

    (A) the narrator has been a slave

    (B) the narrator has worked with love for the Houyhnhnms

    (C) the narrator admires and respects His Honour

    (D) the narrator is being satirical

    (E) His Honour does not want to let the narrator go

53. When he returns home, the narrator chooses not to sleep with his wife but

(A) in the garden in the open air

(B) on the beach for the sound of the waves

(C) in a hammock

(D) in his stables

(E) in a navy cot

QUESTIONS 54–60 are based on the following passage. Read the passage carefully before choosing your answers.

"Charlie, I haven't a cent!" answered Vandover, looking him squarely in the face. "Would I be here and trying to get work from you if I had? No; I gambled it all away. You know I had eighty-nine hundred in U.S. 4 per cents…For a time I got along by work in the paint shop. But they have let me out now; said I was so irregular. I owe for nearly a month at my lodging-place." His eyes sought the floor, rolling about stupidly "Nearly a month, and that's what makes me jump and tremble so. You ought to see me sometimes —b-r-r-r-h!— and I get to barking! I'm a wolf mostly, you know, or some kind of animal, some kind of a brute. But I'd be all right if everything did not go around so slowly, and seem far off. But I'm a wolf….Ah! It's up four flights at the end of the hall, very dark, eight thousand dollars in a green cloth sack, and lots of lights a-burning. See how long my finger nails are — regular claws; that's the wolf, the brute! Why can't I talk in my mouth instead of in my throat? That's the devil of it. When you paint on steel and iron your colours don't dry out true; all the yellows turn green…And when all those eight thousand little lights begin to burn red, why, of course that makes you nervous! So I have to drink a great deal of water and chew butcher's paper. That fools him and he thinks he's eating. Just so I can lay quiet in the Plaza when the sun is out…."

From Vandover and the Brute, by Frank Norris.

228

54. The speaker suffers from

    (A) the delusion he is a dog

    (B) lycanthropy

    (C) misanthropy

    (D) delusions of grandeur

    (E) senility

55. Which best explains what happened to the speaker?

    (A) He refused to get a job because of all his money; now he cannot get a job and is starving.

    (B) He could not do the work in the paint shop and now is homeless and ill.

    (C) He gambled all of Charlie's money away; now that he is out of work he wants Charlie to come to his rescue.

    (D) He gambled all his money away, lost his job and is now suffering from malnutrition.

    (E) He lost his job and had to resort to gambling to pay his bills; now he is starving and ill.

56. Which best answers the speaker's question, "Why can't I talk in my mouth instead of in my throat?"

    (A) Because he is so hungry his voice is getting deeper and deeper.

    (B) Because he is slipping into senility his voice is losing its timbre.

    (C) Because he is growing into manhood (symbolized by the brute motif), his voice is growing gruffer.

    (D) Because gradually the brute inside him is trying to get out.

    (E) Because the brute, not the man, is expressing itself in growling tones.

57. The pronoun in "It's up four flights" refers to

    (A) the money at the end of the hall

    (B) some sort of brute at the end of the hall

(C) the apartment at the end of the hall

(D) the painting of eight thousand eyes at the end of the hall

(E) the wolf at the end of the hall

58. Which best explains the use of the third person pronouns in "That fools him and he think's he's eating"?

(A) The speaker distances himself from the devil inside him.

(B) The speaker considers the brute inside him a totally integrated part of his personality.

(C) The speaker considers the butcher's dog a threat to his way of life.

(D) The speaker considers Charlie as a threat to his way of life and distances himself from him.

(E) The speaker considers the brute inside him as divorced from his true human self.

59. The eight thousand little lights represent

(A) all the guilt the speaker feels at gambling away his money

(B) all the U.S. Bonds the speaker lost

(C) the bonds that the speaker gambled away

(D) the opportunities the speaker missed by gambling away the bonds

(E) all the missed opportunities in a futile life

60. The last line expresses the speaker's

(A) reluctance to give up his human status

(B) laziness

(C) giving in to the way of the brute

(D) acknowledgement that he is a werewolf

(E) sense of humor in trying to get money from Charlie

TEST 5

ANSWER KEY

1.	(B)	16.	(B)	31.	(C)	46.	(C)
2.	(A)	17.	(E)	32.	(C)	47.	(B)
3.	(C)	18.	(D)	33.	(A)	48.	(A)
4.	(D)	19.	(D)	34.	(E)	49.	(B)
5.	(B)	20.	(E)	35.	(B)	50.	(B)
6.	(D)	21.	(D)	36.	(E)	51.	(A)
7.	(A)	22.	(C)	37.	(A)	52.	(C)
8.	(E)	23.	(C)	38.	(C)	53.	(D)
9.	(E)	24.	(E)	39.	(E)	54.	(B)
10.	(C)	25.	(A)	40.	(A)	55.	(D)
11.	(C)	26.	(D)	41.	(C)	56.	(E)
12.	(C)	27.	(A)	42.	(C)	57.	(C)
13.	(E)	28.	(D)	43.	(D)	58.	(E)
14.	(D)	29.	(A)	44.	(D)	59.	(C)
15.	(C)	30.	(D)	45.	(C)	60.	(C)

DETAILED EXPLANATIONS
OF ANSWERS

TEST 5

1.   **(B)**   Deceptively simple because of its meter and rhyme, Blake's poem says a great deal about love and freedom of love from religious laws. The best explanation of the Chapel is (B)...the other alternatives are too specific — Blake is not criticizing commitment in marriage — or too far from the point — pure love is not symbolized but curtailed by the Church in Blake's view.

2.   **(A)**   The answer here is (A) as the most rational of the answers. The others are too extreme for what the poet is saying.

3.   **(C)**   Certainly the poet is not bored by flowers; the verb refers of course to the flowers blooming in the garden when he was young when he "played"; in other words when he felt love as a free emotion. The answer is (C). The others go too far in the interpretation of how he feels now in the garden, or give information about the poet and other people, information not substantiated in the text.

4.   **(D)**   In other poems Blake did condemn the Industrial Revolution and made strong pleas for the workers, especially child laborers, but here his theme is the curtailing of free love, not art or poetry, or individuality. The answer is (D).

5.   **(B)**   Make sure you know the various figures of speech: onomatopoeia: the sound is like the action — oozing, buzzing; internal rhyme when the rhyme comes not in the usual position at the end of the line but within the line; feminine rhyme: two or three syllables where the second or third is unstressed: motion/notion; fortunate/importunate; assonance is the opposite to alliteration: a stressed vowel sounds alike but the consonant sound is unalike: late/make. The answer here is alliteration: the re-

peated consonant sound: binding/briars, often used to give a slowing effect
to the rhythm (B).

6.   **(D)**   Here the effect of the alliteration is not only to slow the rhythm
but also give an effect of speaking with clenched teeth. The answer is (D).
He is annoyed that the priests and rules of the Church have trammeled his
love; the overall tone is one of wistfulness for the past but in the last line
the poet's anger is expressed clearly.

7.   **(A)**   The rhyme scheme of a poem is important very often simply
for any changes which signify "alert" — the scheme is simple: abcb defe
— one would expect ghih with a word rhyming with "be" — instead
Blake provides an internal rhyme briars/desires. This does not give a satisfying conclusion but should make you sit up and think: it does not complete a circle — desires are not the main point of the poem but the tram-
meling of love — the answer then is (A) as a break in the simplicity of the
poem. The last line should make you go back and read the poem again in a
new light.

8.   **(E)**   The answer is (E) — the poet builds to a climax and expresses
his increasing frustration with the priests as the representatives of the
Church...not hatred which is too strong.

9.   **(E)**   The answer is (E). Make sure you know the terms for various
pieces of poetry: allegory is the figurative treatment of one subject dis-
guised under another subject. Blake describes the Garden of love but
really describes the state of free love. A fable uses animals to explain a
human failing or state of mind (the Fox and the Hen is a good example); a
parable is a simple story used by teachers (such as Christ in the Christian
tradition) to explain a complex issue (the Prodigal Son is a good example);
a dramatic monologue is usually longer and gives one side of a conversation in poetic form ("My Last Duchess" by Browning is a good example);
a fabliau is a coarse country tale to amuse yet give a moral (Chaucer's
"Miller's Tale" is a good example).

10. **(C)**   Although from his description, toil and deprivation do belong
in the new time world, Rifkin begins by saying that this pairing should
have been eliminated. . . the answer then is (C). As you read the passage,
all the other pairings are firmly established in the high-tech world.

11. **(C)** The key word here is contrast. Rifkin chooses two natural processes that we are all familiar with, then contrasts such processes with the fast artificial world we have created. The answer is (C) as the closest idea of the natural time process in contrast to the modern world's concept of time.

12. **(C)** The fact that we can make day into night and vice versa shows the ability to tamper with nature (C). We shall never have control over nature (witness earthquakes and hurricanes) nor can we elongate the day no matter what we do with shift work and biological rhythms. Read the passage carefully to gain not just the understanding but also the symbolic quality of what Rifkin has to say.

13. **(E)** Rifkin clearly states "experience can only be simulated but no longer savored" which suggests that in the old time world we could savor life to the fullest…now we simply try to copy life…(E).

14. **(D)** The natural rhythm of the sentence here draws attention to the artificial rhythms Rifkin describes (D); the other answers undercut what Rifkin says about the new time world, or go too far as in suggesting a satisfying climax.

15. **(C)** Rifkin's use of the personal pronoun includes us all in the process of moving into the new time-world away from the natural processes (C). He is not out to make us feel guilty or proud, nor to put himself at any distance or exonerate us. We are all in the change of time processes whether we like it or not.

16. **(B)** (B) clearly makes us sound as if we are part of the high-tech machines Rifkin regrets in the new time world. The other answers express more of the regret…here we sound like little automaton "zipping" along in life.

17. **(E)** Learn words such as misanthropic — hatred of humankind — then you will realize that Rifkin demonstrates perhaps the opposite. Because he loves the world, he worries about its outcome. He is not sentimental and sad about it all; he is not giving us a lecture or being "teacher-like" (pedantic) but he is stern (the voice commands respect) and understanding — he involves himself in the process. The answer is (E).

18. **(D)** Because of the understanding and the concern, Rifkin may rightly be termed a humanist — he cares about what is going to happen to human-kind (D). Doom and gloom is not the message here but "sit up and notice"; not doing good for mankind (philanthropist) but drawing attention to the problems; a misogynist hates women — there is no hint of this hatred here; a scientist would usually have the language and style that would not appeal to the lay reader, as Rifkin's language and style do.

19. **(D)** Thoreau draws a consistent connection between the healthy sentence and the healthy outdoors (D). Analogy simply draws a comparison or connection between two actions or things (nurturing a child/nurturing a tree); horseback riding is mentioned only once; metaphor, simile and personification have specific meanings which need to be learned and understood.

20. **(E)** The first sentence sets up the "hue" and "fragrance" of thought that should be in a healthy sentence then the passage elaborates on the healthy sentence in language that is in itself overblown! However, the gist of the passage comes toward the end with the idea of fact and experience. The best answer is (E).

21. **(D)** Here the horseback riding analogy is helpful. One can ride through Western forests because the tall growth controls the undergrowth...in other words, the forests are more accessible (D). The other answers have something to do with the main point but, in connection with the analogy of the healthy sentence, accessibility is the key.

22. **(C)** Thoreau does not say that Raleigh was admired by other writers but that he admires him among other greats. He does not say that Raleigh expresses facts in a unique way but that he has an excellent style. Thoreau does say there is openness and space in Raleigh's writing with the analogy of horseback riding. The answer is (C).

23. **(C)** The words "false and florid" are your keys here. Thoreau criticizes the modern writers (i.e., of his age) because of wordiness and not enough experience and fact (C). Draw out what Thoreau admires about Raleigh's sentences then contrast with the last sentence of the piece and here is the answer.

24. **(E)**   Nowhere does Thoreau say that Raleigh's contemporaries wrote "beautiful" sentences (E). You may interpret beauty because of the flower association but the main gist of the sentences of Raleigh and his peers was that they were succinct to the point, and contained action, not simply esoteric quality.

25. **(A)**   No doubt the writer was aiming for the word "verdurous" meaning flourishing, green as in verdure. From context the same meaning comes across…the closest word here then is "robust" (A). Venal, of course, means open to bribery, with a more common meaning of being mercenary.

26. **(D)**   Reading between the lines is tempting when one thinks of the motion of riding through a forest, but Thoreau makes quite clear the ease of moving through Raleigh's sentences with their breathing spaces. The analogy of the horse riding simply clarifies the idea further (D).

27. **(A)**   Having read the entire passage, go back to the opening sentence. The answer clearly becomes (A) pulling together the entire notion of writing and nature, flowering and growth.

28. **(D)**   Nowhere does the writer mention regret for the old days (D). Simply describing the old hamlet before the Industrial Revolution does not set up nostalgia for the agrarian way of life.

29. **(A)**   The word "hamlet" means a small village, originally without its own church so it would have to join in the jurisdiction of a larger parish. The writer merely stresses the difference in size since the Industrial Revolution (A).

30. **(D)**   Later of course in the novel, the "he" does feature again but for the writer's purpose here the human being is not important (D). Industry, functionalism is all important.

31. **(C)**   Cleverly the writer places two near opposites together to make his point: essentially alike/formless. Not just specific buildings are described here but the entire place — even perhaps the aura of the place. The closest explanation then is (C).

32. **(C)** The entire passage is in fact built on repetition if you analyze how many words are indeed repeated. Again the human beings are not so important as the place, and the place's deathlike awfulness (C).

33. **(A)** The figure of speech is of course alliteration but the words themselves are ugly in their sound "great and gaudy" to draw attention to the ugliness, crassness of the pub (A).

34. **(E)** Any of the pairs that suggest reminiscing with sadness, nostalgia can be discounted. The tone is devoid of feeling. It is sad only because we have seen or known towns like this. It is depressing to think of what life is like for the inhabitants there but the narrator's tone indulges in neither of these emotions. He remains cold and distant from the place and the people (E).

35. **(B)** The frightening concluding description is visual and psychological: a town should have a centre; it should be a microcosm of the world itself; the use of the word artery suggests human life...this town does not have this, nor any organic formation...it becomes more and more inhuman as the description develops (B).

36. **(E)** An aubade is usually a beautiful greeting of the day. Here Volpone spends one line on the day and the rest on his gold. The passage is a parody of what was a tradition in Renaissance poetry and drama (E).

37. **(A)** We do not know the rest of this world well enough to judge, nor the goodness of Volpone's soul, but we do learn that Volpone puts his gold before the world...the gold has not just replaced the soul, it is his centre (A).

38. **(C)** Even if you do not know the "celestial" signs of the Zodiac and recognize Ram as Aries, spring equinox, the rest of the description of the earth teeming and warming to the sun would supply the answer Spring (C). Easter is too specific and no doubt there would have been further reference to rebirth and resurrection from such a precise writer.

39. **(E)** The entire description makes fun of religion and the worshipping of saints in shrines. Relics were often sold as remains of saints or Christ (found to be totally bogus pieces of cloth or old pig bones as

Chaucer describes in "The Pardoner's Tale"). The answers all have some element of truth but the best explanation is the stressing of Volpone's worshipping of his treasures as if they were actual relics (E).

40. **(A)**   The answer is (A)...a mendicant is a beggar which Volpone definitely is not. All the other words definitely apply to Volpone. If any of these words are new, learn and add them to your vocabulary.

41. **(C)**   Go back to the opening of the previous sentence where Volpone addresses his gold. Trace the Latinate sentence along (verbal part rather than the object at the end) then you will understand that the title must have gold in it somewhere...The Golden Age (C).

42. **(C)**   Volpone continues to address his gold referring to it now as the son of Sun (Sol) but then admits that his gold is brighter than its father i.e., the Sun! (C).

43. **(D)**   Volpone refers to his gold as "Thou" but that is not one of the options. Go back then to the opening when Volpone refers to his gold as "my saint" in the shrine. The answer is (D).

44. **(D)**   Volpone obviously puts all the human attributes of joy far below the love of gold, and believes the rest of the world including the "wise poets" do the same. He has sacrificed humaneness for his gold because for him the joy in his treasures transcends all other joy found on earth (D).

45. **(C)**   The key here is to ponder over the use of the word "Hoof." His Honour, the Master behaves like a human being but has a hoof... so the human words cannot provide the answer...as the pronoun used is masculine the answer cannot be a mare but a horse (C)!

46. **(C)**   The narrator puts himself in the category of travellers receiving favors and as he has written about his exploits the answer is (C).

47. **(B)**   Of course he is making up the story but that is not the narrator's interpretation of the censure. Travellers did not lie about the way they treated *inferiors*...the answer is clearly (B).

48. **(A)** We do not have enough to go on to determine if the narrator is reliable (although we are skeptical of him talking to horses). We do not censure tall tales, we tend to enjoy them. What we do censure is a human being prostrating himself before an animal, behaving in an overly flattering way (A).

49. **(B)** A man who prostrates himself before a horse and then is overwhelmed by the "honour" of the horse raising his hoof to be kissed is not supercilious, nor vain, nor equal. He is certainly not demanding. He is humble and puts himself down in this company...the answer is (B).

50. **(B)** The overwhelming feeling here is the regret at leaving his Honour (B). He is going *to* the islands; his frustration at waiting is very controlled; he never mentions the beauty of the place...the answer can be found through elimination of the facts.

51. **(A)** The illustrious person is still his Honour but as this option is not here, look for a class in which to place "his Honour the horse." The concluding sentence gives you that class as an answer to the detractors who might censure the narrator. The answer then is (A).

52. **(C)** Because of the love expressed for his Honour, the ideas of slavery or satire do not fit here. The narrator has not worked for the Houyhnhnms but respects the Master who does not express here unwillingness at letting him go. The answer then is (C).

53. **(D)** If you have truly grasped the notion of the piece that a human being loves, respects, worships *a horse* the answer is clearly that he will choose to sleep in his stables with his horses (D). Through a process of elimination, there is no mention of love of sea, or fresh air or the life of a sailor.

54. **(B)** The narrator, Vandover, does behave like a dog at times, the last image for example, but he himself says he is more like a wolf...lycanthropy is the delusion when one believes one is a wolf (B). Misanthropy, of course, hatred of humankind; senility the deterioration with old age; Vandover certainly has no delusions of grandeur.

55. **(D)** By reading carefully you gather Vandover's downfall from what

he says. He did have money; he did have a job but no longer has it; the detail of how things go around and seem far off suggest extreme hunger. The answer is (D).

56. **(E)** Once you have grasped the fact of the lycanthropy all the details of the brute become clearer. None of the first three options is viable. The brute is not trying to get out — witness Vandover's passivity — but is there nevertheless, first heard in the guttural nature of words from the throat not the mouth (E).

57. **(C)** Because of the hunger and "brutedom," Vandover is not expressing himself coherently or sequentially. He darts from one subject to the next. Trace back what possibly might be at the end of the hall. "It" then logically refers back to his lodging-place, interpreted here as an apartment (C).

58. **(E)** A change from first person pronoun to third should always signal a distancing. He mentions the devil in connection with his voice but to say the devil is in him is too strong. The brute is not integrated yet but still developing. The butcher's dog is not even mentioned, only the butcher's paper which would have a taste of meat to satisfy the "brute." Charlie at this point is simply listening to Vandover. The answer is (E).

59. **(C)** Mentally, Vandover rounds off his bonds into an even number of dollars which then return to haunt him. The money was not just "lost" but gambled away — herein lies the problem (C).

60. **(C)** Here is the final acknowledgement that the brute is taking over...not the wolf as in the wild werewolf but the animal who sleeps away his day in the sun (C).

Literature

TEST 6

Literature

TEST 6

1. Ⓐ Ⓑ Ⓒ Ⓓ Ⓔ
2. Ⓐ Ⓑ Ⓒ Ⓓ Ⓔ
3. Ⓐ Ⓑ Ⓒ Ⓓ Ⓔ
4. Ⓐ Ⓑ Ⓒ Ⓓ Ⓔ
5. Ⓐ Ⓑ Ⓒ Ⓓ Ⓔ
6. Ⓐ Ⓑ Ⓒ Ⓓ Ⓔ
7. Ⓐ Ⓑ Ⓒ Ⓓ Ⓔ
8. Ⓐ Ⓑ Ⓒ Ⓓ Ⓔ
9. Ⓐ Ⓑ Ⓒ Ⓓ Ⓔ
10. Ⓐ Ⓑ Ⓒ Ⓓ Ⓔ
11. Ⓐ Ⓑ Ⓒ Ⓓ Ⓔ
12. Ⓐ Ⓑ Ⓒ Ⓓ Ⓔ
13. Ⓐ Ⓑ Ⓒ Ⓓ Ⓔ
14. Ⓐ Ⓑ Ⓒ Ⓓ Ⓔ
15. Ⓐ Ⓑ Ⓒ Ⓓ Ⓔ
16. Ⓐ Ⓑ Ⓒ Ⓓ Ⓔ
17. Ⓐ Ⓑ Ⓒ Ⓓ Ⓔ
18. Ⓐ Ⓑ Ⓒ Ⓓ Ⓔ
19. Ⓐ Ⓑ Ⓒ Ⓓ Ⓔ
20. Ⓐ Ⓑ Ⓒ Ⓓ Ⓔ

21. Ⓐ Ⓑ Ⓒ Ⓓ Ⓔ
22. Ⓐ Ⓑ Ⓒ Ⓓ Ⓔ
23. Ⓐ Ⓑ Ⓒ Ⓓ Ⓔ
24. Ⓐ Ⓑ Ⓒ Ⓓ Ⓔ
25. Ⓐ Ⓑ Ⓒ Ⓓ Ⓔ
26. Ⓐ Ⓑ Ⓒ Ⓓ Ⓔ
27. Ⓐ Ⓑ Ⓒ Ⓓ Ⓔ
28. Ⓐ Ⓑ Ⓒ Ⓓ Ⓔ
29. Ⓐ Ⓑ Ⓒ Ⓓ Ⓔ
30. Ⓐ Ⓑ Ⓒ Ⓓ Ⓔ
31. Ⓐ Ⓑ Ⓒ Ⓓ Ⓔ
32. Ⓐ Ⓑ Ⓒ Ⓓ Ⓔ
33. Ⓐ Ⓑ Ⓒ Ⓓ Ⓔ
34. Ⓐ Ⓑ Ⓒ Ⓓ Ⓔ
35. Ⓐ Ⓑ Ⓒ Ⓓ Ⓔ
36. Ⓐ Ⓑ Ⓒ Ⓓ Ⓔ
37. Ⓐ Ⓑ Ⓒ Ⓓ Ⓔ
38. Ⓐ Ⓑ Ⓒ Ⓓ Ⓔ
39. Ⓐ Ⓑ Ⓒ Ⓓ Ⓔ
40. Ⓐ Ⓑ Ⓒ Ⓓ Ⓔ

41. Ⓐ Ⓑ Ⓒ Ⓓ Ⓔ
42. Ⓐ Ⓑ Ⓒ Ⓓ Ⓔ
43. Ⓐ Ⓑ Ⓒ Ⓓ Ⓔ
44. Ⓐ Ⓑ Ⓒ Ⓓ Ⓔ
45. Ⓐ Ⓑ Ⓒ Ⓓ Ⓔ
46. Ⓐ Ⓑ Ⓒ Ⓓ Ⓔ
47. Ⓐ Ⓑ Ⓒ Ⓓ Ⓔ
48. Ⓐ Ⓑ Ⓒ Ⓓ Ⓔ
49. Ⓐ Ⓑ Ⓒ Ⓓ Ⓔ
50. Ⓐ Ⓑ Ⓒ Ⓓ Ⓔ
51. Ⓐ Ⓑ Ⓒ Ⓓ Ⓔ
52. Ⓐ Ⓑ Ⓒ Ⓓ Ⓔ
53. Ⓐ Ⓑ Ⓒ Ⓓ Ⓔ
54. Ⓐ Ⓑ Ⓒ Ⓓ Ⓔ
55. Ⓐ Ⓑ Ⓒ Ⓓ Ⓔ
56. Ⓐ Ⓑ Ⓒ Ⓓ Ⓔ
57. Ⓐ Ⓑ Ⓒ Ⓓ Ⓔ
58. Ⓐ Ⓑ Ⓒ Ⓓ Ⓔ
59. Ⓐ Ⓑ Ⓒ Ⓓ Ⓔ
60. Ⓐ Ⓑ Ⓒ Ⓓ Ⓔ

LITERATURE

TEST 6

TIME: 60 Minutes
60 Questions

DIRECTIONS: *This test consists of selections from literary works and questions on their content, form, and style. After reading each passage or poem, choose the best answer to each question and blacken the corresponding space on the answer sheet.*

NOTE: Pay particular attention to the requirement of questions that contain the words NOT, LEAST, or EXCEPT.

<u>**QUESTIONS 1–6**</u> are based on the following poem. Read the poem carefully before choosing your answers.

The Prologue

1

To sing of wars, of captains, and of kings,
Of cities founded, commonwealths begun,
For my mean pen are too superior things;
Or how they all, or each, their dates have run;
5   Let poets and historians set these forth;
My obscure lines shall not so dim their worth.

2

But when my wond'ring eyes and envious heart
Great Bartas' sugared lines do but read o'er,

Fool, I do grudge the muses did not part
10   'Twixt him and me that overfluent store.
A Bartas can do what a Bartas will;
But simple I according to my skill.

3

From schoolboy's tongue no rhet'ric we expect,
Nor yet a sweet consort from broken strings,
15   Nor perfect beauty where's a main defect.
My foolish, broken, blemished Muse so sings;
And this to mend, alas, no art is able,
'Cause nature made it so irreparable.

4

Nor can I, like that fluent, sweet-tongued Greek
20   Who lisped at first, in future times speak plain.
By art he gladly found what he did seek;
A full requital of his striving pain.
Art can do much, but this maxim's most sure:
A weak or wounded brain admits no cure.

5

25   I am obnoxious to each carping tongue
Who says my hand a needle better fits;
A poet's pen all scorn I should thus wrong,
For such despite they cast on female wits.
If what I do prove well, it won't advance;
30   They'll say it's stol'n, or else it was by chance.

"The Prologue," by Anne Bradstreet

1.   From the context the word "mean" (line 3) can be interpreted as

  (A) judgmental   (D) unknown

  (B) unimportant   (E) angry

  (C) aged

2.   The best paraphrase of stanza one is

(A) the author is not interested in writing about ancient things

(B) the author thinks that wars, captains, kings, and dates are not worthy topics for poets

(C) events and people in history make superior subjects for poetic contemplation

(D) many little-known poets have chosen to write about significant events from the past

(E) the author feels unable to use important past events as subjects for verse

3. Which of the following is descriptive of the author's feelings toward the poet Bartas?

(A) The author aspires to imitate Bartas' poetic imagination.

(B) The author feels Bartas had more freedom to express himself openly.

(C) Reading Bartas' poetry engenders feelings of inadequacy in the writer.

(D) The author thinks Bartas' poetry is suitable for casual reading.

(E) Bartas' poetry is overly flowery and sweet.

4. Which of the following is NOT a contrast found in the poem?

(A) "Bartas' sugared lines" (line 8) and "that overfluent store" (line 10)

(B) "schoolboy's tongue" and "rhet'ric" (line 13)

(C) "sweet consort" and "broken strings" (line 14)

(D) "perfect beauty" and "main defect" (line 15)

(E) "Muse so sings" (line 16) and "this to mend" (line 17)

5. What is the best meaning of stanza 4?

(A) The author feels she, like the Greek poet, will find peace through poetry.

(B) Through his writing, the Greek poet found an outlet for his suffering.

(C) The early poetry of the Greek author was weaker than his later efforts.

(D) If she continues to write, the author's poetry will become better.

(E) The Greek poet, though unable to speak correctly, wrote beautiful poetry.

6. Which stanza does NOT close with a comment on the author's failings as a poet?

(A) stanza 1

(B) stanza 2

(C) stanza 3

(D) stanza 4

(E) stanza 5

7. Which of the following is an observation the author makes about her own writing?

I. She will never be a good writer because men will not give her the opportunity.

II. She will never be a good writer because she lacks the inspiration and noble subjects of her predecessors.

III. She will never be a good writer because she lacks the skill.

IV. She will never be a good writer because she does not have adequate knowledge of poetic forms.

(A) I only

(B) III only

(C) I and II only

(D) III and IV only

(E) I, II, III, and IV

8. As used in the poem, the word "it" (line 30) refers to

(A) "I am obnoxious" (line 25)

(B) "each carping tongue" (line 25)

(C) "my hand a needle better fits" (line 26)

(D) "despite they cast on female wits" (line 28)

(E) "what I do prove well" (line 29)

9. What is the main criticism expressed by men of the poet's time?

   (A) Any good poetry produced by the poet is stolen or an accident.

   (B) Just as there were no good female Greek poets, so there cannot be good contemporary female poets.

   (C) Women should be used as inspiration for poetry.

   (D) Women carp too much to pay attention to the finer details of good poetry.

   (E) The poet should stick to her needlework.

10. The attitude the author displays is one of

   (A) overwhelming despair   (D) fierce anger

   (B) bitter irony   (E) subtle satire

   (C) gentle complaint

QUESTIONS 11–20 are based on the following poem. Read the poem carefully before choosing your answers.

> How many paltry, foolish, painted things,
> That now in coaches trouble every street,
> Shall be forgotten, whom no poet sings,
> Ere they be well wrapped in their winding sheet?
> 5 Where I to thee eternity shall give
> When nothing else remaineth of these days,
> And queens hereafter shall be glad to live
> Upon the alms of thy superfluous praise.
> Virgins and matrons, reading these my rhymes,
> 10 Shall be so much delighted with thy story
> That they shall grieve they lived not in these times
> To have seen thee, their sex's only glory;
> So shalt thou fly above the vulgar throng,
> Still to survive in my immortal song.

by Michael Drayton.

11. According to the context of the poem, what is the best meaning of "well wrapped" (line 4)?

    I.   They will be securely wrapped.

    II.   They will be cared for properly.

    III. They will be better off wrapped.

    (A) I only   (D) I and III only

    (B) II only   (E) I and II only

    (C) III only

12. Which phrase does NOT directly contribute to the tone of the first four lines?

    (A) "paltry, foolish, painted things" (line 1)

    (B) "now in coaches" (line 2)

    (C) "trouble every street" (line 2)

    (D) "whom no poet sings" (line 3)

    (E) "they be well wrapped" (line 4)

13. What is the subject of the first four lines?

    (A) fancy coaches   (D) fearsome death

    (B) inferior women   (E) short memories

    (C) false poets

14. According to the context of the poem, what is the best definition of "winding sheet"?

    (A) curtains

    (B) bed covers

    (C) lies told to hide misdeeds

    (D) delusions of the rich

    (E) wrapping for a dead body

15. What is the best paraphrase of lines 5–6?

    (A) The poet will live forever.

    (B) The poet will give his sweetheart gifts forever.

    (C) The poet will immortalize his sweetheart.

    (D) The poet will look back on these days as the best he has known.

    (E) The poet knows that time is fleeting.

16. All of the following provide contrast to the poet's sweetheart EX-CEPT

    (A) "painted things" (line 1)

    (B) "queens" (line 7)

    (C) "virgins and matrons" (line 9)

    (D) "their sex's only glory" (line 12)

    (E) "the vulgar throng" (line 13)

17. All of the following refer to the verse of the poet EXCEPT

    (A) "every street" (line 2)

    (B) "eternity" (line 5)

    (C) "alms" (line 8)

    (D) "thy story" (line 10)

    (E) "immortal song" (line 14)

18. According to the context of the poem, what is the best meaning of "vulgar" (line 13)?

    (A) common   (D) obscene

    (B) cruel   (E) tawdry

    (C) boring

19. What does the poet say will be the attitude of other women?

    (A) They will wish for a poet to sing their praises.

    (B) They will wish to see the poet's sweetheart.

(C) They will hope to improve themselves according to her example.

(D) They will be grateful not to feel in competition with such a famous beauty.

(E) They will be duly impressed with her because she is the object of such praise.

20. Which of the following best describes the author's approach and attitude toward his subject?

(A) ordinary amusement   (D) gentle satire

(B) direct appreciation   (E) artful sentimentality

(C) mild self-deprecation

QUESTIONS 21–28 are based on the following passage. Read the passage carefully before choosing your answers.

As time went by our need to fight for the ideal increased to an unquestioning possession, riding with spur and rein over our doubts. Willy-nilly it became a faith. We had sold ourselves into its slavery, manacled ourselves together in its chain-gang, bowed ourselves to
5   serve its holiness with all our good and ill content. The mentality of ordinary human slaves is terrible — they have lost the world — and we had surrendered, not body alone, but soul to the overmastering greed of victory. By our own act we were drained of morality, of volition, of responsibility, like dead leaves in the wind.
10   The everlasting battle stripped from us care of our own lives or of others'. We had ropes about our necks, and on our heads prices which showed that the enemy intended hideous tortures for us if we were caught. Each day some of us passed; and the living knew themselves just sentient puppets on God's stage: indeed, our task-
15   master was merciless, merciless, so long as our bruised feet could stagger forward on the road. The weak envied those tired enough to die; for success looked so remote, and failure a near and certain, if sharp, release from toil. We lived always in the stretch or sag of nerves, either on the crest or in the trough of waves of feeling. This
20   impotency was bitter to us, and made us live only for the seen horizon, reckless what spite we inflicted or endured, since physical sensation showed itself meanly transient. Gusts of cruelty, perver-

sions, lusts ran lightly over the surface without troubling us; for the
moral laws which had seemed to hedge about these silly accidents
25 must be yet fainter words. We had learned that there were pangs too
sharp, griefs too deep, ecstasies too high for our finite selves to
register. When emotion reached this pitch the mind choked; and
memory went white till circumstances were humdrum once more.

Reprinted from The Seven Pillars of Wisdom *by T.E. Lawrence, by permission of*
Doubleday, a division of Bantam, Doubleday, Dell Publishing Group, Inc.

21. The narrator is writing a justification of his exploits as a participant in

    (A) a hanging   (D) slave-trading

    (B) a voyage   (E) a prison camp

    (C) an army

22. This passage is developed primarily by which method?

    (A) reasons   (D) narration

    (B) examples   (E) description

    (C) cause and effect

23. The author of this passage justifies his participation in this venture by

    (A) detailing how he was coerced into it

    (B) showing that he was merely a victim of circumstances

    (C) explaining which methods he used to extricate himself from it

    (D) stressing his devotion to a cause greater than himself

    (E) observing the great rewards he received from being a participant

24. Which is NOT an image which develops the author's perception of his
    own actions?

    (A) "riding with spur and rein" (line 2)

    (B) "manacled ourselves together in its chain-gang" (line 4)

    (C) "puppets on God's stage" (line 14)

(D) "either in the crest or trough of waves of feeling" (line 19)

(E) "reckless what spite we endured or inflicted" (line 21)

25. As used by the narrator, the phrase "meanly" (line 22) can be construed to mean which of the following?

    I.   Halfway between extremes, moderate

    II.   Low in value

    III. Malicious

    IV. Ignoble

    (A) I only   (D) I and II only

    (B) II only   (E) III and IV only

    (C) IV only

26. The passage indicates that the men who accompanied the narrator were

    (A)   stronger than most men

    (B)   weak-minded to be led so easily

    (C)   afraid of being captured

    (D)   innately cruel and perverted

    (E)   grief-stricken at their own actions

27. What explanation does the author give for his swings of emotion?

    (A)   He felt the need to experience the bizarre in order to feed his ever-growing need for new sensations.

    (B)   He was looking for a victory in a battle for ideals that transcended ordinary mortal feelings.

    (C)   He was running as a fugitive from justice and fully expected to be killed if caught.

    (D)   He became morally depraved due to his perception that he was unable to control events.

    (E)   He ceased to appreciate each day's victories and lived only for what might happen in the future.

28. Which of the following best presents the central paradox of the author's argument?

   (A) "Willy-nilly it became a faith." (line 3)

   (B) "The mentality of ordinary human slaves is terrible." (lines 5–6)

   (C) "By our own act we were drained of morality, of volition, of responsibility." (lines 8–9)

   (D) "We lived always in the stretch or sag of nerves." (lines 18–19)

   (E) "When emotions reached this pitch, the mind choked; and the memory went white till the circumstances were humdrum once more." (line 27–28)

QUESTIONS 29–35 are based on the following passage. Read the passage carefully before choosing your answers.

   'Now came the difficulties of our position. I am proud. I say nothing in defence of pride, but I am proud. It is also my character to govern. I can't submit; I must govern. Unfortunately, the property of Madame Rigaud was settled upon herself. Such was the insane act of
5 her late husband. More unfortunately still, she had relations. When a wife's relations interpose against a husband who is a gentleman, who is proud, and who must govern, the consequences are inimical to peace. There was yet another source of difference between us. Madame Rigaud was unfortunately a little vulgar. I sought to im-
10 prove her manners and ameliorate her general tone; she (supported in this likewise by her relations) resented my endeavours. Quarrels began to arise between us; and, propagated and exaggerated by the slanders of the relations of Madame Rigaud, to become notorious to the neighbours. It has been said that I treated Madame Rigaud with
15 cruelty. I may have been seen to slap her face — nothing more. I have a light hand; and if I have been seen apparently to correct Madame Rigaud in that manner, I have done it almost playfully.'

   by Charles Dickens.

29. The most probable motive Monsieur Rigaud had in marrying Madame Rigaud was that he

(A)   hoped to improve her manners

(B)   desired a mate as playful as he was

(C)   was attracted to the wealth she had inherited

(D)   greatly admired her late husband

(E)   wanted to marry a refined lady

30.   The chief source of difficulties between the husband and his wife was the

(A)   will of Madame Rigaud's late husband

(B)   slight vulgarity of Madame Rigaud

(C)   nature of Monsieur Rigaud to be in charge

(D)   slanders of the relations

(E)   interposition of the relations

31.   What is the best analysis of Monsieur Rigaud's personality?

(A)   avaricious   (D)   genteel

(B)   domineering   (E)   cruel

(C)   obsequious

32.   Madame Riguad can best be described as

(A)   vulgar and lacking in polite social graces

(B)   quarrelsome and shrewish even in public

(C)   submissive and meek except when goaded by her relatives

(D)   abused and struggling to maintain her dignity

(E)   notorious and disloyal to her husband

33.   Who was most at fault in exacerbating the problems between the two married people?

(A)   the late husband   (D)   the relatives

(B)   Madame Riguad   (E)   Monsieur Rigaud

(C)   the neighbors

34. Why did Madame Riguad's relations interfere in her marriage?

    I.   To protect her financial status

    II.   To protect her from physical abuse

    III. To protect the family's good name

    (A) I only   (D) I and III only

    (B) II only   (E) I, II, and III

    (C) I and II only

35. The tone of this passage is best described as

    (A) argumentative   (D) contemptuous

    (B) ironic   (E) pragmatic

    (C) defensive

QUESTIONS 36–41 are based on the following passage. Read the passage carefully before choosing your answers.

Their encreasing passion quite terrified us; and Mrs. Mirvan was beginning to remonstrate with the Captain, when we were all silenced by what follows.

'Let me go, villain that you are, let me go, or I'll promise you I'll
5 get you put to prison for this usage; I'm no common person, I assure you, and, *ma foi*, I'll go to Justice Fielding about you; for I'm a person of fashion, and I'll make you know it, or my name i' n't Duval.'

I heard no more: amazed, frightened, and unspeakably shocked,
10 an involuntary exclamation of *Gracious Heaven*! escaped me, and, more dead than alive, I sunk into Mrs. Mirvan's arms. But let me draw a veil over a scene too cruel for a heart so compassionately tender as yours; it is sufficient that you know this supposed foreigner proved to be Madame Duval, — the grandmother of your Evelina!
15 O, Sir, to discover so near a relation in a woman who had thus introduced herself! — what would become of me, were it not for you, my protector, my friend, and my refuge?

My extreme concern, and Mrs. Mirvan's surprise, immediately betrayed me. But I will not shock you with the manner of her
20 acknowledging me, or the bitterness, the *grossness* — I cannot

otherwise express myself, — with which she spoke of those un-
happy past transactions you have so pathetically related to me. All
the misery of a much-injured parent, dear, though never seen, regret-
ted, though never known, crowded so forcibly upon my memory,
25 that they rendered this interview — one only excepted — the most
afflicting I can ever know.

When we stopt at her lodgings, she desired me to accompany her
into the house, and said she could easily procure a room for me to
sleep in. Alarmed and trembling, I turned to Mrs. Mirvan, 'My
30 daughter, Madam,' said that sweet woman, 'cannot so abruptly part
with her young friend; you must allow a little time to wean them
from each other.'

'Pardon me, Ma'am,' answered Madame Duval, (who, from the
time of her being known somewhat softened her manners) 'Miss
35 can't possibly be so nearly connected to this child as I am.'

by Fanny Burney.

36. Which is the best evaluation of Evelina's personality?

   (A) She is as refined as her grandmother.

   (B) She is ladylike but has occasional lapses.

   (C) She is rude in her private life but restrained in public.

   (D) She is timid as a result of being reared in a sheltered environ-
        ment.

   (E) She is slow to understand what is expected of her in new situ-
        ations.

37. Mrs. Duval's threat of sending the Captain to prison is

   (A) justified, given the Captain's behavior

   (B) unjustified, as the Captain is obviously teasing

   (C) a sign to the others that they should interfere in the escalating
        hostilities

   (D) something that undermines her protests of not being a common
        person

   (E) absurd because she is only making an idle threat

38. To whom is Evelina probably writing?

   (A) Mrs. Mirvan's son

   (B) her grandfather

   (C) her guardian

   (D) the father of her closest friend

   (E) her own father

39. What piece of information suggests that the meeting between Madame Duval and the others had been planned?

   (A) the shocking grossness with which her grandmother speaks of the past

   (B) Madame Duval's failure to be surprised at discovering her granddaughter

   (C) Madame Duval's already having lodgings and being easily able to procure a room for Evelina

   (D) Mrs. Mirvan's plea to let Evelina spend one more night with the Mirvans'

   (E) the Captain's not being able to apologize gracefully for his rudeness

40. Evelina's reaction to meeting Madame Duval makes it clear that

   (A) Evelina has known of Madame Duval's existence but has not cared to seek her out

   (B) Madame Duval has merely pretended to be a foreigner

   (C) this scene is the worst one Evelina has ever endured

   (D) Evelina is prepared to love her newly-found relative

   (E) everyone involved would have been better off if the meeting had never taken place

41. Which of the following best characterizes Madame Duval's behavior?

   (A) It is admirable because she is frank and open

   (B) It is honest but a bit intimidating to weaker personalities

(C)   It reveals little of her true nature

(D)   It betrays her inner coarseness and insensitivity

(E)   It shows that her suffering has driven her into bitterness

QUESTIONS 42–51 are based on the following poem. Read the poem carefully before choosing your answers.

The Lovers of the Poor
arrive. The Ladies from the Ladies' Betterment
League
Arrive in the afternoon, the late light slanting
In diluted gold bars across the boulevard brag
5   Of proud, seamed faces with mercy and murder hinting
Here, there, interrupting, all deep and debonair,
The pink paint on the innocence of fear;
Walk in a gingerly manner up the hall.
Cutting with knives served by their softest care,
10 Served by their love, so barbarously fair.
Whose mothers taught: You'd better not be cruel!
You had better not throw stones upon the wrens!
Herein they kiss and coddle and assault
Anew and dearly in the innocence
15 With which they baffle nature. Who are full,
Sleek, tender-clad, fit, fiftyish, a-glow, all
Sweetly abortive, hinting at fat fruit,
Judge it high time that fiftyish fingers felt
Beneath the lovelier planes on enterprise.
20 To resurtect. To moisten with milky chill.
To be a random hitching-post or plush.
To be, for wet eyes, random and handy hem.
Their guild is giving money to the poor.

"The Lovers of the Poor," by Gwendolyn Brooks.

42.   Which of the following does NOT indicate the wealth of the ladies from the Ladies' Betterment League?

(A) "the late light slanting/In diluted gold bars" (lines 3–4)

(B) "Of proud, seamed faces with mercy and murder hinting/Here, there" (lines 5–6)

(C) "Sleek, tender-clad, fit" (line 16)

(D) "hinting at fat fruit" (line 17)

(E) "high time that fiftyish fingers felt/Beneath the lovelier planes of enterprise" (lines 18–19)

43. What does the phrase "pink paint" (line 7) reveal about the ladies from the Ladies' Betterment League?

    I.   They are flushed with embarrassment.

    II. They are afraid of being harmed.

    III. They are not showing their true feelings.

    (A) I only   (D) II and III only

    (B) II only   (E) I, II, and III

    (C) III only

44. The paradox of "mercy and murder" (line 5) can be best understood as which of the following?

    (A) The ladies must be cruel in order to be kind.

    (B) The ladies are afraid of being murdered in spite of their charity.

    (C) The ladies' lack of honesty in their kindness is cruel.

    (D) The ladies make kind remarks while not giving very much to the poor they have come to serve.

    (E) The ladies' chill reserve is cruel.

45. The narrator's tone can be identified as one of

    (A) self-serving pity

    (B) patronizing understanding

    (C) bitter derision

    (D) incredulous disappointment

    (E) shocked amusement

46. Which of the following pairs of words or phrases does NOT illustrate the contrast of intention and reality of the ladies' actions?

   (A) "deep" and "debonair" (line 6)

   (B) "barbarously" and "fair" (line 10)

   (C) "coddle" and "assault" (line 13)

   (D) "Anew" and "dearly" (line 14)

   (E) "Sweetly" and "abortive" (line 16)

47. The people the ladies have come to help are metaphorically compared to which of the following?

   (A) "boulevard" (line 4)

   (B) "knives" (line 9)

   (C) "stones" (line 12)

   (D) "wrens" (line 12)

   (E) "fruit" (line 17)

48. What is significant about the age of the ladies?

   (A) Women that old have no business traipsing about town in late afternoon.

   (B) Before that age, women are not mature enough to deal with such a different lifestyle.

   (C) At that age, women have accumulated enough wealth to be able to help others.

   (D) The women are ashamed of themselves for not having become concerned sooner in their lives.

   (E) The women should have been concerned with the plight of others long before that age.

49. What is the best interpretation of the title, "Ladies' Betterment League"?

   (A) The ladies in the league primarily wish to feel better about themselves.

   (B) The ladies in the league wish they could improve the hopeless conditions they see.

(C) The ladies of the league have decided to stop the encroachment of the poor neighborhood.

(D) The ladies of the league would help if they could receive cooperation from the poor.

(E) The ladies of the league would like to improve the plight of women in the poor neighborhood.

50. The meaning of the word "random" in line 21 is best understood as which of the following?

    I. the ladies' periodic inspections of their work to make sure nothing goes astray

    II. the picture the ladies have in their minds of themselves helping a deserving, grateful person or two

    III. the inability of anyone to achieve an organized plan of action for assistance

    (A) I only   (D) I and II only

    (B) II only   (E) II and III only

    (C) III only

51. According to the narrator, what do the ladies consider to be their own motive in coming to the poor neighborhood?

    (A) to give money to the poor

    (B) to assuage their own guilt about their wealth

    (C) to lift others out of their poverty and despair

    (D) to make things along the boulevard more colorful

    (E) to be as fair to all involved as possible

QUESTIONS 52–60 are based on the following passage. Read the passage carefully before choosing your answers.

He entered the tavern, and was guided by the murmer of voices and the fumes of tobacco to the public-room. It was a long and low apartment, with oaken walls, grown dark in the continual smoke, and a floor which was thickly sanded, but of no immaculate purity.

263

5 A number of persons — the larger part of whom appeared to be mariners, or in some way connected with the sea — occupied the wooden benches, or leather-bottomed chairs, conversing on various matters, and occasionally lending their attention to some topic of general interest. Three or four little groups were draining as many

10 bowls of punch, which the West India trade had long since made a familiar drink in the colony. Others, who had the appearance of men who lived by regular and laborious handicraft, preferred the insulated bliss of an unshared potation, and became more taciturn under its influence. Nearly all, in short, evinced a predilection for the Good

15 Creature in some of its various shapes, for this is a vice to which, as Fast Day sermons of a hundred years ago will testify, we have a long hereditary claim. The only guests to whom Robin's sympathies inclined him were two or three sheepish countrymen, who were using the inn somewhat after the fashion of a Turkish caravansary;

20 they had gotten themselves into the darkest corner of the room, and heedless of the Nicotian atmosphere, were supping on the bread of their own ovens, and the bacon cured in their own chimney-smoke. But though Robin felt a sort of brotherhood with these strangers, his eyes were attracted from them to a person who stood near the door,

25 holding whispered conversation with a group of ill-dressed associates. His features were separately striking almost to grotesqueness, and the whole face left a deep impression on the memory.

"My Kinsman Major Molineaux," by Nathaniel Hawthorne.

52. The best description of the tavern would be

 (A) quite a popular place for couples to meet

 (B) old but comfortable

 (C) dark and somewhat dirty

 (D) a meeting place for travelers

 (E) a place where Robin would want to rent a room

53. According to the context, we can conclude that "Nicotian" (line 21) means pertaining to

 (A) a Turkish bath

 (B) filled with smoke

(C) gloom and darkness

(D) talkative cheerfulness

(E) frugality born from poverty

54. Of all the people in the room, Robin would be most inclined to strike up a conversation with the

(A) tavern-keeper

(B) mariners

(C) day laborers

(D) countrymen

(E) person standing near the door

55. From all indications, which of the following is probably true of the men eating their home-cooked food?

I. They are from the countryside.

II. They are uncomfortable being in the tavern.

III. They are resented by the rest of the men in the tavern.

(A) I only   (D) I and II only

(B) II only   (E) II and III only

(C) III only

56. What is the main recreation of the men in the room?

(A) sitting by the chimney and watching the fire

(B) dozing quietly

(C) observing the other people

(D) discussing topics of general interest

(E) smoking and drinking bowls of punch

57. What is the drink in the bowls of punch?

(A) rum   (D) beer

(B) Scotch   (E) ale

(C) wine

58. Taken in context of the passage, the best interpretation of "Nearly all, in short, evinced a prediliction for the Good Creature" (lines 14–15) is that nearly all the

    (A) mariners looked as if they might be pirates

    (B) mariners are celebrating a successful voyage to the West Indies

    (C) people in the tavern are drinking an alcoholic beverage

    (D) people in the tavern had been reformed by turning to religion

    (E) men in the tavern were known for seeking out the enjoyable things of life

59. To what does the author say "we have a long hereditary claim" (lines 16–17)?

    (A) seafaring   (D) gossiping

    (B) drinking   (E) fasting

    (C) smoking

60. Which of these is the location for the tavern described in this passage?

    (A) West India   (D) Cuba

    (B) British Isles   (E) United States

    (C) Turkey

TEST 6

ANSWER KEY

1.	(B)	16.	(D)	31.	(A)	46.	(A)
2.	(E)	17.	(A)	32.	(D)	47.	(D)
3.	(C)	18.	(A)	33.	(E)	48.	(E)
4.	(A)	19.	(E)	34.	(E)	49.	(A)
5.	(C)	20.	(E)	35.	(B)	50.	(B)
6.	(E)	21.	(C)	36.	(D)	51.	(C)
7.	(B)	22.	(A)	37.	(D)	52.	(C)
8.	(E)	23.	(D)	38.	(C)	53.	(B)
9.	(A)	24.	(E)	39.	(B)	54.	(D)
10.	(C)	25.	(B)	40.	(A)	55.	(D)
11.	(D)	26.	(A)	41.	(D)	56.	(E)
12.	(B)	27.	(B)	42.	(B)	57.	(A)
13.	(B)	28.	(C)	43.	(D)	58.	(C)
14.	(E)	29.	(C)	44.	(C)	59.	(B)
15.	(C)	30.	(A)	45.	(C)	60.	(E)

DETAILED EXPLANATIONS
OF ANSWERS

TEST 6

1. **(B)** The word "mean" is in contrast to "superior" in line 3; the opposite of superior is inferior or unimportant. Although the subjects of the poetry are historical events or figures, "aged" (C) does not modify the author's pen. The author is making a judgment, but "judgmental" (A) or "angry" (E) is not the intended meaning. The author's lines of verse are "obscure" (line 6) or unknown (D), not the pen that produces them.

2. **(E)** The meaning of the first stanza is that poems about wars, leaders, and beginnings of cities are better left to better writers. Choice (C) is certainly true, but not the main thrust of meaning for the stanza. Choice (B) is directly contradicted by the phrase "superior things" (line 3). There is no mention of little-known poets (D), nor does the poet indicate disinterest (A) in historical subjects.

3. **(C)** There is no evidence of Bartas' poetry being suitable for casual reading (D); indeed, the reverse can be inferred from the formality of the verse, the topics for "great" verse, and the allusions in the poem. The reverse is also true of choice (E) because Bartas' skill at creating "sugared lines" is envied by the author. The poet grudges the muses did not give her a larger portion of the poetic talent allocated to Bartas, and she calls her skill "simple." Choice (A) is therefore contradicted. It is likely that the poet Bartas had greater freedom to express himself openly (B), but that is an issue not addressed in this stanza.

4. **(A)** Both items listed in choice (A) refer to the same thing—Bartas' beautiful poems and his talent in poetry. All other choices contrast the author's inadequacies with the abilities or products of better writers. The author contrasts her childish verse with rhetoric (polished language) in choice (B); her "broken strings" will not produce beautiful music ("sweet consort") in choice (C); her defect prohibits "perfect beauty" in choice (D);

and her Muse of poetry is "foolish, broken, blemished" (line 16) so that nothing can "mend" it in choice (E).

5.   **(C)**   The Greek poet "spoke" through his verse, so choice (E) is not the correct choice. At first the Greek poet "lisped" or had trouble "speaking plainly," but in later times he spoke "plain"; the logical conclusion is that the author considers the Greek's later poetry better and worth "his striving pain" (line 22). The phrase "striving pain" does not necessarily mean suffering (B). Because the poet views her abilities as weak, she is not saying her poetry will become better (D) or peace will be hers (A) as a writer.

6.   **(E)**   Each of the first four stanzas closes with a reference to being a weak writer: "obscure lines" (stanza 1); "simple I" (stanza 2); "irreparable" (stanza 3); "weak or wounded brain" (stanza 4). Only stanza 5 closes by giving a male commentary on the good poems produced by the author: the male critics say her good verse is "stol'n" or created "by chance" (line 30).

7.   **(B)**   The poet has obviously created her own opportunity to write poetry, so (A), (C), and (E) can be eliminated. Choices (C) and (E) can also be eliminated because the author lists several subjects inspiring to poets. Twice the poet makes reference to skills or "art" of poetry that "can do much" (line 23), but "no art is able" (line 17) to mend lack of talent portrayed by the "blemished Muse" (line 16) and "weak or wounded brain" (line 24). This line of reasoning eliminates choices (D) and (E).

8.   **(E)**   The last two lines are one sentence. The sentence begins with a subordinate clause, "If what I do prove well." The next three independent clauses contain the pronoun "it," and antecedent of "it" can only be what is in the first part of the sentence: "what I do prove well" (write good poetry).

9.   **(A)**   Men of the author's time say women should stick to their needlework (E). The strongest criticism is, however, contained in the last two lines which say that any good poetry written by the woman poet is "stol'n" or was written "by chance." There is no mention of Greek poets (B) or of inspirations for poetry (C). The carping (D) referred to in this stanza is done not by women but by men complaining about women poets.

10.   **(C)**   The author may despair at not having greater talent (A), but the tone is not one of overwhelming despair. There is no satire of social wrongs

(E), nor is there evidence of a fierce anger (D). The irony (B) of men mistaking good poetry for stolen work or poems created by chance is simply stated and does not appear to be bitter. All the way through the poem the author complains of her lack of talent in a gentle way that betrays the sense of her "place" in society.

11. **(D)** In the first quatrain, the author is describing inferior women who will be forgotten after their death. The phrase "well wrapped" refers to their being securely wrapped for burial; also, the phrase hints that these women will be better off dead as they cannot possibly compete with the woman described later in the poem. There is no indication that anyone cares for these women, alive or dead.

12. **(B)** The first four lines ironically describe women who are not in the least desirable. The expression "painted" (A) literally means the women are wearing make-up, but since it is paired with "paltry, foolish," the women's efforts are made to seem ridiculous and futile. The verb "trouble" (C) indicates that the women should stay at home since they merely clog the streets. No poet (D) thinks the women are worthy of verse, and these ladies would be as well off dead (E) as alive. That the women travel about in coaches (B) is a neutral statement.

13. **(B)** All of these choices are mentioned in the first quatrain. However, the main thrust of the discussion is indicated by the main subject, "things" (line 1), and the verb "shall be forgotten" (line 3), so the subject is inferior women (B). These women ride in coaches (A), have no poet to praise them (C), so memory of them (E) will not last after their death (D).

14. **(E)** A winding sheet is a wrapping for a dead body. This meaning can be inferred from the fact that the women "shall be forgotten" (line 3) who "now in coaches trouble every street" (line 2). Although the women may well be rich, as evidenced by their travel in coaches, they do not appear to be deluded (D) as to their eternal importance. None of the other choices is viable.

15. **(C)** Lines 5-6 can be rephrased as, "When nothing remains of these days, I shall give you eternity." Because the poet does know that time is fleeting (E), he makes the poem so his love will be immortalized (C). These lines do not say he will live forever (A), although his memory certainly has

not died because we still read his verse. There is not any mention of "gifts" (B) other than the one mentioned above. Choice (D) is probably true but not a subject brought up in lines 5-6.

16. **(D)** The poet refers to his love as the female sex's "only glory." All other women are inferior, "painted things" (A) or "the vulgar throng" (E). Even "queens" (B) and "virgins and matrons" (C) pale in comparison to this woman. Queens will be grateful to live on the leftovers, "the alms" of what they glean from her "superfluous praise" (line 8). Virgins and matrons will sorrow that they did not live in her lifetime so as to be able to see her.

17. **(A)** The poet's verse is an "immortal song" (E) that will make the "story" (D) of his love live for "eternity" (B). Queens will be glad to live on the leftovers, "alms" (C), of the poet's praise of his love. The inferior ladies travel "every street" (A).

18. **(A)** Since the others are so inferior, the lovely woman will "fly above the vulgar throng" (line 13). These other women, by contrast, are common (A) and ordinary. They are probably boring (C) as well, but "common" is the better answer. There is no indication of cruelty (B); indeed, the other women are grateful to have known her or wish they could have known her. The others are not portrayed as obscene (D) or tawdry (E) in any way, even though these two definitions might apply to "vulgar" in another situation or setting.

19. **(E)** Other women are impressed with the beauty of the poet's sweetheart (E). All the other choices might be true under these circumstances, but there is no direct evidence to support them. The subject of the poem surpasses in beauty the others to the extent that they do not even consider themselves in competition (D) with her, nor do they hope to attain that perfection of beauty (C). Accordingly, there is no desire to have a poet of their own (A).

20. **(E)** The author does not appear to be amused (A) at his subject or self-deprecating (C). Possibly, he satirizes the other ladies in the first quatrain (D). His appreciation, rather than direct (B), is more artful than anything else (E). The best description of his approach is artful sentimentality because of the exaggerated contrasts and the lofty language.

21. **(C)** The author is afraid of being captured and hanged (A), but it would be a result of his participation in an army (C) engaged in fighting "for the ideal" (line 1). He views his devotion to this cause as a form of voluntary slavery, not slave-trading (D) or a prison camp (E). Lines 18–19 give the indication of a voyage (B) but are a metaphor.

22. **(A)** Although there is some cause and effect (C) in the passage, the main method of development is reasons (A) to justify his deeds while in the army. There is much abstract metaphor that might seem description (E) or examples (A) but is not based on anything concrete. As there is no movement through time or a story line, narration (D) must be eliminated.

23. **(D)** The author stresses in different ways that he became devoted to a cause greater than himself. He fought for an "ideal" (line 1); he served its "holiness" (line 5). Although he indicates that he surrendered to the cause, he does not indicate he was coerced (A) or that he tried to extricate himself from the battles (C). Instead of being a victim of circumstances (B), the author willingly dedicated his life and fortunes to the cause. Once in the struggle, the author abandoned himself totally to the ideal. Rather than rewards (E), the author paints an emotional portrait of the suffering and often painful extremes of emotions he experienced.

24. **(E)** Choice (E) is the only one listed that is not an image, a verbal picture of something visual. Choice (A) is an image of a horse and rider; choice (B), a chain-gang; choice (C), puppets on a stage; choice (D), a ship on rough waters. All of the first four, then, are things which can be visualized as specific pictures in the mind of the reader.

25. **(B)** All the definitions listed could be viable options for "meanly" in different contexts. In this passage, however, the author intends that physical sensation was low in value (B) because it did not last long. All highs and lows of ecstasy and suffering were fleeting sensations and not to be trusted as the true measure of the men's existence.

26. **(A)** The men involved in the campaign had to be strong (A) in order to endure what they did. One of the fears they endured was the threat of capture and hanging (C), but this fear was not enough to deter the men from their goal. Although they endured "gusts of cruelty, perversions, lusts" (lines 22–23) the author indicates these were to be endured and excused for

the sake of a "success" (line 17) which seemed so remote at times. There is no evidence that the men were innately cruel or perverted (D), nor that they were grief-stricken (E) at their own actions.

27. **(B)** Because he was fighting for an ideal, the author's fears and hopes swung to extremes. Rather than seeking out bizarre experiences (A), the experiences brought about by battle inflicted themselves upon him. Incidents of cruelty and perversion are termed "silly accidents" (line 24), and even though he admits giving up control of his will to the cause, he never admits becoming depraved (D) as a result of giving up his control. There is no evidence to support (C), although as a prisoner he could expect to be executed. He never discusses how he feels about any successes the men might have experienced.

28. **(C)** A paradox represents two opposite but equally true things. The central paradox of the passage is that in choosing to fight the war wholeheartedly, the author gives up a sense of volition and control over his own life. He refers to the fighters in the cause as "dead leaves in the wind" (line 9) something without a life of their own and totally at the mercy of something larger than themselves. All the other statements show how the soldiers felt, and most are contrasts, but they do not express paradox.

29. **(C)** Monsieur Rigaud was undoubtably attracted to the "property" (line 3) her late husband settled upon her. Rigaud calls this the "insane act of her late husband" (lines 4–5), so (D) is hardly likely. Monsieur Rigaud was not desirous of improving his wife's manners nor was he playful (B): he was abusive. The husband's desire to marry into money had no bearing on the "refinements" he says he desired (E).

30. **(A)** The will was designed to protect the widow from fortune hunters such as Monsieur Rigaud. Problems between the husband and wife most certainly stemmed from the woman's refusal to give Rigaud control of all the money, so the chief cause of difficulty was not the husband's "character to govern" (C), but his anger at being thwarted by the will (A). Monsieur Rigaud's assessment of his wife as "a little vulgar" (B) can be credited to her protests and refusal to hand over control of the money. The slanders of the relations (D) doubtless came after their interposition (E) on behalf of Madame Rigaud, attempting to protect her from this man she had married.

31. **(A)** Monsieur Rigaud's dominant trait is his overwhelming greed (A). It is true that he is domineering (B) and cruel (E), but those two traits appear as a side result of his avariciousness. He is never obsequious (C) or genteel (D), although he would make himself out to be the injured party. Obviously, Monsieur Rigaud is an unreliable narrator who is twisting the events to favor himself.

32. **(D)** Madame Rigaud was publically slapped by her husband — it is likely he hit her harder in private. The narrator says, "It has been said that I treated Madame Rigaud with cruelty" (lines 14–15). Doubtless, she was struggling to maintain her dignity and control over her money. It may be that the descriptions listed as choices (A), (B), and (E) were applicable to Madame Rigaud, but it is highly unlikely since they are listed as her faults by her husband. Probably, he used these as excuses to hit her, or these were reactions she had to his demand. There is no evidence of (C).

33. **(E)** Monsieur Rigaud was the one at fault. The late husband (A) was merely protecting his widow, and it is likely to assume the relatives (D) would never have intervened in such a strong manner if the second husband had not been abusive of his wife (B). If there had been no beatings or public quarrels, the neighbors would probably have found something to gossip about, but they can hardly be the biggest problem.

34. **(E)** The two obvious reasons for interfering were to protect Madame Rigaud from physical abuse, as well as to protect the family's good name from becoming an object of scandal and ridicule among the neighbors. As there is no mention of children and as Monsieur Rigaud seems to expect all the money to pass to him, the relatives may also have been fighting to protect the woman's financial status. Monsieur Rigaud apparently has no money of his own, or has squandered any money he may have had. It is therefore logical to assume that with all the money in his control, he would either immediately abandon his wife or he would spend all the money and continue to make her life miserable in other ways. As he appears to be a thoroughly unpleasant and dangerous fellow, his wife would have a terrible existence with no money of her own.

35. **(B)** The tone is definitely ironic (B) as Monsieur Rigaud is an unreliable narrator. Everything he says is suspect as being the opposite of what he means or as being a severe understatement of the true conditions.

Monsieur Rigaud is argumentative (A) and defensive (C), and the reader may well feel contemptuous (D) toward this man who views cruelty in a pragmatic (E) fashion. None of these choices, however, reflect the tone of the passage.

36. **(D)** Evelina is timid and easily shocked. She almost faints at meeting her grandmother in an unexpected manner. Therefore, it can be concluded that Evelina has been reared in a sheltered environment (D). Evelina is unsure of what is expected of her in this new situation (E), but this is not the best evaluation of Evelina's personality. Madame Duval is anything but ladylike, so (A) is not applicable. Evelina is presented as always ladylike in her reactions — her strongest expression is "Gracious Heaven!" — so (C) and (B) can be eliminated.

37. **(D)** Although Mrs. Duval claims not to be "common," the fact that she says it betrays her lack of breeding; a true lady never would feel constrained to declare herself a "person of fashion" (line 7) or threaten to send another to prison for insulting her. The Captain's verbal abuse (A) is insufficient for a threat of prison, even if it is obvious he is not teasing (B). She might or might not be making an idle threat (E), but the chances are that Justice Fielding would take her demands with a grain of salt. The increasing hostilities (C) alarm the others, but only to the extent that Mrs. Mirvan feels constrained "to remonstrate with the Captain" (line 2), not physically interfere, so the conflict has not been terribly serious.

38. **(C)** It is likely Evelina is writing to her guardian. She refers to herself as "your Evelina" (line 14), and addresses the man as "my protector, my friend, and my refuge" (line 17). If Evelina were writing to Mrs. Mirvan's son, she would refer differently to Mrs. Mirvan (A) and probably include a phrase such as "you mother" somewhere in the narrative. Evelina's father (E) and grandfather (B) would be addressed in more familiar, familial terms, and likely some reference to the family connection to Mrs. Duval would be made. The least likely answer is (D), as there is no reference to the "closest friend"; also, Evelina would probably be writing the friend and not the father if this were a viable option.

39. **(B)** The lack of surprise on Madame Duval's part is the most telling piece of evidence for presuming the meeting had been planned. Another clue is the passionate argument she has with a supposed stranger, the

Captain, and the fact that Evelina does not describe or even mention any apology of the Captain's (E) to Madame Duval, an apology certainly due a stranger. It is likely the Captain already despises Madame Duval. As a stranger in town, Madame Duval would certainly have rooms let (C).

40. **(A)** Because Evelina has such a severe reaction to the mention of the woman's name, it is obvious that the girl had known of Madame Duval's existence (A) but had not wanted to seek her out. It is true Madame Duval (B) is a "supposed foreigner" (line 13) but this is not the critical thrust of the scene. This scene may or may not be the worst one Evelina has endured (C) and perhaps everyone would have been better off if it had never taken place (E), but there is no evidence for either of these answers. Evelina thinks her newly-found relative is gross in expression, and the girl refuses to spend the night with her grandmother, so there is evidence to contradict (D).

41. **(D)** Madame Duval is coarse and insensitive (D) to confront her granddaughter in such a fashion. The quarrel with the Captain was not a good beginning to the relationship, but then to attack Evelina's guardian so strongly shows a severe lack of sensitivity. Madame Duval's frankness and openness (A) is suspect because the meeting is probably a planned one prepared to look like an accident. Choice (B) is true — she is intimidating to weaker personalities — but it is not the best interpretation. Madame Duval's true nature is revealed, so choice (C) is inaccurate. There is no evidence to support (E).

42. **(B)** The golden rays of light (A) are symbolic of the fiftyish women (E) just now becoming conscious of their social obligations to poorer people. The ladies have been well tended (D) and have not wanted for anything. That the women spend their days in preserving their bodies and being well dressed instead of working and suffering is indicated by (C). The proud faces (B) could belong to rich or poor women.

43. **(D)** The ladies are "deep and debonair" (line 6), so they are covering their true feelings. The pink paint also covers "the innocence of fear" (line 7). There is no indication in the poem of any embarrassment shown by the Ladies' League members.

44. **(C)** The cruelty of the ladies is in their true lack of feeling for the people they intend to serve. The ladies are prepared to treat the poor as they

would an animal such as the wrens. They are not prepared to distinguish the good from the desperate from the criminal in the poor people they encounter: this "barbarously fair" (line 10) love is cruel because it is so impersonal. Also, because the ladies are out to make themselves feel better about having money, they are convinced it is their "social obligation" to serve those worse off.

45. **(C)** The narrator has nothing but contempt for the ladies of the league. The narrator does not reveal self-serving pity (A) nor patronizing understanding (B). There is disappointment (D) and shock (E) but no amusement. The overriding tone is one of bitter derision for the ladies from the Ladies' Betterment League.

46. **(A)** The intention of the ladies is good, but the reality is that their actions hurt. The ladies intend to be fair, but their fairness is barbarous (B). Their sweetness is abortive to their efforts (E). They coddle but assault anew (C) and (D) in their efforts. Choice (A) shows no contrast as the intentions and feelings of the ladies are deep and smoothed over by a comfortably thick facade.

47. **(D)** The mothers of the ladies taught their daughters to be fair, not to throw stones upon the already "helpless" — the wrens or the poor. The boulevard is where the poor live (A). Knives (B) and stones (C) are used metaphorically by the ladies to injure the poor. Fruit (E) is a metaphor for the ladies of the league.

48. **(E)** The ladies should have had a social consciousness long ago. Age fifty is a bit late for turning "moral." Probably the women have been wealthy all their lives, as evidenced by their dress and sleek bodies, so (C) is not a viable answer. Choice (B) is not a good choice because even children can deal with different lifestyles. There is no evidence the ladies are ashamed of themselves (E), and (A) is never a good excuse for not helping others.

49. **(A)** The ladies wish to feel better about themselves. Their arrival in late afternoon, symbolic of their late start in life in giving charity to others, as well as the description of the ladies as sleek and complacent and cruel shows the true concern is with themselves, not with others. Although highly probable interpretations, there is no evidence of any of choices (C) and (E)

in this selection. Hopeless conditions (B) and lack of cooperation from the poor (D) are not mentioned in this selection.

50. **(B)** The ladies wish "to be a random hitching-post" (line 21), an occasional place for someone to seek help. The also wish to be a "random and handy hem" (line 22) for someone who is crying, "for wet eyes" (line 22). There is no sense of an organized or steady help for the poor, just an occasional visit or commiseration.

51. **(C)** The ladies from the league feel it is high time they did something besides garden club activities: "high time that fiftyish fingers felt/Beneath the lovelier planes of enterprise" (lines 18–19). The people whom the ladies would help would be grateful and improve themselves, so the ladies can view themselves as going "to resurrect" (line 20) some deserving poor. Of course, this resurrection will be done by giving money (A), but the ladies are there themselves, so giving money is not what they see as their primary activity. In helping, the ladies probably intend to be as fair as possible (E) and may wish to improve the appearance of things (E), but these are not mentioned in the poem. The ladies themselves seem unaware of (B), but this is the subconscious motive the author makes clear to the reader.

52. **(C)** The tavern is "long and low"(line 2), "grown dark" (line 3), and has a floor "of no immaculate purity" (line 4). The main impression of the tavern at the outset is that it is dark and dirty (C). One may assume it is old and comfortable (B) by the attitudes of some of the patrons; however, not all the patrons are comfortable because the countrymen are "sheepish" (line 18) and huddled into a dark corner. Travelers do come here (E), but Robin does not seem singularly impressed with the tavern and its occupants as a whole.

53. **(B)** "Nicotian" comes from nicotine (B); the atmosphere of the tavern is filled with "continual smoke" (line 3). It is the smoke that has made the oaken walls grow "dark" (line 3). The travelers use the tavern "after the fashion of a Turkish caravansary" (line 19), a rest stop along the way of their journey, but there is no mention of baths (A). The men are hardly portrayed as cheerful (D) and their financial background (E) is never discussed.

54. **(D)** Most of the guests are men who seem older and rougher (B) and (C), "mariners" (line 6) and "men who lived by regular and laborious handicraft" (11-12). Robin does not feel attracted to these, and the narrator states

that the "two or three sheepish countrymen" (line 18) are the "only guests to whom Robin's sympathies inclined him" (Lines 17–18). The tavern-keeper (A) is not mentioned. Although the man at the door draws Robin's attention, he does not seem that kind of person with whom Robin would feel comfortable striking up a conversation.

55. **(D)** The author states these men are "countrymen" (line 18). That they feel uncomfortable is apparent by their position in the "darkest corner of the room" (line 20), a place where they can hope to escape the notice of anyone else in the tavern. The other men in the tavern are not portrayed as hostile, but mariners and day laborers might not be the gentlest folk in dealing with outsiders, so one can assume the countrymen hope to avoid undue attention.

56. **(E)** The author states that "nearly all" (line 14) are drinking and that the smoke is "continual" (line 3). It is true many of the men are talking (D), but others are become "taciturn" (line 13) under the influence of the drink. There are not any men mentioned as watching the fire (A) or dozing (B). Robin appears to be the only one observing other people (C).

57. **(A)** The men are drinking bowls of rum punch. This is a drink made with liquor "which the West India trade had long since made a familiar drink in the colony" (lines 10–11). This trade of sugar, tobacco, rum, and slaves among America, West Africa, and the West Indies islands should be a familiar reference for students of American history and literature.

58. **(C)** Almost everyone in the tavern is drinking (C) an alcoholic beverage of some kind: "nearly all, in short, shared a prediliction for the Good Creature in some of its various shapes" (lines 14–15). The "Good Creature" is the punch "long since made a familiar drink in the colony" (lines 10–11). Also, some men prefer the "insulated bliss of an unshared potation" (lines 12–13); a "potation" is an alcoholic beverage. The author does not indicate where the mariners might have traveled (B), nor that they look as if they might be pirates (A). That the men have not been reformed by religion is apparent (D) because they are still drinking alcohol. Although it can be assumed the men enjoy drinking, smoking, and talking, these things are not referred to as the "enjoyable things of life" (E).

59. **(B)** "We have a long hereditary claim" (lines 16–17) to the "vice"

(line 15) of drinking. Seafaring (A) is hardly a vice. The men are smoking (C) and talking (D), but the author does not describe these activities as vices. Fasting (E) is associated with religious activities and a partner to alcoholic temperance, something these men are not exhibiting.

60. **(E)** From context, it can be assumed the tavern is set in a colony which trades with the West Indies and which had Fast Day sermons a hundred years before this passage was composed. Since the colony trades with the West Indies, choice (A) can be eliminated, as well as (D) because Cuba was one of the islands in the West Indies group of islands. Turkey (C) is the least probable answer, and (B) can be eliminated because it is not a colony.

LITERATURE INDEX

This index lists all of the literary works mentioned in this book, in both the tests and the reviews, with references to where each work appears. The works are listed alphabetically by author's last name. This index also serves as a list of suggested reading material. By reading these works for both study and pleasure, your knowledge of literature will be expanded as well. The works are listed by page number.

Allen, Woody. "The Kugelmass Episode," 8
Aristotle. *Poetics*, 51
Arnold, Matthew. "Requiescat," 144–45
Asprin, Robert. *Hit or Myth*, 17
Auden, W. H. "Hearing of Harvests Rotting in the Valleys," 38
    "Musee des Beaux Arts," 71
Bacon, Francis. "Of Love," 12
Barrie, J. M. "The Admirable Chrichton," 16
Barth, Roland. "Lost in the Funhouse," 8
Beckett, Samuel. *Waiting for Godot*, 180
Bishop, Elizabeth. "Sestina," 38
Blake, William. "The Chimney Sweeper," 19, 32
    "The Garden of Love," 211–12
    "London," 31
Boccaccio, Giovanni. *The Decameron*, 3
Bolt, Robert. *A Man For All Seasons*, 49, 54–55, 56
Bradstreet, Anne. "The Prologue," 245–46
Brooks, Gwendolyn. "Lovers of the Poor," 260
Burney, Fanny. *Evelina*, 258
Byron, George Gordon, Lord. "Stanzas," 24, 25, 26
Capote, Truman. "A Christmas Memory," 9–10, 11
Charles, Dorthi. "Concrete Cat," 36
Chaucer, Geoffrey. *The Canterbury Tales*, 37, 38
Chopin, Kate. "The Story of an Hour," 8
Coleridge, Samuel Taylor. "The Rime of the Ancient Mariner," 30, 37–38
Dickens, Charles. *Martin Chuzzlewit*, 108, 148–49
Dickinson, Emily. "After Great Pain," 139–40
    "Hope is the thing with Feathers," 185
    "Narrow Fellow in the Grass," 19
Donne, John. "19," 76
    "The Flea," 34
    "For Whom the Bell Doth Toll," 157, 183–84
Douglas, Keith. "Vergissmeinnicht," 111
Drayton, Michael. "How many paltry, foolish, painted things," 249
Eliot, George. *Middlemarch*, 20
Eliot, T. S. "Hamlet and his Problems," 65–66

"Journey of the Magi," 25
Faulkner, William. "A Rose for Emily," 9
Fitzgerald, F. Scott. "The Rich Boy," 101-02
Ginsberg, Allen. "A Supermarket in California," 36
Golding, William. *Lord of the Flies*, 4, 7
Gray, Thomas. "Elegy Written in a Country Churchyard," 38
    "Ode on a Distant Prospect of Eton College," 29–30
Hardy, Thomas. "The Darkling Thrush," 154–55
Hawthorne, Nathaniel. "My Kinsman, Major Molineaux," 264
Heller, Joseph. *Catch-22*, 16–17
Herbert, George. "Easter Wings," 36
Hesse, Hermann. *Siddhartha*, 4
Holinshed, Raphael. *Chronicles*, 54
Hollander, John. "Swan and Shadow," 36
Homer. *The Iliad*, 37
    The Odyssey, 37
Hopkins, Gerard Manley. "The Caged Skylark," 26–27
    "Hurrahing in Harvest," 150
    "Pied Beauty," 33
    "Sprung Rhythm," 26
Hughes, Langston. "Dream Deferred," 187
Ibsen, Henrik. *A Doll's House*, 43
    The Wild Duck, 20
Jennings, Elizabeth. "Happy Families," 20, 21
Jonson, Ben. *Volpone*, 223
Joyce, James. *A Portrait of the Artist as a Young Man*, 38
    "Araby," 9, 11
Keats, John. "Ode to a Grecian Urn," 33
    "Ode to a Nightengale," 30–31
    "Ode to Psyche," 33
    "To Autumn," 20, 34
Koch, Kenneth. "Variations on a Theme by William Carlos Williams," 16
Lawrence, D. H. *The Rainbow*, 220
Lawrence, T. E. *The Seven Pillars of Wisdom*, 252–53
Lee, Harper. *To Kill a Mockingbird*, 5
Malory, Sir Thomas. "Morte d'Arthur," 3
Mansfield, Kathleen. "Bliss," 9
Mather, Cotton. Meditation 146, Second Series, 99–100
Miller, Arthur. "Death of a Salesman," 41, 42, 49, 56, 57–58
Milton, John. *Paradise Lost*, 25, 37
Nemerov, Howard. "Boom," 16
Norris, Frank. *Vandover and the Brute*, 228
O'Connor, Flannery "Good Country People," 9
Orwell, George. "Shooting an Elephant," 12, 13–14, 61–62
Paton, Alan. *Cry, the Beloved Country*, 113–14

Pope, Alexander. "The Rape of the Lock," 33, 37, 63–64

Rifkin, Jeremy. *Time Wars*, 214

Shakespeare, William. *Hamlet*, 39, 40, 42, 43, 48

    Henry V, 54

    Henry VIII, 54

    King Lear, 42, 54

    Macbeth, 27, 42, 54

    The Merchant of Venice, 49

    A Midsummer Night's Dream, 48

    Othello, 49, 52–53

    Romeo and Juliet, 42

    Sonnet 18, 173

    Sonnet 22, 158

Shaw, George Bernard. *Pygmalion*, 43

Shelley, Percy Bysshe. "Ozymandias," 34

Sheridan, Richard. *The Rivals*, 73

Sophocles. *Antigone*, 43, 44–47

    Oedipus at Colonus, 43

    Oedipus Rex, 42

Southwell, Robert. "The Author to his Loving Cosen," 78

Steinbeck, John. *The Grapes of Wrath*, 4, 5, 15

Swift, Jonathan. *Gulliver's Travels*, 15, 16, 225–26

    "A Modest Proposal," 15

Tennyson, Alfred, Lord. "In Memoriam A. H. H.," 146–47

Thomas, Dylan. "Do Not Go Gentle into that Good Night," 38

Thoreau, Henry David. *Walden*, 177–78

    "A Week on the Concord and Merrimack Rivers," 217

Twain, Mark. *A Connecticut Yankee in King Arthur's Court*, 172

    The Adventures of Huckleberry Finn, 5, 17

    Tom Sawyer, 5

    "Roughing It," 95–96

Updike, John. "A & P," 9, 10–11

Voltaire. *Candide*, 16

Vonnegut, Kurt, Jr. *Cat's Cradle*, 68

    Slaughterhouse-Five, 188–89

Waller, Edmund. "Of the Last Verses in the Book," 105

Wheatley, Phillis. "On Being Brought From Africa to America," 181–82

White, E. B. "The Ring of Time," 12, 13

Wilde, Oscar. *The Importance of Being Earnest*, 16, 49–51

Williams, Tennessee. *The Glass Menagerie*, 40, 56

Williams, William Carlos. "That is Just to Say," 16

Wordsworth, William. "To Daffodils," 19, 21, 38

    "The World is Too Much With Us," 175

Wycherley, William. *The Country Wife*, 117–18

Available at your local bookstore or order directly from us by sending in coupon below.

THE BEST TEST PREPARATION FOR THE

AP*

ADVANCED
PLACEMENT
EXAMINATION

ENGLISH
Language & Composition

3 Full-Length Practice Exams

Based on official exams released by the College Board

Detailed explanations to every exam question

Far more comprehensive than any other test preparation book

Includes a **COMPREHENSIVE REVIEW COURSE** of the topics covered on the exam. This book can be used for self-study or by any class preparing for the exam.

RE A *Research & Education Association*

* AP is a registered trademark of the College Entrance Examination Board, which does not endorse this book.

Available at your local bookstore or order directly from us by sending in coupon below.

REA's **Problem Solvers**

The "PROBLEM SOLVERS" are comprehensive supplemental text-books designed to save time in finding solutions to problems. Each "PROBLEM SOLVER" is the first of its kind ever produced in its field. It is the product of a massive effort to illustrate almost any imaginable problem in exceptional depth, detail, and clarity. Each problem is worked out in detail with a step-by-step solution, and the problems are arranged in order of complexity from elementary to advanced. Each book is fully indexed for locating problems rapidly.

ACCOUNTING
ADVANCED CALCULUS
ALGEBRA & TRIGONOMETRY
AUTOMATIC CONTROL
   SYSTEMS/ROBOTICS
BIOLOGY
BUSINESS, ACCOUNTING, & FINANCE
CALCULUS
CHEMISTRY
COMPLEX VARIABLES
DIFFERENTIAL EQUATIONS
ECONOMICS
ELECTRICAL MACHINES
ELECTRIC CIRCUITS
ELECTROMAGNETICS
ELECTRONIC COMMUNICATIONS
ELECTRONICS
FINITE & DISCRETE MATH
FLUID MECHANICS/DYNAMICS
GENETICS
GEOMETRY
HEAT TRANSFER

LINEAR ALGEBRA
MACHINE DESIGN
MATHEMATICS for ENGINEERS
MECHANICS
NUMERICAL ANALYSIS
OPERATIONS RESEARCH
OPTICS
ORGANIC CHEMISTRY
PHYSICAL CHEMISTRY
PHYSICS
PRE-CALCULUS
PROBABILITY
PSYCHOLOGY
STATISTICS
STRENGTH OF MATERIALS &
   MECHANICS OF SOLIDS
TECHNICAL DESIGN GRAPHICS
THERMODYNAMICS
TOPOLOGY
TRANSPORT PHENOMENA
VECTOR ANALYSIS

*If you would like more information about any of these books,
complete the coupon below and return it to us or visit your local bookstore.*

REA's Test Preps
The Best in Test Preparation

- REA "Test Preps" are **far more** comprehensive than any other test preparation series
- Each book contains up to **eight** full-length practice tests based on the most recent exams
- **Every** type of question likely to be given on the exams is included
- Answers are accompanied by **full** and **detailed** explanations

REA publishes over 60 Test Preparation volumes in several series. They include:

Advanced Placement Exams (APs)
Biology
Calculus AB & Calculus BC
Chemistry
Computer Science
English Language & Composition
English Literature & Composition
European History
Government & Politics
Physics
Psychology
Spanish Language
Statistics
United States History

College-Level Examination Program (CLEP)
Analyzing and Interpreting Literature
College Algebra
Freshman College Composition
General Examinations
General Examinations Review
History of the United States I
Human Growth and Development
Introductory Sociology
Principles of Marketing
Spanish

SAT II: Subject Tests
Biology E/M
Chemistry
English Language Proficiency Test
French
German
Literature

SAT II: Subject Tests (cont'd)
Mathematics Level IC, IIC
Physics
Spanish
United States History
Writing

Graduate Record Exams (GREs)
Biology
Chemistry
Computer Science
General
Literature in English
Mathematics
Physics
Psychology

ACT - ACT Assessment

ASVAB - Armed Services Vocational Aptitude Battery

CBEST - California Basic Educational Skills Test

CDL - Commercial Driver License Exam

CLAST - College-Level Academic Skills Test

ELM - Entry Level Mathematics

ExCET - Exam for the Certification of Educators in Texas

FE (EIT) - Fundamentals of Engineering Exam

FE Review - Fundamentals of Engineering Review

GED - High School Equivalency Diploma Exam (U.S. & Canadian editions)

GMAT - Graduate Management Admission Test

LSAT - Law School Admission Test

MAT - Miller Analogies Test

MCAT - Medical College Admission Test

MTEL - Massachusetts Tests for Educator Licensure

MSAT - Multiple Subjects Assessment for Teachers

NJ HSPA - New Jersey High School Proficiency Assessment

PLT - Principles of Learning & Teaching Tests

PPST - Pre-Professional Skills Tests

PSAT - Preliminary Scholastic Assessment Test

SAT I - Reasoning Test

SAT I - Quick Study & Review

TASP - Texas Academic Skills Program

TOEFL - Test of English as a Foreign Language

TOEIC - Test of English for International Communication

RESEARCH & EDUCATION ASSOCIATION
61 Ethel Road W. • Piscataway, New Jersey 08854
Phone: (732) 819-8880   **website: www.rea.com**

Please send me more information about your Test Prep books

Name _____

Address _____

City _____ State _____ Zip _____

REA's Test Prep Books Are The Best!

(a sample of the <u>hundreds of letters</u> REA receives each year)

" I am writing to congratulate you on preparing an exceptional study guide. In five years of teaching this course I have never encountered a more thorough, comprehensive, concise and realistic preparation for this examination. "
Teacher, Davie, FL

" I have found your publications, *The Best Test Preparation...*, to be exactly that. "
Teacher, Aptos, CA

" I used your *CLEP Introductory Sociology* book and rank it 99% — thank you! "
Student, Jerusalem, Israel

" Your GMAT book greatly helped me on the test. Thank you. "
Student, Oxford, OH

" I recently got the French SAT II Exam book from REA. I congratulate you on first-rate French practice tests."
Instructor, Los Angeles, CA

" Your AP English Literature and Composition book is most impressive."
Student, Montgomery, AL

" The REA LSAT Test Preparation guide is a winner! "
Instructor, Spartanburg, SC

(more on front page)